D1600985

Socialism before Sanders

Jake Altman

Socialism before Sanders

The 1930s Moment from Romance
to Revisionism

Jake Altman
Saline, MI, USA

ISBN 978-3-030-17175-9   ISBN 978-3-030-17176-6   (eBook)
https://doi.org/10.1007/978-3-030-17176-6

Cover illustration: Everett Collection Historical/Alamy Stock Photo

This Palgrave Macmillan imprint is published by the registered company Springer Nature
Switzerland AG
The registered company address is: Gewerbestrasse 11, 6330 Cham, Switzerland

For Audrey, always.

ACKNOWLEDGEMENTS

I am grateful for the time and ideas that friends, colleagues, and mentors have shared with me while I worked on this project. I benefited from many friendships and much scholarly engagement at the University of Iowa. I'm grateful to Jake Hall, Josh Cochran, Matt Hodler, Avi Michael, Janet Weaver, John McKerley, Jason Whisler, Meghan Metler, Matt Mettler, Faye Bartram and many, many others for their friendship and help thinking through ideas in all the stages of this project. I am very fortunate to have great teachers. Shel Stromquist encouraged me throughout this project, and his patient and thoughtful efforts improved my craft. Landon Storrs provided very sound analysis of the work and pushing me to make it better. Doug Baynton, to whom I am also thankful for suggesting this title, Tina Parratt, and Charles Connerly all offered valuable help, and I greatly benefited from their seminars. Kristin Anderson-Bricker, Lee Zhu, David Salvaterra, Mark Kehren, Cindy Smith, and John Eby all deserve thanks for making me a historian. My friends in the labor movement, from whom I also learned much, deserve thanks: Kathy, Bill, and Ellen from Massachusetts and the fantastic staff of the Labor Center at the University of Iowa. I owe a debt to the many archivists and librarians who preserved and organized the records vital to this project and helped me use them. The Reuther Library and Archives and the University of Iowa's Department of History and Graduate College provided research and writing support for this project. Thanks also to my family for their support. They help me put work in perspective and make sure that I focus on what really matters. And finally, Audrey, to whom this book is dedicated, know that this would not have been possible without your constant support and many kindnesses.

CONTENTS

CHAPTER 1

Introduction

Before 2015, few in the mainstream of American political thought could have imagined that a socialist revival would reinvigorate the social-democratic left in the United States, threaten the dominant faction within a Democratic Party skeptical of the ameliorative effects of the New Deal and the Great Society, and put a national health insurance program on the political agenda for the American people in a way that had been almost unimaginable just a few years earlier and had not been seriously considered since the days of Harry S. Truman and Walter Reuther.[1] The ruling economic and political orthodoxy is now besieged on all sides. The person at the center of this latest socialist revival is a self-proclaimed democratic socialist of longstanding, Bernie Sanders.

Sanders drew his inspiration, at least in part, from Eugene V. Debs, one of several founders of the Socialist Party of America (SP), and the subject of Sanders's 1979 documentary and subsequent Folkways album. On the album, Sanders applies his mid-twentieth-century Brooklyn accent to the words of a late-nineteenth-century labor leader from Terre Haute, Indiana.[2] This combination of Terre Haute, Indiana, and Brooklyn, New York,

[1] Kevin Boyle, *The UAW and the Heyday of American Liberalism, 1945–1968* (Cornell University Press, 1995), 53–54, 68–69; Jill Quadagno, *One Nation, Uninsured: Why the U.S. Has No National Health Insurance* (Oxford University Press, 2006), 110–111.

[2] Bernard Sanders and Huck Gutman, *Outsider in the House* (Verso, 1997), 22.

© The Author(s) 2019
J. Altman, *Socialism before Sanders*,
https://doi.org/10.1007/978-3-030-17176-6_1

1

may seem a cultural oddity to the early-twenty-first-century observer. The Terre Haute-Brooklyn connection reflects the vitality and diversity of early-twentieth-century socialism in the United States, and its ability to cut across divides that may seem unbridgeable today. It brought together the small town railroad worker from the Midwest and the needle trade worker from the Northeast with a common dream of a better, more equitable world. Sanders's vision of a new social-democratic movement in America relies on an idea that the waitress from New York City and the firefighter from Terre Haute can be connected by a common set of concerns and the social-democratic politics of the New Deal made real again.

Socialism was no isolated movement. Its appeal cut across the country, attracting hundreds of thousands of voters. Beginning in the 1900s and reaching a pinnacle in the early 1910s, this Socialist Party of rural hamlets, small towns, and urban enclaves was the core of socialism's first major period of success in the United States. Of the two congressmen that socialists sent to Washington during this heyday, one hailed from Wisconsin and the other from New York's Lower East Side.[3] There were socialist state legislators scattered across the country in states that included Nevada, Utah, Oklahoma, California, Washington, Montana, Wisconsin, North Dakota, Kansas, Illinois, and Pennsylvania. Socialists elected local officials in the industrial towns of the Northeast right across the prairie and out to the Pacific Northwest, including mayors in Schenectady, New York; Cedar City, Utah; Butte, Montana; Boone, Iowa; Winslow, Arkansas; Grand Junction, Colorado; Brainerd, Minnesota; Broken Bow, Nebraska; Berkeley, California; Fairhope, Alabama; Coeur d'Alene, Idaho; Antlers, Oklahoma; Lima, Ohio; New Castle, Pennsylvania; Bicknell, Indiana; Minneapolis, Minnesota; Traverse City, Michigan; and many, many other cities and towns.[4] Eugene Debs polled six percent of the vote in his 1912 run for president. In 1920, he ran from a prison cell after being convicted of anti-war speech under the Espionage Act and won more than 900,000 votes.[5]

---

[3] James Weinstein, *The Decline of Socialism in America, 1912–1925* (Rutgers University Press, 1984), 107; Sally M. Miller, *Victor Berger and the Promise of Constructive Socialism, 1910–1920* (Greenwood Press, 1973), 39.

[4] See Appendix B in Jack Ross, *The Socialist Party of America: A Complete History* (University of Nebraska Press, 2015); Weinstein, *The Decline of Socialism*, 116–118.

[5] Nick Salvatore, *Eugene V. Debs: Citizen and Socialist* (University of Illinois Press, 2007), 264.

Although socialism was an intellectually diverse movement in the Debs era, socialists shared a belief that capitalism would be replaced by a better, more cooperative system. Some were reformers insistent that they could build an alternative to capitalism, and others were Marxists who debated the preconditions of capitalism's downfall and imagined a fundamental rupture. There were romantic revolutionaries and hard-headed strategists who took a longer view. They were all committed anti-capitalists. United by a belief that capitalism's days were numbered, they disagreed on the how, the why, and the when of capitalism's collapse.[6]

Socialism's first period of success in American life lasted roughly twenty years.[7] Its failure to mature into a durable, independent political party has been attributed to many forces: repression, social mobility, political alliances between Democrats and Republicans, the ability of preexisting political movements to absorb elements of the socialist appeal, and internecine conflict within the socialist movement.[8] But this was all retrospective. It appeared at specific moments in history that socialism was on the upswing or soon would be again; it's upward boundaries not yet demarcated.[9] Although socialism never returned to the independent electoral strength of the Debs era, it has never gone completely and has remained a persistent and influential thread. The 1930s offered new opportunities, challenges, and a new and persistent relevance for socialists.

The socialist revival of the 1930s demonstrates that socialism's contribution to American political life lived well beyond the Socialist Party of America's heyday in the 1910s.[10] During the socialist revival, socialists built institutions, organized the unemployed, extended aid to the labor movement, developed local political movements, and built networks that would remain

---

[6]Weinstein, *The Decline of Socialism in America*, 4–16.

[7]Ibid., ix.

[8]Ibid., xi–xii, 326–332; Richard William Judd, *Socialist Cities: Municipal Politics and the Grass Roots of American Socialism* (State University of New York Press, 1989), 26.

[9]Salvatore, *Eugene V. Debs*, 264–265.

[10]Judd, *Socialist Cities*, 3; James Weinstein, *The Decline of Socialism*, 93–103, 108, 230, 231. Daniel Bell largely discounts the continued significance of socialists and the role of a social-democratic tradition in shaping the orientations of former Socialist Party members in positions of power. Daniel Bell, *Marxian Socialism in the United States* (Princeton University Press, 1967), 191; Frank A. Warren, *An Alternative Vision: The Socialist Party in the 1930's* (Indiana University Press, 1974), 3–4; and Weinstein, *The Decline of Socialism*, 338.

active in the struggle against injustice throughout the twentieth century.[11] The 1930s revival also served as a space in which women claimed leadership roles, though divergent gender ideologies and expectations provoked tensions within the socialist movement.[12] Reincorporating socialists into the history of the American left and the history of the labor movement adds an important dimension to our understanding of the struggles for power in the Congress of Industrial Organizations (CIO) and the development and interplay of diverse anti-communisms.[13] It brings this history out from under the shadow of Cold War historiography and moves scholarly debate toward a more honest appraisal of the histories of the socialist and labor movements. This work, while not a definitive history of American socialism in these years, is a piece of that larger project to bring complexity to histories shaped by the Cold War and suggests the vibrancy and diversity of the labor movement in the United States during the 1930s. Highlander Folk School's socialist roots, the attraction of revolutionary ideas, women's important role in the SP, and the shift from revolutionary rhetoric to gradualism demonstrates the complexity and importance of this history.

Histories of socialism in the 1930s have focused on the SP and its institutional life and internecine struggles.[14] The SP began to evaporate from 1936 onward. As members left to join the New Deal coalition, the SP became largely irrelevant. Yet, the socialist movement had life

[11] There are a number of works that step outside of the institutional, interparty framework. See Roy Rosenzweig, "'Socialism in Our Time': The Socialist Party and the Unemployed, 1929–1936," *Labor History* 20, no. 4 (1979), 478. Rosenzweig offers a good critique of Daniel Bell's emphasis on the internal struggles of the socialist movement at the expense of their practical organizing work; Cecelia Bucki, *Bridgeport's Socialist New Deal, 1915–1936* (University of Illinois Press, 2001), 135–193; James R. Green, *Grass-Roots Socialism: Radical Movements in the Southwest, 1895–1943* (Louisiana State University Press, 1978), 396–437; James N. Gregory, "Upton Sinclair's 1934 EPIC Campaign: Anatomy of a Political Movement," in *Labor: Studies in Working-Class History of the Americas* 12, no. 4 (2015), 51–81.

[12] Accounts of socialist women in the 1930s remain scant. A notable exception is William C. Pratt, "Women and American Socialism: The Reading Experience," *Pennsylvania Magazine of History and Biography* 99, no. 1, (1975).

[13] Shelton Stromquist, "Introduction: Was All (Cold War) Politics Local?" in *Labor's Cold War: Local Politics in a Global Context*, ed. Shelton Stromquist (Illinois University Press, 2008), 5.

[14] Bell, *Marxian Socialism in the United States*, 190–191, 193; Warren, *An Alternative Vision*, 123–124, 189.

and relevance beyond the SP. [15] Socialists migrated into the New Deal coalition and the Democratic Party, where they retained some coherence as a force for social democracy and a thoughtful variant of anti-communism.[16] This redefinition of socialism complicates assertions that socialists were too idealistic and inflexible to be relevant in the United States. They, and socialism itself, underwent political and ideological transformations. No longer would most socialists continue to vote or soapbox for the SP's candidates. President Roosevelt and the success of the New Deal coalition reshaped their political allegiances.

Taken together, the chapters that follow establish the significance and scope of the socialist revival in the 1930s, the importance of its most radical elements, the limitations and successes of the revival at the local level, and the ways in which its participants evolved through the 1930s, 1940s, and beyond. The prologue and "Radical Incubators" set the scene, explaining the economic and social moment in New York City at Union Theological Seminary where socialism attracted important young people, including the founders of Highlander Folk School. "The Revolutionary Policy Committee" looks at one particularly radical manifestation of socialism. The RPC was a product of the 1930s. It was an effort to find a conduit for militancy and radicalism that remained compatible with democratic socialism. "Fruits of the Socialist Revival" focuses on two key institutions, Highlander Folk School and Soviet House. This chapter raises the profile of Soviet House and emphasizes the importance of socialism in shaping Highlander Folk School during its formative years. "Their Party, Their Power" explores the revival in the context of women's participation in the SP and underscores the importance of their efforts. "While the Men Played Revolution" builds on the previous chapter by examining the life of Elizabeth "Zilla" Hawes and the conflicts that developed around gender in the SP and at Highlander Folk School. "'A Mighty River'" examines the change among socialists from a chiliastic socialism to a more pragmatic embrace of social democracy.

Just as the Terre Haute of the 2010s is no longer the Terre Haute of the 1910s, the socialism of Bernie Sanders is not the socialism of Eugene Debs. The experiences of socialists in the 1930s provided an important waypoint

---

[15] Bell, *Marxian Socialism in the United States*, 5.

[16] Landon R.Y. Storrs, *The Second Red Scare and the Unmaking of the New Deal Left* (Princeton University Press, 2013), 9–11.

between the era of Debs and the resurgence of socialism in the United States after 2015. The 1930s moment helped shape a Sanders coalition built on concrete social-democratic demands. Socialists came to see capitalism as a force that could be contained, channeled, and blunted. They also lost the certainty that it could be completely replaced. While utopian strains remain within the socialist movement, they are no longer dominant. Instead, owing to the experience of the 1930s and the decades that followed, socialists have come to accept social democracy as a pragmatic ameliorative to capitalism's destructive rapaciousness.

CHAPTER 2

Prologue: The Promise of Revival

The United States witnessed a revival of the socialist movement during the Great Depression. Although its membership and activities had declined during the First World War, the economic and political upheavals of the late 1920s and early 1930s created a moment in which socialist ideology inspired an engaged and influential core of intellectuals and activists. Socialist parties showed signs of success internationally and in key municipalities in the United States, giving socialists hope that a political revolution was dawning. Pro-capitalist institutions and their leaders were unable to offer adequate explanations or solutions for the unemployment crisis facing the United States. Socialists, especially in the person of Norman Thomas, the Socialist Party's perennial presidential candidate and the de facto leader of the party, provided a viable alternative that was particularly attractive to those suffering from unemployment and its accompanying social upheavals. New York City was a focal point for both the unemployment crisis and the revitalized socialist movement. It was here that Norman Thomas voiced vociferous opposition to the city's establishment politics, giving socialism a national stage. It was here that young socialist leaders, under the tutelage of Norman Thomas, experienced the harsh realities of the Great Depression and began to form their own political consciousness.

In the 1930s, American socialists looked across the Atlantic and found successful socialist movements. Socialists gained electoral ground across Europe. In 1931 socialists took the largest share of seats in Spanish parlia-

© The Author(s) 2019
J. Altman, *Socialism before Sanders*,
https://doi.org/10.1007/978-3-030-17176-6_2

ment and were a significant force in the coalition government that resulted from the election.[1] Despite a severe loss of seats in the House of Commons in the 1931 election, the Labour Party in Britain constituted the principal opposition to the National Government.[2] In Romania, socialists remained marginal in national politics in the 1930s. Yet, the Social-Democratic Party was reconstituted after left factionalism split the socialist movement and elected several deputies.[3] They won nine seats in a parliament of several hundred.[4] The two social democratic parties in Czechoslovakia achieved greater success. Both parties improved their overall share of the vote with the Czech party becoming the second largest in the country with 739,411 votes. The other Czechoslovakian social-democratic party polled just over 400,000 votes. The total increase in votes for the social-democratic parties in Czechoslovakia was over 150,000.[5] Local elections in Finland also heralded socialist victories. Socialists took control of sixty-six municipalities by winning nearly eighty new council seats.[6] In Palestine, socialist David Bloch-Blumenfeld had been mayor of Tel Aviv, and a correspondent from *The New Leader*, a socialist weekly published in New York, reported, "the Socialist city of Telaviv is eminently successful." The correspondent—warmed by the charms of Mayor Bloch-Blumenfeld and Goldie Meyerson—was pleased that "no exploitation and no such thing as private charity" existed in Tel Aviv.[7] Socialists in America looked to these successes and imagined their movement might achieve widespread electoral success.

Events in the United States reaffirmed hope for a successful socialist political movement. Electoral victories in Reading, Pennsylvania, raised

---

[1] Stanley G. Payne, *Spain's First Democracy: The Second Republic, 1931–1936* (University of Wisconsin Press, 1993), 50–51.

[2] Ben Pimlott, *Labour and the Left in the 1930s* (Cambridge University Press, 1977), 1, 12–13.

[3] William Brustein, *Roots of Hate: Anti-Semitism in Europe Before the Holocaust* (Cambridge University Press, 2003), 315.

[4] "9 Socialists Win Seats in Roumania," *The New Leader*, 12 January 1929, 3.

[5] Franz Soukop, "Big Victory for Czech Socialists," *The New Leader*, 5 January 1929, 2.

[6] "Socialists Make Notable Gains in Finnish Cities," *The New Leader*, 5 January 1929, 2.

[7] Gertrude Weil Klein, "Socialism in the Holy City: Socialist Mayor Bloch Tells of Administration's Progress and Problems," *The New Leader*, 5 January 1929, 4. Goldie Meyerson was future prime minister of Israel Golda Meir.

socialists' expectations for the future of their party. The SP captured the mayoralty, two of four council seats, two seats on the school board, and the office of controller in a November 1927 election.[8] J. Henry Stump, the new socialist mayor of Reading, reflected the ebullient mood: "As sure as Socialism is the remedy for capitalism, so sure will the people eventually be forced to turn from capitalist political parties and seek justice in a political party of their own."[9] Those who witnessed the growing crisis of capitalism, which challenged official claims of prosperity, shared the certainty of purpose in Stump's statement. It appeared that the SP's strategies of "education and propaganda" as well as institution building were paying dividends in Reading.[10] The local Reading branch had a weekly paper—including its own printer—a labor lyceum, founded in 1904, and ran a "successful cooperative cigar factory."[11] James Oneal, editor of *The New Leader*, credited "persistent and continuous" education for the socialist victory in Reading.[12] Reading provided proof that socialists could win elections.

Although some historians argue that socialists were sometimes successful as a "good government" alternative to corrupt machine politics, socialist victory in Reading was rooted in class politics. What may appear as a "good government" campaign against the corrupt old parties in Reading can in fact be read as class struggle with anti-capitalist elements when one considers the distribution of tax burdens. The SP had championed efficient city government and relief from high tax assessments for homeowners. Socialists pointed out that high assessments on homeowners had been used to offset years of very low assessments given to influential "downtown property own-

---

[8]James Oneal, "Workers Hold Celebration at Inauguration," *The New Leader*, 7 January 1928, 1. In November 1930, the SP took complete control over the council when the remaining non-Socialist council members were defeated; For a full accounting of socialism in Reading see William Pratt's "'Jimmie Higgins' and the Reading Socialist Community" in *Socialism and the Cities*, ed. Bruce Stave (Kennikat Press, 1975).

[9]"Party Organization Made Victory Possible Is Mayor Stump's Word to Comrades," *The New Leader*, 7 January 1928, 1.

[10]Oneal, "Workers Hold Celebration at Inauguration," 1.

[11]Oneal, "Workers Hold Celebration at Inauguration," 1; "Reading Labor Lyceum Petitions to End 60-Year History and Divide $75,000," *Reading Eagle*, 5 June 1964, 34.

[12]James Oneal, "Workers Hold Celebration at Inauguration," *The New Leader*, 7 January 1928, 1.

ers" by non-socialist administrations.[13] James H. Maurer, a socialist who served several terms in the Pennsylvania State Legislature and as president of the Pennsylvania Federation of Labor, was also elected to Reading's city council in the socialist victory of 1927. Attacked as "red" throughout the election, Maurer could later joke that he and his comrades were indeed a "red menace" when they reversed the previous administration's tax regime: "Up to 1928 Reading was a city of home-owners, fully half of the workers holding title, though often under mortgage. We found that gradually the assessments of these little fellows had been jacked up, while the big ones got theirs reduced. We reversed the process, which made the once-favored absolutely sure that we were indeed the 'red menace.'"[14] With the victory in Reading adding to continued socialist success in Milwaukee and great hopes for the future in New York City, it was not unreasonable to expect a resurgence of socialism in the United States. Milwaukee had long been a socialist stronghold, and in 1932, the SP reelected its longtime socialist mayor, Daniel Hoan. Hoan achieved a 39,000-vote majority, garnering over 101,500 votes to his opponent's 62,500.[15] Ambitious young people who witnessed economic deprivation during the Great Depression and what they thought could be the unraveling of capitalism came to similar conclusions.

Well before Black Tuesday in October 1929 signaled what was later to be seen as the start of the Great Depression, the SP warned that growing unemployment, stagnant wages, and declining industrial production contradicted official claims of prosperity. In New York City, Norman Thomas fought to make the SP a serious party of opposition on this economic ground. Thomas disputed claims of widespread prosperity. He highlighted the unemployment crisis that captured the attention of New Yorkers in 1928 as proof that all was not well with capitalism. Launching a salvo against New York City's lively and dissolute elites, Thomas wrote: "In the wild and extravagant revelry of New Year's Eve, up and down crowded

[13]"Made Success Ruling City: Reading Has Confidence in Socialists," *The Florence Times-News*, 15 January 1931; "Socialists in Power in Reading City Government," *The Lewiston Daily Sun*, 3 January 1928, 7; and "Firing of Old Party Assessor of Taxes Is First Official Action by Mayor Stump," *The New Leader*, 7 January 1928, 2.

[14]James Hudson Maurer, *It Can Be Done: The Autobiography of James Hudson Maurer* (New York: The Rand School Press, 1938), 297–298.

[15]"Socialist Sweep in Milwaukee: Hoan Wins Record Majority—Party Elects Treasurer and City Attorney, Gains Nine Local Seats," *The New Leader*, 9 April 1932, 1.

Broadway in New York, marched a brave little group of 100 of the unemployed, men to whom the cost of one night's party along the great White
Way [Broadway] would have meant a decent living for a year."[16] Thomas
set himself to the task of debunking claims of ever-growing prosperity:
"the little group which dared to advertise what the dying of another year
of Coolidge prosperity had meant to them was only a tiny fraction of the
great army of the unemployed in the United States. To meet their desperate needs something more is required than the professional optimism of
Herbert Hoover."[17] Thomas set out his vision of "something more" early
in the crisis. The alternative, expressed in Thomas's direct and erudite fash-
ion, was compelling in the face of growing uncertainty. He used the issue
of unemployment to put forward a bold socialist plan that included public works, coordinated public employment programs, immediate relief to
feed the hungry, and municipal housing programs to provide safe homes.[18]
Thomas and the socialists were in good form. The crisis boosted their confidence and revealed the wisdom of their critique: "When some months
ago, we Socialists caused a little rift in the prosperity lute by stating on
every occasion that for the great mass of workers this prosperity talk was
sheer bunkum, we were accused of being sour-bellied pessimists."[19] The
socialists celebrated a small victory as politicians including Governor Al
Smith of New York, a soon to be candidate for the Presidency, clamored to
address the unemployment issue. Unemployment could not be ignored.

Their critiques of capitalism seemingly confirmed by the economic crisis,
socialists set about the task of providing opposition and offering their alternative. Thomas attacked capitalists and their promoters for their platitudi-
nous remarks about growing prosperity shared by all classes while denying
the growing social crisis apparent on the streets in the rising numbers of
the unemployed. Thomas drew together a list of economic indicators that
suggested the economy was under threat. Wages had been stagnant for four
years and average weekly pay had declined between October and November of 1927, numbers which Thomas took from the National Industrial
Conference Board (NICB), hardly a radical body.[20] Railroad traffic was

[16] Norman Thomas, "Timely Topics," *The New Leader*, 7 January 1928, 1.
[17] Ibid.
[18] Norman Thomas, "Timely Topics," *The New Leader*, 11 February 1928, 1.
[19] "Washington Discovers Unemployment," *The New Leader*, 18 February 1928, 8.
[20] Norman Thomas, "Timely Topics," *The New Leader*, 4 February 1928, 1.

on the decline by double digits. Steel production, too, was declining at a similar rate. Most important from the perspective of the workers, and not unsurprising given the direction of the other economic indicators that Thomas cited, the rate of unemployment was growing quickly.[21]

Socialists were hopeful about their chances for rebuilding the party, the movement, and creating new electoral strongholds.[22] They believed that workers' natural sympathy for socialism was hampered by the power that employers held over their livelihoods. With this obstacle to mass support removed by rising unemployment, socialists anticipated a resurgence of support: "one-tenth of the working population of the county are walking the streets of our cities with dark despair gnawing at their hearts," wrote an anonymous correspondent for *The New Leader*, "add to them the 1,800,000 aged men and women thrown on the industrial dump-heap and dependent upon their children or charity for a meagre existence, and add again the farmers fast sinking to peasant level, and you have a picture of the blessings which the capitalist system bestows."[23] Socialists, confronted with an economic crisis, were in their element, their critiques of capitalism given new luster.

Socialists addressed rising unemployment, an issue that had captivated New Yorkers beginning in the early months of 1928. In February, *The New Leader* ran a huge headline: "Worst Depression in Years Stalks the South-West." The article, written by Murray King, detailed the social dislocation caused by unemployment and new mobility allowed by automobile ownership. King pointed out that the "hobo" no longer fit the popular image of a single, male itinerant worker. Families now moved across the land together. King shared mainstream fears about the "degeneracy" of workers and dispossessed smallholders into a "tramp class." The majority of "hobo families" were dispossessed farmers. These desperate souls, huddled around the dying light of campfires, were to be part of the clay from which socialists crafted a new challenge to the increasingly distressed capitalist order.[24]

Unemployment, and its accompanying social upheavals, was *the* social concern in New York City by the early months of 1928. The deaths of

---

[21]Norman Thomas, "Timely Topics," *The New Leader*, 7 January 1928, 1.

[22]"Socialist NEC in Session in Philadelphia," *The New Leader*, 14 January 1928, 1.

[23]"Washington Discovers Unemployment," *The New Leader*, 18 February 1928, 8.

[24]Murray E. King, "Worst Depression in Years Stalks the South-West," *The New Leader*, 4 February 1928, 1.

unemployed workers from starvation and exposure served as the impetus for Mayor Jimmy Walker's involvement with the Committee on Unemployment Relief. The frigid cold that descended on New York City in the winter of 1928 contributed to the growing crisis and pushed impoverished people to the very edge of desperation. Reports of starvation and related illnesses were not uncommon in 1928, as New York City's unemployment problem went unresolved. In February, an unemployed carpenter was found unconscious on Third Avenue. He died of heart failure in Harlem Hospital. Doctors ruled starvation was the underlying cause.[25] Three unemployed men were taken to hospitals in New York on one day in early March 1928. One of the men had crawled into a tunnel near Grand Central station, as the steam pipes in the tunnel provided some protection against the wind. Two of the three men died moments after arriving at the hospital. The ultimate cause of death for all three cases was attributed to the men's unemployment. One accused bootlegger arrested in February 1928 confessed to the police that he had turned to the illegal trade in liquor because he had been unable to secure legal employment after a six-month search.[26] A purse-snatcher and a coat thief told similar stories of unemployment leading to desperation and want to explain their crimes.[27] In July, Earl Dodd, a twenty-three-year-old unemployed cook, died in Bellevue hospital after enduring six weeks with little food. On the same day, a twenty-six-year-old women collapsed in the street from "malnutrition" while looking for work.[28] New York's charitable institutions were under increasing strain, but could not ascertain the causes of rising unemployment.[29] In conjunction with New York's governor and its industrial commissioner, they launched an inquiry to solve the mystery of New York's growing "army" of the unemployed.[30]

The immediate reasons for the growing presence of the unemployed in New York City were not mysterious even if the ultimate causes seemed more

---

[25] "Jobless, Starves to Death," *New York Times*, 17 February 1928, 3.

[26] "Starvation Kills Two Jobless Men," *New York Times*, 6 March 1928, 2.

[27] "Seized as Purse Snatcher: Prisoner, Captured After 2-Mile Chase, Says He Was Jobless," *New York Times*, 5 February 1928, 27; "78, Jobless, Admits Stealing Coat," *New York Times*, 5 January 1928, 60.

[28] "Starved Six Weeks, Dies," *New York Times*, 29 July 1928.

[29] "Reports More Jobless: Bowery Y.M.C.A. Aided 600 More Men in 1927 than in 1926," *New York Times*, 15 January 1928, 7.

[30] "City Seeks Source of Homeless Here: Charities Aid in Survey to Determine Whence Comes Army of Unemployed," *New York Times*, 15 February 1928.

difficult to grasp. Manufacturers were discharging workers. By November 1927, the number of workers in manufacturing had fallen by nearly 13% from a high point in November 1923. This represented a dip in manufacturing employment of a little over seven and a half percent from 1926.[31] In early 1928, the Labor Department reported that for every one hundred jobs in New York, there were two hundred and fifteen job seekers. They also reported that 66,000 workers in the state suffered from layoffs in 1927.[32] Officials of the Bowery Mission stated that New York had not seen such a demand in the breadlines since 1916, and the Charity Organization Society had to borrow $44,000 dollars to provide for the influx in newly unemployed workers.[33] In February 1928, AFL Vice President Matthew Woll laid out the source of the problem as he saw it: "our problem is not one of overproduction but of underconsumption."[34] In Woll's view, higher wages were the solution for unemployment and necessary to stabilize the economy.

New York City's officials voiced different explanations for the unemployment crisis that did not call the overall health of the economy into question. Commissioner Bird Coler, who ran the Department of Public Welfare in New York City, blamed "undesirables and unfortunates" for the increased demand on charitable services in New York. Coler sent the police to interrogate hundreds of unemployed women and men as they stood in line to receive shelter at various institutions. They were asked about their employment searches. Those whose answers did not satisfy the police were sent to the workhouse as vagrants. The goal of Coler's action was to expel from New York City all of the "out-of-town vagrants." On their first night, the police found only a handful of "out-of-town vagrants" in the long lines. Despite the claims of Coler and of Colonel Edward Underwood of the Salvation Army, there was not an army of "tramps usurping the cots of more worthy persons."[35]

[31] "November Record for Unemployment: Jobless Most Numerous and Payrolls Smallest Since 1924," *New York Times*, 26 January 1928, 38.

[32] "State and City Act to Aid Jobless," *New York Times*, 9 February 1928, 26.

[33] "Call for Breadlines Longest Since 1916," *New York Times*, 13 February 1928, 21; "Ranks of Jobless Found on Rise Here," *New York Times*, 6 February 1928, 25.

[34] "Weisbord Rallies Jobless in Passaic," *New York Times*, 5 February 1928, 2.

[35] "Free Bed Seeks Under Official Fire," *New York Times*, 5 January 1928, 24.

Labor unions did not escape blame for the crisis. Colonel Underwood said, "Many of the homeless are striking miners from Pennsylvania."[36] In fact, hundreds of striking miners and their families had been evicted from company-controlled housing around Pittsburgh in early January. The coal company hoped the cold would break the miners' spirits. The United Mine Workers of America (UMWA), under the leadership of Philip Murray, future president of the Congress of Industrial Organizations, hastily erected dwellings or found accommodations in disused churches and halls to protect the miners from the winter. Murray said that the UMWA housed all of the miners.[37] While some miners did eventually move on to other states, Colonel Underwood offered no corroborating evidence that a large stream of evicted miners moved into Manhattan.[38]

The housing infrastructure of the New York's private charities was overwhelmed, and this was well before the worst years of the economic crisis had hit. Yet, New Yorkers, including charity directors, could find no explanation that fit with their notion that the economic system was sound. The State Board of Charities investigated the "army of homeless men" and was forced to conclude that most of the unemployed workers in New York City were "normal, unemployed men who were looking for work."[39] They did not, however, predict a worsening crisis or question the enduring stability of their economic system. Rather, the report of the State Board of Charities concluded that the upsurge in jobless people had "some undefinable reason, elusive and yet existent."[40]

The unemployment crisis drew the attention of leading figures including Senator Robert F. Wagner, who was settling into his first term, and Secretary of Labor James Davis. Wagner pressed for a national commission to investigate rising unemployment. He revealed that workers also faced wage cuts, as a result of the growing crisis. "Apparently the threat of unemployment has already been used to hammer down the employee's wage level," Wagner pointed out, "The total paid out in wages has shrunk even more

---

[36] Ibid.

[37] "Families of 800 Miners Are Evicted," *The New Leader*, 7 January 1928, 1; "Berger Assails Pennsylvania Coal Barons," *The New Leader*, 28 January 1928, 4.

[38] Irwin M. Marcus, James P. Dougherty, and Eileen M. Cooper, "Confrontation at Rossiter: The Coal Strike of 1927–1928 and Its Aftermath," *Pennsylvania History* 59, no. 4 (October 1992), 315–316, 322–323.

[39] "Free Bed Seekers Under Official Fire," *New York Times*, 5 January 1928, 24.

[40] Ibid.

than the number of employees, at the same time that the laborer has been producing steadily more and more per hour."[41] Wagner feared that the rational economic behavior of individual employers would have profound consequences for American society. While trying to allay fears about rising unemployment, James Davis warned that a reduction of pay rates would spark a deeper economic crisis: "Above all we need not reduce the wages of those now operating automatic machines. To do so would lower the purchasing power of the American people to a point that would hit all business a fearful blow." Beyond stable wage rates, Davis's solution was continued support for and strengthening of a tariff designed to protect and foster American manufacturing against foreign competition.[42] Critics of the "wonder-working tariff" pointed out that it had failed to prevent rising unemployment even in industries that received special protections.[43]

Unemployment became a national political issue in 1928. As national elections approached, the Republicans drew fire from Democrats. Norman Thomas and the socialists denounced both parties and their collective inaction. Republicans and Democrats squabbled over the number of unemployed and the depths of the crisis.[44] At the low end, Secretary of Labor Davis stated that 1,874,050 American workers were unemployed in the early months of 1928. In response and using the same sources of information as Davis, Senator Wagner argued that at least 4,000,000 workers were unemployed.[45] Senator Shipstead of the Farmer-Labor Party looked at all years since 1920 and argued that 8,331,170 workers were unemployed.[46] What was not in dispute was that the number of employed persons had shrunk by nearly seven and a half percent from 1925 to 1928.[47] Even the corporation-oriented NICB, concluded that the government's numbers

[41] "Asks Davis Inquiry on Unemployment," *New York Times*, 16 February 1928, 2.

[42] "Davis Asks Labor to Uphold Tariff," *New York Times*, 17 February 1928, 21.

[43] "How Not to Do It," *New York Times*, 18 February 1928, 16.

[44] "Wagner Hits Figure Repeated by Davis," *New York Times*, 23 July 1928, 36. The cautious language of Secretary of Labor Davis throughout 1928 makes apparent that he, too, regarded unemployment and its larger economic implications from a position of grave concern. He was likely constrained from presenting a worrying picture by others members of the Coolidge administration, who put forward much more hopeful visions of the American future. This group included Secretary of Commerce Hoover.

[45] "Calls Davis Wrong on Unemployment," *New York Times*, 21 April 1928, 16.

[46] "8,000,000 Jobless, Shipstead Asserts," *New York Times*, 3 April 1928, 8.

[47] Ibid.

were wrong. The NICB's president, Magnus Alexander, put the number of unemployed at 3,500,000.[48]

The SP had found a new voice in Norman Thomas and a new issue in the unemployment crisis. Socialists in New York City articulated compelling opposition to the establishment's inadequate response to early symptoms of economic crisis that would culminate in the Great Depression. Norman Thomas blasted the housing failures of Mayor Walker, a Tammany Democrat. If the city was serious about eliminating slums and providing affordable housing, Thomas argued, it must provide a municipal housing program that charged rents at cost—no profiteering on the backs of working families. In the midst of a burgeoning unemployment crisis, the robust municipal housing program put forward by Thomas could have eased the suffering of the increasing numbers who found themselves without work and unable to make rent.[49] Thomas defied expectations when he received over 174,000 votes in the 1929 mayoral election in New York City.[50] The SP received hundreds of membership applications in response to Thomas's vote total, which improved upon the SP's previous highpoint in New York's mayoral contest, set in 1917, by nearly 30,000 votes.[51] Still, in 1929 Thomas took just over 12% of the vote and Walker, the Democratic candidate, won reelection.[52]

Despite his electoral defeat, Thomas kept up his opposition, advocating for better food relief, housing, and employment programs. By late November 1930, food relief provided by the Mayor Walker's Committee on Unemployment Relief was inadequate to meet the rising demand. A few months later, Frances Perkins, the future secretary of labor and onetime SP member, wrote of the meagerness of food on which "eight unemployed girls" tried to subsist.[53] As these "unemployed girls" discovered,

---

[48] "Sees Jobless Crisis Slowly Improving," *New York Times*, 12 March 1928, 10.

[49] "Municipal Housing Urged by Thomas," *New York Times*, 12 December 1930, 37; "Thomas Plea for Housing Called 'Red'," *The New Leader*, 25 February 1928, 1.

[50] "Socialist Peak Set by Thomas's Vote," *New York Times*, 6 November 1929, 5.

[51] "Socialists Winning New Party Members," *New York Times*, 8 November 1929, 12; "Socialist Peak Set by Thomas's Vote," 5.

[52] "Final Results of the Election on Tuesday," *New York Times*, 7 November 1929, 20.

[53] "Eight Girls Found Living on Bananas," *New York Times*, 19 March 1931, 6; Melvyn Dubofsky, *Hard Work: The Making of Labor History* (University of Illinois Press, 2000), 16.

relief services often served only those with young children. In late 1931, shortfalls in relief were huge. The chairman of the Emergency Unemployment Relief Committee anticipated a need of $65,000,000 to meet the basic needs of the unemployed. New York City had allocated only $15,000,000.[54] Private charity was completely overwhelmed by the scope of need. The executive secretary of the Knights of Columbus in New York reported that his organization received "between 800 and 1,000 applications every day for work and that its employment service was unable to find more than twenty or thirty jobs."[55] When Norman Thomas and Lewis Waldman put forward the case for an accelerated public works program, a subway expansion to fight unemployment, Mayor Walker and his allies rebuffed them.[56] Thomas's call for free school lunches was also rebuffed by the associate superintendent of schools, who implied that private contributions from teachers and principals ensured that no children went hungry in New York's schools. Another official from the Board of Education went well beyond the associate superintendent when he issued an outright denial that children went hungry in New York City's schools: "He said that sometimes malnutrition was confused with lack of food, and declared malnutrition could be found among the best families."[57] It was much the same on the issue of public housing projects. Mayor Walker cited the law as a barrier to more public development. Thomas told Walker to change the law. Walker scoffed or snidely dismissed Thomas's demands. Thomas, however, continued to present a real and aggressive opposition to Walker's government.

The young social reformers who ventured to New York City in the late 1920s and early 1930s saw the unemployed queuing for food, work, or housing. The situation would worsen during their time in the great and troubled city, and the experience forged their political ideologies. They witnessed Norman Thomas's spirited and persuasive efforts to construct an effective opposition to the political status quo in New York City, and they embraced socialism.

[54]"City's Relief Fund in Held Inadequate," *New York Times*, 25 October 1931, 3.
[55]"Mayor and Thomas Clash on Jobs Plans," *New York Times*, 26 March 1930, 1.
[56]Ibid.
[57]Ibid.

CHAPTER 3

Radical Incubators: New York City and Union Theological Seminary

A teeming metropolis greeted the students who arrived in New York City in the late 1920s and early 1930s to begin their studies at Union Theological Seminary (UTS). The incredible wealth of a privileged society—manifest in the marvelous colonnades they passed as they disembarked from Penn Station—stood in stark contrast with the poverty and dislocation of the unemployed. They must have been overcome with the sheer majesty of Penn Station—its lofty ceilings, granite and bronze statuary, wrought iron archways, and neoclassical façade. Even those arriving by bus were ushered into the city under the shadow of the mighty train terminal.[1] Penn Station stood as a testament to collective human achievement. When they ventured about the city, as bright students with social concerns, they witnessed unemployed workers—who were keen to keep hold of their shaving kits and maintain their dignity—makeshift bivouacs that housed the unem-

---

[1]Frank E. Wrenick, *The Streamline Era Greyhound Terminals: The Architecture of W.S. Arrasmith* (McFarland, 2007), 100; Berenice Abbott, "Greyhound Bus Terminal, 33rd and 34th Streets Between Seventh and Eighth Avenues, Manhattan," Changing New York: Photographs by Berenice Abbott, 1935–1938, WPA Federal Art Project Images, Photography Collection, Miriam and Ira D. Wallach Division of Art, Prints and Photographs, New York Public Library [CNY]; "Link Bus and Rail Service," 2 April 1930, *New York Times*, 60; "New Buses Start Service to North," 14 October 1928, *The Washington Post*, 10; and Berenice Abbott, "Penn Station, Interior, Manhattan," 1935, CNY.

© The Author(s) 2019
J. Altman, *Socialism before Sanders*,
https://doi.org/10.1007/978-3-030-17176-6_3

ployed, and the despair that accompanied life on the political and economic margins of the great city.[2]

The human capacity for collective achievement signified by Penn Station and the dire want of the unemployed was jarring to the young people fresh from the South or Midwest, including Myles Horton, James Dombrowski, and Franz Daniel. These students came to New York City to study at UTS, a progressive, nondenominational graduate college. Professors at UTS and SP mentors encouraged radical thought, an intellectual process further fueled by the visible economic distress and stoked by the knowledge that collective action could change society. Reinhold Niebuhr was both professor and SP mentor. Other important influences for the radical socialists were Harry Ward, Norman Thomas, and Roger Baldwin. These leaders set out to attract professional, college-educated young people to radical politics, as part of an explicit plan to establish a new generation of leadership for the SP specifically and the radical movement in the United States more generally. They were incredibly successful—due in large part to the economic circumstances that gave a new and urgent legitimacy to their critiques—in developing a new layer of leadership. Encouraged and fostered at UTS, Horton would go on to found Highlander Folk School (HFS), a school for labor activists in Tennessee that was essential to the mission of the SP and the development of socialist thought in the United States. Dombrowski and Daniel would serve as influential leaders of HFS. These men and a host of other socialists were radicalized at UTS amidst the economic turmoil of New York City.

In the late 1920s and early 1930s, New York City was a place to discover and to witness the great contradiction at the heart of capitalism—the existence of poverty and economic desperation in the very midst of so much wealth. The attraction of radicalism was bolstered by the widespread acceptance that capitalism was facing imminent collapse, revolutionary upheaval, or both. Niebuhr captured the social intensity of the period when he wrote about the bourgeoisie's response to a march of the unemployed on Washington in 1931. "The outlook in America was so dark and the morale of the powerful groups so low," wrote Niebuhr, "that badly scared men in Wall Street ordered their summer homes to be stocked with edibles as a precautionary measure, and men and women speculated in the drawing-

---

[2]"Police Guard Jobless Sleeping on Grass," *New York Times*, 15 August 1928, 11; Berenice Abbott, "Huts and Unemployed, West Houston and Mercer St., Manhattan," 25 October 1935, CNY.

rooms on the best kind of poison as a means to oblivion from the horrors of revolution."[3] The fear of Washington's elite was apparent in the city's overreaction to the relatively small protest march and the inflation of supposed threats to law and order. The entire police force of 1400 officers was called out to protect Washington society from the unemployed marchers. Additional reserves were ordered to guard important sites around the city, including the White House. If the rich hoped to meet "oblivion before the horrors of revolution," the radical socialists who emerged in the late 1920s and early 1930s envisioned not a revolution of "horrors" but a revolution for justice.[4]

Norman Thomas saw the contradiction for what it was, a gap for socialists to conquer, a space to be overcome, and a revelation to be spread among workers. Thomas explained what had changed in society and why capitalism had to give way to a new and more just system of social organization. He saw the "age of scarcity" as past. A time of abundance for all had arrived and "the enormous scientific and mechanical process which... accompanied capitalism" had brought humanity out from a time of the "grim decrees of Nature" and into a world of "potential abundance." Thomas argued that the means to maintain "our whole population with a standard of living about equivalent to that which can be maintained by a family with an income of $20,000 a year" was an achievable and necessary goal. He regarded the alternative as anathema to a civilized society. "The alternative to shared abundance," he wrote, "is a continuance of economic insecurity and a deadliness of strife which will make the world a hell worse than Dante ever imagined." For Thomas, humanity was confronted with two potential futures: "Either we must deliberately and consciously manage machinery for collective life or let it become the instrument of wholesale death."[5] Socialists were determined to pursue the former option.

---

[3] Reinhold Niebuhr, "Catastrophe or Social Control? The Alternatives for America," *Harper's Magazine*, June 1932, 117. There were a series of marches on Washington, DC by unemployed workers from large cities prior to the Bonus March in 1932. "Unemployed Hunger Marchers in Protest March on Washington," *The Pittsburgh Courier*, 12 December 1931, 2; "Jobless Army in Capital to Make Demands Today," *Los Angeles Times*, 7 December 1931, 1; and "Senate Hears Hunger Threat: Jobless Marchers' Leader Warns Committee," *Los Angeles Times*, 31 December 1931, 2.

[4] Niebuhr, "Catastrophe or Social Control?" 117.

[5] Norman Thomas, review of *Moral Man and Immoral Society*, by Reinhold Niebuhr, *The World Tomorrow*, 14 December 1932, 266.

Myles Horton, James Dombrowski, and Franz Daniel joined the SP during their time at UTS and in response to their experiences in New York
City. They were more than rank-and-file Socialist Party members. They
were leaders. They stood on street corners preaching the socialist gospel,
traveled to organize for the movement, and developed an increasingly radical vision for the future of human society. The world they witnessed in New
York City and elsewhere confirmed their suspicion about the immorality of
capitalism and its potential for inflicting unnecessary horrors on humanity.
With a stark social reality set before them, they found an explanation for
the crisis in their exposure to socialism and the writings of Karl Marx at
UTS. Socialism helped them explain the contradictions they witnessed in
New York City, and it was Marx who caught the attentions of their teachers
and mentors in New York City. Marxists pursued, in the words of Reinhold
Niebuhr, "the most rational possible social goal, that of equal justice."[6] In
Thomas's SP, they found a program and a solution.

UTS was an extraordinary place in the 1920s. It was an institution open
to free expression, experimentation, and political discovery. Students who
arrived at UTS found an environment in which socialism was an accepted
part of political and religious discussions. As liberalism and the social gospel
lost their appeal, radical ideas filled the vacuum. At a conference hosted by
UTS in 1926, forty clergymen trooped around Manhattan for meetings
with leaders of the Socialist Party, communists, anarchists, and members
of the Industrial Workers of the World (IWW). On their first stop, at the
Socialist Rand School of Social Science, they listened intently to Norman
Thomas, who, as a former minister, was cut from the same pious cloth as
his audience. Thomas instructed them on the joint mission of Christianity
and the labor movement, and, of course, on the practical accomplishments
of socialism.[7]

Thomas was not satisfied with a passive role for America's clergy.
He chastised Christian society before his very Christian audience, "You
cannot prove that any of the great improvements of society have been
brought about by preaching. It is through socialism and not through the
churches that our great social progress has been made." Then, perhaps
remembering his audience, he softened, "Christianity is doing something,

---

[6]Reinhold Niebuhr, *Moral Man and Immoral Society: A Study in Ethics and Politics*
(Charles Scribner's Sons, 1932), 171.

[7]"Churchmen Listen to Radical Talks: Theological Conferees Visit the Local Headquarters of Various Groups," *New York Times*, 4 June 1926.

but Christianity can do a lot more."[8] To round out his lecture, Thomas challenged his ecclesiastical congregation with a critical analysis of capitalism and outlined the possibilities of socialism:

Society is wasteful, unethical and provocative of war... We have plenty of power, tools and means today amply to feed and clothe the world with much less effort than we expend. The trouble is the production of wasteful luxuries, the waste of human energies in fields where co-ordination is needed. But how is co-ordination possible among industries where each manager thinks, not of the ways of developing natural resources, but of ways of bringing the largest income to his stockholders?[9]

The clergymen retained some skepticism, asking about "the failure of socialism to grow as rapidly [in the United States] as in Europe."[10] This episode reveals the extent to which the grounds for radical discussion at UTS were verdant, even prior to the Depression. If they remained unconvinced by Thomas, these church leaders were not closed off to discussions of the future, even if such discussions led in radical directions. The unraveling social world decreed that students and clergy find answers to the problems of capitalism.

Conservatism and revolt stood side-by-side at UTS. While radical leaders and faculty members stoked the intellectual fires of revolution, the Reverend Dr. Henry Sloane Coffin, theologically liberal in orientation, attempted to guide UTS away from the attractions of left radicalism, a task at which he failed.[11] Coffin was popular among the students—if seen as a bit stodgy in his political views and responses to radicalism at UTS.[12] Coffin had little to offer in the place of their burgeoning radicalism. His concern for the students' political choices deepened as they embraced left politics. In 1930, he cautioned students and faculty in a sermon, which failed to persuade many members of his young audience.[13] The subject

[8] Ibid.

[9] Ibid.

[10] Ibid.

[11] "Sees Church Peril If Liberals Lose: Dr. Coffin Warns of Dangers of Modernist Controversy in General Assembly," *New York Times*, 18 May 1925, 8.

[12] Berthe Daniel to Grossmama, 26–31 December 1929, Box 13, Folder 6, FDC.

[13] Professor Harry Ward—still the leading ethics teacher at Union—certainly would not have been convinced and did not change course politically despite the anxieties

of the sermon was accepting the "undesired inevitable."[14] Its arguments ran against the grain of his students' intellectual development and political proclivities. He began with a dry series of choices that "men" could make when confronted with the "undesired inevitable."

Coffin limited his range of options to five responses. Revolt, the first option, he thoroughly castigated. The other options were less relevant to his revulsion toward the growing radicalism of his students and ranged from a broad category that included drug use to "the stoic, or the red Indian—self-controlled endurance."[15] The final option, Coffin's preference, was an acceptance of the inevitability of God's will. "My father," said Coffin, quoting Jesus in the Christian Gospels, "if this cannot pass away, except I drink it, Thy will be done." Coffin's commentary came next: "His prayers were questions asked His wiser Father."[16] Here, Coffin, drew a paternalistic parallel between God and himself. At Union he was the wiser father whose benevolent plan students and faculty should accept. The parallel continued, "The curriculum of our life and death is mostly made up of required courses."[17] Coffin's argument for "acquiescence" to the world as it was, or rather as it was made by men like Coffin, made the Marx-reading youth in the audience even more suspicious of mainstream of Christian thought in the United States.[18] They questioned the premise that Christianity was meant to force men into obedience of an authority that considered its own interests above their own. Coffin had shaken their faith in the institutional churches.

Reinhold Niebuhr and Harry Ward, known as "the radicals" on UTS's faculty, offered an alternative faith.[19] Niebuhr, a member of the SP, connected his students to a burgeoning movement. One socialist student remembered UTS's important role in his political formation. "If I hadn't

---

voiced by Coffin. Reinhold Niebuhr, Union's other prominent political radical, was opposed to Coffin not only politically but also in theological terms. Niebuhr resisted any efforts to moderate his views or the views of his students, though he showed some sympathy for Coffin's position.

[14]"Dr. Coffin Urges Accepting Fate: Tells Congregation at Union Theological Chapel That Revolt Is Wrong," *New York Times*, 31 March 1930, 14.

[15]Ibid.

[16]Ibid.

[17]Ibid.

[18]Ibid.

[19]Berthe Daniel to Grossmama, 26–31 December 1929, Box 13, Folder 6, FDC.

gone to Union," he wrote decades later, "my world would be much smaller. I wouldn't have gotten to know faculty and student social activists and become involved in all the issues I didn't know existed."[20] The same student remembered long discussions about socialism among the students and faculty, Niebuhr's prominent affiliation with the SP, and the presence of Norman Thomas.[21] Another of Niebuhr's students, who spent Christmas with his professor in 1929, credited UTS with giving him "an opportunity to get first hand information of the workers' problems and their organizations." At Union, he said, "I became acquainted with many leaders. By the time I had finished my graduate work, I was convinced that I desired a more active role in the labor movement than I had hitherto contemplated..."[22] Niebuhr and UTS anchored the students to a new world of social engagement.

James Dombrowski, a Polish-American student from a middle-class family who had attended Emory, realized that much of the popular rhetoric about the egalitarian nature of the United States was patently, painfully false.[23] Harlem was the hardest hit by relief shortfalls. Hundreds of Harlem families struggled without adequate food. Those who could not afford to pay rent found little help.[24] The dire economic need in Harlem was not lost on James Dombrowski. He spent his free hours in late October 1930 speaking at a series of street corner meetings organized throughout Harlem by the SP in preparation for New York's elections in early November.[25] He witnessed Harlem's despair from atop his soapbox.[26]

[20] Myles Horton with Judith Kohl and Herbert Kohl, *The Long Haul: An Autobiography* (Teachers College Press, 1998), 36.

[21] Ibid., 35–36, 59.

[22] Franz Daniel, "Labor Experience," 1942–1943, Box 6, Folder 23, FDC; Berthe Daniel to Grossmama, 26–31 December 1929, Box 13, Folder 6, FDC.

[23] Frank T. Adams, *James A. Dombrowski: An America Heretic, 1897–1983* (University of Tennessee Press, 1992), 9, 24–25.

[24] "Needy Get 450 Tons of Food From City," *New York Times*, 27 November 1930, 1, 28.

[25] "Street Meetings," *The New Leader*, 25 October 1930, 3; "Vote Orderly Here; Few Are Arrested," *New York Times*, 5 November 1930, 7.

[26] For a survey of Harlem's woes during the Great Depression, see Cheryl Greenberg's *"Or Does It Explode?": Black Harlem in the Great Depression* (Oxford University Press, 1997).

Dombrowski had seen despair before and it crystallized his political commitments. In 1929, at the urging of Professor Harry Ward, Dombrowski had gone to Elizabethton in eastern Tennessee to learn about the textile strike that was unfolding in and around the rayon mills.[27] His "tour" through mill country "prompted only a depressed feeling a dark picture of the future." The trip bolstered Dombrowski's nascent commitment to a Marxist interpretation of social relations. He found no mention of the ongoing strike—what he called "a life-and-death struggle"—in the Elizabethton's newspaper. As Dombrowski was beginning to understand, the interests of the mill owners and the professional classes prohibited direct reference to the workers' struggles. He did find reference to a meeting, hosted by the Chamber of Commerce, on the topic of "the better enforcement of the law." The audience at the meeting, which Dombrowski attended, was made up of the Elizabethton's business and civil leaders, as well as clerks and shopkeepers. They spoke of doing violence to the striking workers, of machine guns, and referred to the strikers as an "unholy evil."[28]

Class interest shaped the discussions he had with Elizabethton's social elite. When Dombrowski spoke of a greater human interest at the meeting, members of the audience verbally threatened him. The following day he was arrested on a murder charge.[29] Dombrowski was released without charge after a short stay in jail. The experience was instructive. For Dombrowski, it was becoming clear that no arguments or appeals would restrain the capitalist class from defending the exploitation that fueled their wealth and power. A few months later, back in New York City, Dombrowski spoke about his experiences in Elizabethton at LID events hosted in Norman Thomas's home and at UTS.[30] Dombrowski was ensconced within the network of New York City's socialists.

In 1928, in the midst of New York's unemployment crisis, Franz Daniel had a revelation about his family's fortunes. The grandson of prosperous German immigrants, Daniel recognized his family's economic security was due, in large part, to an accident of geography. Fortuitously his

---

[27] Adams, *An America Heretic*, 29.

[28] James Dombrowski, "From a Mill-Town Jail," *The New Republic*, 2 October 1929, 171.

[29] Ibid., 172.

[30] Lawrence J. Rogin, "Students and Industry," *The New Leader*, 4 January 1930, 8.

grandparents had settled in Osceola, Missouri and not in New York City. In New York, Daniel met German immigrants who reminded him of his grandparents.[31] He imagined his own family trapped in a New York slum. "You were very wise and fortunate," Daniel wrote to his grandfather, "[that] you didn't stop in New York when you came to this country. I had in my parish here a good number of German and Irish people who came over about the same time you did. Practically all that they have ever seen is dark tenements and dirty streets."[32] His realizations became much starker as the Depression took its toll on New York City's working class.

Overwhelmed by the suffering he witnessed in New York City, Daniel spoke of "the unhappiness and misery" that confronted all who dwelled in the city, as if it was foul cloud of despair. For the socially conscious person, there was no escape from the economic crisis. He could not retreat to dinner parties or holiday festivities. Thoughts of privation lingered. Even if he wanted to escape, his conscience held sway. "There is so much suffering here," he wrote to his grandmother, "that I can't stand to stay around, and yet when I go away I feel that I am running from it."[33] Socialism was an antidote for this despair. It was also a loud declaration that marked a willingness to fight against capitalism's inadequacies. Franz Daniel joined the SP and the League for Industrial Democracy in 1928. He became a leader of the Morningside Heights Branch (MHB) until he was hired as a SP organizer in the summer of 1930 and sent to Philadelphia.[34]

Before he arrived at UTS in the fall of 1929, Myles Horton had read and thought more about socialism than his soon-to-be-comrades, Daniel and Dombrowski. Horton's commitment to socialism was formalized at UTS, where he joined the SP. In 1930, Horton traveled northwest from Manhattan to the Finger Lakes in Upstate New York. Along with two other socialist comrades, Horton was on a two-week campaign trip for Louis Waldman, the SP's candidate for governor. He witnessed the despair of the unemployed alongside the terror of still-employed workers who had to cope with the realities of speedup, wage cuts, and the threat of unemployment. Horton and his comrades found town after town ruled by one or two industries, few unions, and immigrant workers "segregated to [the] poorest

[31] Franz Daniel to Grosspapa, 12 September 1928, Box 14, Folder 18, FDC.
[32] Ibid.
[33] Franz Daniel to Grossmama, 23 December 1929, Box 14, Folder 18, FDC.
[34] Franz Daniel to Gerald Bonham, 2 March 1976, Box 15, Folder 2, FDC.

section" of town.[35] Employers paid misery wages. Yet, even in the most difficult of times, workers were bolstered by memories of past struggles and victories. One worker recollected, "some years ago, striking employees of the Columbian Rope Co. threatened the owner with death and he was so frightened that a few months later he did die."[36]

The trip through New York State helped Horton and his comrades recognize that the cause of the unemployment crisis was capitalism itself. The socialist trio witnessed a fundamental contradiction of capitalism—vast wealth, idle machines, and willing workers all sidelined in abject poverty. Capitalists employed simple logic as revenues fell. They fired workers, cut wages, and imposed productivity increases to stay competitive as prices were squeezed lower by an inability to consume. Both actions placed severe limits on capitalism's ability to reproduce itself effectively. Fewer workers labored for lower wages, further eroding effective demand. Andrew Steiger, one of Horton's comrades on the trip, wrote,

> In all the communities [we] visited there is a serious problem of finding employment to keep a majority of the population busy a majority of the time. Employers assume this to be desirable, yet the majority of the time they can only employ a minority of the available workmen and still produce more than enough goods to meet the current demand. All industries, even the Oneida Community Plate Co., a silverware factory, run by people nurtured in a Utopian-socialistic tradition, have had to not only reduce their working force from one-quarter to one-half but have also cut down the working day from six per week to three and four and five per week.[37]

Market imperatives and the prerogatives of private property kept machines idle, workers unemployed and hungry.[38] As they passed Utica, the socialist

---

[35] Andrew J. Steiger, "On Tour for Socialism," *The New Leader*, 27 September 1930, 4.

[36] Ibid.

[37] Ibid.

[38] Rapid technological advance (and the strain of forced productivity increases, the infamous "stretch-out" system) at the expense of employment, structural changes to the economy, and the collapse of buying power for the vast majority of workers fueled the crisis. There were predictions that a shift in technology at the expense of employment would, in short order, result in a much more serious crisis, or possibly herald an end to labor. See Michael A. Bernstein, "Why the Great Depression Was Great: Toward a New Understanding of the Interwar Economic Crisis in the United States," in *The Rise and*

trio saw abandoned farmsteads, a sign of migration to the cities. They also saw the "reduced… consumptive capacity of most people."[39]

Despite all of the despair, dereliction, and fear they encountered, the socialists did not lose hope. They were the troubadours of a solution. Horton had chased a solution to social ills for several years, and yet the remedy had been unknown to him before he discovered organized socialism. He had seen poverty that predated the Great Depression in the hills of his native Tennessee, the inadequacies of private charity, and the caprice of employers whose only concerns were keeping wages low and workers malleable.[40] Socialism offered a different world.

Once at UTC, Dombrowski, Daniels, and Horton refined their political consciousness within a local branch of the SP. Growing out from UTS's "gothic" campus, Morningside Heights, a neighborhood in Upper Manhattan, was the site of young socialists' radical awakenings.[41] It was home to one of the more energetic branches of the SP. The MHB grew quickly, and had, at its height in 1931, 180 members.[42] Friends, classmates, teachers, and Norman Thomas recruited talented potential leaders to the branch from among UTS's students. Dombrowski, who had been lured to UTS by Professor Harry Ward's ideas and encouragement, joined because his friends invited him into MHB.[43] Daniel enthusiastically participated in Norman Thomas's 1929 mayoral campaign in New York City, gaining Thomas's "trust and confidence."[44] Morningside Heights was, in the words of one writer for *The New Leader*, a "feeder-branch."[45] Talented young members were chosen from this branch to continue work on behalf of the SP, and its peripheral institutions, in other cities and regions. Daniel,

---

Fall of the New Deal Order, 1930–1980, ed. Steve Fraser and Gary Gerstle (Princeton University Press, 1989), 35–36, 39–40. On the "stretch out", see Landon R. Y. Storrs, *Civilizing Capitalism: The National Consumers' League, Women's Activism, and Labor Standards in the New Deal Era* (University of North Carolina Press, 2000), 65.

[39] Steiger, "On Tour for Socialism," 4.

[40] Horton, *The Long Haul*, 31.

[41] "The New Home of the Union Theological Seminary," *Outlook*, 10 December 1910, 802.

[42] Leon Gibson, "The Morningside Heights Branch," *The New Leader*, 10 February 1934, 2A–2B.

[43] Adams, *An America Heretic*, 40.

[44] Berthe Daniel to Grossmama, 26–31 December 1929, Box 13, Folder 6, FDC.

[45] Gibson, "The Morningside Heights Branch," 2A–2B.

who would become an important labor leader in a few years, was identified in this way and was hired as an organizer by the SP. Horton and J. B.
Matthews, who later worked for the House Un-American Activities Committee and investigated former members of the MHB, were also members.

The branch was lively, youthful, and confident. The energy of its young
members was captured by an observer who wrote that there was a belief
within the SP that it was "on the high road to becoming *the* revolutionary
working class party in the United States, and that in a very brief period
of time."[46] Confidence in the SP was also apparent in the massive organizing effort that led up to its election efforts. As the party expanded, so,
too, did the hopes and ambitions of its members.[47] In 1930, members
of the MHB, working with socialists from the Harlem Branch, staged an
impressive fundraising event at the Ambassador Theatre on 49th Street.
Funds from ticket sales were used to organize food for families suffering as
a result of the Depression and for "the establishment of a permanent free
employment and legal aid bureau." Two theatres had already promised to
use the potential bureau for hiring and at least one lawyer had volunteered
to offer legal services without charge through the new bureau. The acts for
the event included Adele and Fred Astaire, the Yiddish theatre sensation
Molly Picon, and Ginger Rogers.[48] To inaugurate the opening of the MHB
headquarters in the first month of 1932, members held a housewarming
dance for SP members from across New York City. It was part fundraising
event and part social gathering for the members.[49]

Guided by its members' personal experiences and by the encouragement of their mentors, the MHB fostered diverse political interests, including in international developments and affinities for the labor movement.
Those who read Norman Thomas's weekly column in *The New Leader* saw
his attacks on racism and lynch mobs, his repudiation of war reparations
for Germany—a punishment, Thomas argued, that was paid for by the

---

[46]Shachtman, "Right Face in the Socialist Party," *New International* (December
1934): 131.

[47]Bernard K. Johnpoll, *Pacifist's Progress: Norman Thomas and the Decline of American
Socialism* (Greenwood Press, 1970), 88; Seymour Martin Lipset and Gary Marks, *It
Didn't Happen Here: Why Socialism Failed in the United States* (Norton, 2000), 205.

[48]"Harlem-Morningside Socialists to Stage Gala Theatre Party," *The New Leader*, 13
December 1930, 2.

[49]"Morningside Heights Branch Will Hoof It," *The New Leader*, 30 January 1932,
4.

working class—and his opposition to US military and economic interven-tion in Latin America.[50] In addition to building the MHB, UTS students volunteered for labor organizing drives, participated in anti-imperialist demonstrations, and spoke on street corners.[51] They ventured out to hear to a lecture and discussion of the British Labour Party hosted by the League for Industrial Democracy, an educational organization aimed at college stu-dents and headed by Norman Thomas.[52] Labor's political strength in the United Kingdom bolstered hopes for socialism in the United States. They were also exposed to their socialist comrades' fears of a world that had given birth to new and repressive regimes. They came to view American politics through the prism of European politics. Editors and speakers com-pared "rightwing" leaders of the American Federation of Labor to fascist and Bolshevik dictators in their intolerance for dissent from the anointed path of whatever brand of autocracy they practiced.[53]

Manifesto to the Middle Class

Prominent left thinkers connected to UTS undertook an effort to organize the middle class and bring it into the socialist movement. These thinkers included Norman Thomas, Harry Ward, and Roger Baldwin, a noted radi-cal and director of the American Civil Liberties Union. Aided and encour-aged by propitious circumstances in New York City and conscious of their successes at UTS and in the MHB, they projected a new vision for orga-nizing among the professional middle class. The organizing missive to the middle class included specific instructions for the development of a pro-gram for young, middle-class radicals. The socialists who developed out of UTS and the MHB were an early effort to develop protégés who could work in the radical movement. Older radicals delegated responsibility for this program to Roger Baldwin, who had connections with Myles Horton and the other members of the socialist group at UTS and MHB.[54] The rea-

[50]Norman Thomas, "Timely Topics," *The New Leader*, 12 January 1929, 8.

[51]Horton, *The Long Haul*, 36–37; Adams, *An America Heretic*, 40–41, 43.

[52]"New York L.I.D. Chapter to Hear Strachey, Starr," *The New Leader*, 12 January 1929, 2; For a discussion of LID, see Robert Cohen, *When the Old Left Was Young: Student Radicals and America's First Mass Student Movement, 1929–1941* (Oxford University Press, 1993), 31–33.

[53]"Professor Dewey vs. Matthew Woll," *The New Leader*, 12 January 1929, 8.

[54]Harry F. Ward to Reinhold Niebuhr, 13 January 1931, Box 13, RNP.

son for a special program directed at young collegiate professionals spoke to the fear that "organizations like Bell Telephone Company are picking off the cream of the colleges and tying them in with the system."[55] The older radicals, recognizing the strategic brilliance of the capitalists, wished to do a little creaming of their own. They were keen to connect their mentees to organizations that could use their talents for "social transformation."[56] Some of the radical young professionals, such as Myles Horton, may have gotten a push and ultimately funding in order to "provide education for leaders in revolutionary change." The older radicals hoped that Horton and his fellows would create alternatives to existing programs, which tended to capitulate to the "practical measures" of the trade union movement.[57] They were keen to develop "training centers for young people" and cited "I.W.W. Schools" and "various Workers' Schools" as examples. They wanted to "get college students to help educate the workers and farmers."[58] It is hardly surprising that several of their protégés went on to help build an explicitly revolutionary school for workers.

Their missive was bold and more than a little quixotic; it was, however, meant to be a beginning. It was a start in that it represented a serious effort to both build a broad-based radical movement oriented to usher in a new social system, and also to collectively quantify the crisis in wider social terms. The mentors and teachers grasped for language to describe what they saw as "the end of an epoch."[59] In the early 1930s, radicals did not yet think in terms of "the Great Depression." This descriptor came later, though it had roots in the language used to describe the crisis. Rather, they described the crisis as an "unemployment situation," an "unemployment crisis," or more productively as a world economic crisis, which, under whatever designation, was hurting various components of the middle class either through the experience of unemployment or as a result of falling demand. Importantly, however, they did not approach the middle class in terms of an "unemployment crisis" alone but sought to put the crisis in the larger context of the history of capitalism.[60]

[55]"Meeting Notes," 31 December 1930, Box 13, RNP.
[56]Ibid.
[57]Ibid.
[58]Ibid.
[59]Ibid.
[60]Ibid.

Although their efforts to organize the working class had begun infor-
mally in the late 1920s, they were officially codified in January of 1931
in the "manifesto to the working class." Roger Baldwin; Harry Laidler,
a representative of Norman Thomas; Cedric Long; Scott Nearing; and
Harry Ward met on December 31, 1930, to discuss the potential for "en-
lightening and motivating the middle class."[61] Norman Thomas certainly
approved of the drafting of a manifesto to the middle classes, as Harry Laidler, his friend and comrade in the League for Industrial Democracy, was
present at its writing.[62] Thomas likely delegated this task to Laidler. Harry
Ward informed Reinhold Niebuhr of the event and solicited his opinions by
mail.[63] Niebuhr took a negative view of the potential of middle-class liberalism and social reform. During this period, he argued that the appeal of class
interest was too great to foster cooperation across social groups. The tension between the urgency of capitalism's crisis and Niebuhr's understanding
of the irreconcilable nature of class interests may have been resolved, tem-
porarily, in the necessity for action. The group's language reveals a focus
on middle-class professionals, which may have eased some of Niebuhr's
doubts, as he extended much of his criticism to those engaged directly in
capitalist pursuits.[64]

The group that met to organize the middle class was concerned with how
to divide their movement's limited economic resources and time. Emphasis
could be placed on organizing among the middle class. It could be dedicated to a program directed at the working class, or they could split their
resources between the two groups.[65] The group voiced arguments to support each position, but the weight of the discussion emphasized a program
to organize among the middle class. They cited recent British history as
an example of the failure of the working class, despite the motivation of

[61]"Meeting Notes," 31 December 1930, Box 13, RNP.

[62]Robert Cohen, *When the Old Left Was Young: Student Radicals and America's First
Mass Student Movement, 1929–1941* (Oxford University Press, 1993), 31.

[63]"Meeting Notes," 31 December 1930, Box 13, RNP; Harry F. Ward to Reinhold
Niebuhr, 13 January 1931, Box 13, RNP.

[64]Niebuhr's thinking on the middle class would harden. He viewed the petty-
bourgeoisie as particularly prone to reaction, and, in general, viewed even wealthy capitalists as not far removed from a petty-bourgeois ideology. See Niebuhr's "Pawns for
Fascism—Our Lower Middle Class," *The American Scholar* 6, no. 2 (Spring 1937),
145–152.

[65]"Meeting Notes," 31 December 1930, Box 13, RNP.

economic depression, to move toward revolution. One unnamed partici-
pant denounced the middle class as reactionary and the working class as
hopeless. Certain that capitalism would collapse, they concluded that "the
present need is to detach as many of the middle class as possible from the
capitalist psychology and so lessen their resistance to a new order."[66] This
detachment from "capitalist psychology" had happened in Niebuhr's and
Ward's classes at UTS, and Norman Thomas had experienced it as young,
college-educated professionals flowed into the ranks of the SP.

They argued that the best way to appeal to the middle class—and here
they betrayed their penchant for the rational, educational approach to organizing—was "by demonstrating through the factual method the break-
down of capitalism." They acknowledged the success of the unemployment crisis, and their own successes in the classroom, in already creating a
"minority" of middle-class professionals "ready to be educated in the values and initial steps of a new order."[67] To further their goals, the group
drafted a manifesto to the middle class, which was to be released to the
public. The fact that the authors of the document constituted a coherent
group, which they called "a central planning group," was to be hidden
from the public. They were eager to keep the existence of the group "un-
noticed" because they wished "to avoid resentment and antagonism" of
some unnamed group.[68] The manifesto was to be issued and signed by
other people. They were unsure about whether or not they would include
their own names.

The manifesto, developed in early 1931, took shape as an explicit effort
to organize the middle class, by whom the radical mentors and teachers
meant the professional classes, around the issue of unemployment and radical economic policies. It reflected their conceptions of middle-class ideals,
including an acknowledgment of the middle class's supposed penchant for
rationalization and efficiency, to which the radicals hoped to appeal. The
epistle also included a few notes of laudatory recognition that reveal why
the older radicals wanted to appeal to the middle classes. There was, for
instance, an acknowledgment of the middle class's "technical" knowledge
and its broader social responsibility as the arbiter of this expertise.[69] They

[66] Ibid.
[67] Ibid.
[68] Ibid.
[69] "To the Middle Class," January 1931, Box 13, RNP.

directly appealed to the middle class, for whom security was quickly evap-orating, as important and necessary allies for the working class and small-holders in a cooperative society.[70] They also acknowledged that money from the middle class would finance new protest movements. While recog-nizing the value of organizing the middle class, their letter "to the middle class" read, at times, more like an ultimatum than an invitation to join the struggle.[71] One plank included the phasing out of "property rights by destroying their prestige through propaganda, and their legal power through legislation."[72] Another plank told the middle class to "abandon capitalistic psychology and standards of value." It gave no clear path to achieve this goal beyond the widespread cooperation of the middle class, whose values were to be cast aside. Education, not violence, was the means by which they hoped to radicalize the middle class and bring them into the socialist movement.[73]

The teachers and mentors regarded capitalism as responsible for a crisis in which millions were unemployed despite industry's capacity to provide them with work, goods, and livelihoods. They shared Niebuhr's view that capitalism had floundered and wanted to convey this message to the middle class. They wanted the middle class to "recognize, proclaim, and demon-strate the impossibility of capitalism."[74] Their main argument and appeal to the middle classes was put forward on the grounds that capitalism was inefficient and a better system could be organized using modern techno-logical advances and sound management and planning. The manifesto was filled with arguments for abandoning capitalism in favor of a system not riddled with "economic inefficiency."[75] They identified lack of centralized planning, dictated by the laissez-faire economic policy of the government, as a leading cause of the crisis, and an inhibitor to effective relief and recov-ery. The absence of systematic planning prevented appropriate distribution of wealth and ensured that the weight of relief was not placed upon those

---

[70] Ibid.

[71] "Meeting Notes," 31 December 1930, Box 13, RNP; "To the Middle Class," Jan-uary 1931, Box 13, RNP.

[72] "To the Middle Class," January 1931, Box 13, RNP.

[73] "Meeting Notes," 31 December 1930, Box 13, RNP.

[74] Ibid.

[75] Ibid.

who most benefited from the exploitation of labor.[76] They hoped that a managerial middle class would seize the moment and help to enforce much-desired rationality onto an economic system that increasingly failed to fulfill its social functions. They appealed to the middle classes on ethical grounds as well; capitalism was an exploitative system that did harm, though this appeal was secondary.

The absence of Christianity or a well-developed moral appeal in the manifesto to the middle class suggests that religion was less central during the early organizing of the early 1930s. Rationalism, efficiency, and education were at the center of their program. The program for the middle class was a radical mélange for the collegian, or, perhaps, for an accountant. Capitalism, the older radicals argued, was bad for society's account books. The misdistribution of wealth lay at the heart of this inefficiency. Capitalism soaked up wealth made through toil—"by hand or brain"—and left "the good life" beyond the reaches of "the middle class let alone the wage earners and farmers." Given that theologians' hands lay behind the drafting pen of these ideas, it is surprising that so little is made of capitalism's underdeveloped moral attitudes. Even the ethical claims made by older radicals who appealed to the middle class were framed in terms of efficiency rather than standing solely on the grounds of what is "good" or "just." "The ethical nature of capitalism[,] its exploiting power, its insistence upon inequality, is revealed even in the distribution of the costs of relief," they wrote. This is capitalism rendered unethical by lack of efficiency, by lack of economy. This was a high modernist's anti-capitalism. The surety of the historical claims confirms this point. "The general recognition that something is wrong with capitalism," the group concluded, "marks the end of an epoch—capitalism has passed its peak in economic and cultural capacity but not in power to exploit and coerce."[77] While recognizing the historical inevitability of capitalism's demise, the older radicals were not wont to sit quietly as suffering engulfed their communities. They envisioned—through the favorite tool of the socialist, education—a revolutionary change in social organization brought about, in part, by "the middle class as a powerful technical group." While the crux of their argument was calculated rationalism, there was a profound humanity in their engagement with history. They wanted to "lessen the shock of change." These were valiant

[76]Ibid.
[77]Ibid.

thinkers, humanitarians. Their goal was not unending class struggle but "a classless society," and their means for accomplishing this end were peaceful and included propaganda, legislation, the extension of civil liberties, and a cessation of the middle-class crusade to reform a "backwards" working class.[78]

Minor disagreements over content and possibility were easily overcome. While the UTS students and MHB Socialists were busy with their studies, debates, and branch activities, the older men drafted a manifesto for the middle classes, which included a section dedicated to developing the radical youth.[79] Their thinking on the middle class was equivocal; they both denounced the ideology of the middle class, and made appeals to those whose ideology they denounced. This ambiguity owed much to the class statuses of Niebuhr, Thomas, Ward, and Baldwin. They had all brought components of middle-class identity into their efforts, while at the same time rejecting the "educational and purely moral means" for social suasion advocated by middle-class reformers.[80] They turned their fiery rhetoric and attention to those they understood most, the group to which they belonged.

REINHOLD NIEBUHR'S PESSIMISTIC RADICALISM

Niebuhr incorporated ideas about revolution, history, and class struggle from Marx into his works throughout the 1930s. For Niebuhr, it was the ineluctability of class interest that made coercion and violence a political reality. His ideas and teaching in the 1930s reveal the intellectual importance of Marx in that decade, and give clues as to which ideas percolated among the radicals at UTS. Despite incorporating much of Marx's thought into his own analysis, Niebuhr included Marx in the pantheon of utopian thinkers. Niebuhr also rejected the "romantic ideas of the educationalists," by whom he meant the non-radical progressives, and embraced the centrality of class struggle in human societies.

---

[78] Ibid.

[79] Harry Ward to Reinhold Niebuhr, 13 January 1931, Box 13, RNP.

[80] Reinhold Niebuhr, "Is Peace or Justice the Goal?" *The World Tomorrow*, 21 September 1932, 276; Duke, *In the Trenches with Jesus and Marx*, 3–8; Travis Hoke, "Red Rainbow: Describing Roger N. Baldwin," *The North American Review* (November 1932), 431; and Gregory, *Norman Thomas*, 11.

To replace the Enlightenment vision of ever-greater rationality and civic advance, Niebuhr argued that class struggle, which entailed the use of power to achieve a class-interested end, resulted in violence and social upheaval. In the context of Niebuhr's conception of class struggle, his students learned about strikes and other "covert" uses of coercion. Niebuhr argued that these were more productive forms of political action than the utopianism of the liberal "educationalists." His students also learned about the "communist doctrine" of violence, as Niebuhr explained why revolution had been necessary in Russia. Niebuhr used the word "inevitability" to describe violence in Russia, and his references to economic determinism explain why he thought revolution had been unavoidable. He agreed that Russia, failing to advance toward modern capitalism, lacked democratic institutions, which might have allowed the workers to seize control of the state without resorting to violence. Instead, the economic conditions in the Russian Empire made violence necessary—or perhaps, drawing on Niebuhr's notion of class struggle, it was the "intransigent privileged communities" who in their drive to maintain dominance exacerbated social conflict to the point of violence. Niebuhr was sure to remind his students that violence had limitations, and his students were keen to establish themselves as realistic thinkers, non-utopians. From Niebuhr's perspective, however, his students retained much of the utopian taint that he was quick to critique.[81] This was one of the reasons that he rejected their offer to become leader of their left-wing faction, what would become the Revolutionary Policy Committee, within the SP.

Niebuhr's attraction to socialism was built upon his desire to limit what he saw as the inextricable "brutality of life." If utopia represented a total impossibility for Niebuhr, the mitigation of suffering remained his motivation for socialist action. Reinhold Niebuhr, a young professor of just thirty-six years when he took up his post at UTS in 1928, agonized alongside his students, as he participated in a society that operated in contravention of human welfare. Niebuhr was busy preparing for married life in late 1931. This meant finding an apartment for the family he envisioned. Despite the economic crisis, Niebuhr struggled to find an affordable apartment that met his requirements. When he was able to find a suitable home, Niebuhr was aware that his good fortune stemmed from the acute distress of another. "Just had a call from the Columbia University Residence Bureau

---

[81] Reinhold Niebuhr, "Ethics for Social Change," 16 July 1931, Box 57, RNP.

offering me a nice four room studio apartment on 115th street," he wrote, "It sounds very good and I am going over to see it this afternoon." The vacancy was a product of the Depression. "The poor mother and daughter," Niebuhr reported, "are being driven out by the daughter losing her job. It's rather terrible to gain something at other peoples' expense like that." "I have of late grown quite morbid over the terrible brutality of life," he admitted, "it seems to me that brutality is a kind of inevitable part of life and that about all we can do is to reduce it to a minimum without abolishing it."[82] Niebuhr expressed the desperation of the Depression and his deep pessimism, a mood not shared by his best students, in a letter to Ursula Keppel-Compton, his fiancé: "The world situation seems to be so terrible that I have special difficulty in speaking about anything because it seems so futile trying to awaken America before it is too late. We will probably skate to our doom and never know what happened."[83] Niebuhr's pessimism and sense that humanity was forced into its misanthropy shaped his 1934 study *Moral Man Immoral Society.*

Niebuhr was the moral man trapped by a social system that necessitated immorality. The mother and daughter thrown out of their home by lack of work must have lingered in his mind as an example of the dichotomy that shaped his book. It was a moment that could have encompassed, in personal experience, the thesis of *Moral Man and Immoral Society*: "man as an individual, has developed ethical aspirations, ethical codes, and even ethical practices which are fairly adequate. He has not been able to extend them to society."[84] This was confirmed by his experiences throughout the Depression. Niebuhr's less fortunate friends pleaded with him for help. In late 1931, Reinhold Niebuhr again wrote Ursula Keppel-Compton. He told her, "An old newspaper friend came into borrow money. The misery of this town [New York City] is terrible."[85] He meant it. The terror and

[82] Reinhold Niebuhr to Ursula Niebuhr, 24 November 1931, Box 58, Reinhold Niebuhr Papers [RNP], Manuscript Division, Library of Congress, Washington, DC Reinhold Niebuhr sent two letters to his future wife on this date. This is from the second letter written on that date.

[83] Ursula Niebuhr to John and Alice Herling, 7 January 1986, Box 63, RNP. Ursula Niebuhr quotes Reinhold Niebuhr's letter of 24 November 1931.

[84] Norman Thomas, review of *Moral Man and Immoral Society*, by Reinhold Niebuhr, *The World Tomorrow*, 14 December 1932, 265.

[85] Ursula Niebuhr to John and Alice Herling, 7 January 1986, Box 63, RNP. Ursula Niebuhr quotes Reinhold Niebuhr's letter of 22 November 1931.

dread of the Great Depression descended on Niebuhr. He felt helpless, as if the world was teetering on the edge of a precipice ready to plunge into ruin and the end of civil society. A sense of the "terrible" pervaded his work during this period.

And yet, Niebuhr translated his angst, terror, and sense of helplessness into an intellectually stimulating, critical environment to the benefit of his students. He taught with an energetic passion that lit a fire in the hearts and minds of his students. King Gordon, a Canadian student who would co-author the 1933 Regina Manifesto of the Cooperative Commonwealth Federation, remembered walking into the Common Room at UTS to find a coterie of students, including the intellectually pugnacious Myles Horton, arrayed around Reinhold Niebuhr. Gordon encountered an intense debate punctuated with laughter and shrouded in tobacco smoke. He described these conversations, in which he often participated, as "intense, vivid, and exciting."[86]

The radical students had little choice but to gravitate toward Niebuhr and Harry Ward. UTS's other faculty members inspired little political confidence. If any action put Niebuhr's pessimism at rest, it was the willingness of his students to sacrifice what little they had for others: "We have just had our campaign for unemployment. Most of the students are so aroused by the sorry state of the unemployed that they gave more than last year, some going on a more meager diet to do it."[87] Niebuhr's and his students' animosity was directed at the faculty of a seminary who gave as if they were miserly capitalists rather than Christian teachers: "Meanwhile the professors gave less than last year though their salaries are worth 20% more than two years ago. It makes some of the students quite cynical. Students with meager incomes of $1,000 per year give $25 and professors with incomes of $8,000 give $35 and $50 at the most."[88] Niebuhr and Ward, as well as their students, were radicals in the academy of the 1930s and knew it: "When I think of [the professors' unwillingness to give] I feel like giving up all pretension of being a scholar. I never will be anyway and I don't like the

---

[86] J. King Gordon, "Reinhold Niebuhr: The Portrait of a Christian Realist," unpublished paper, June 1971. Box 48, RNP, 2–3. For an account of Gordon's role in the CCF's history, see Eileen Janzen, *Growing to One World: The Life of J. King Gordon* (McGill-Queen's University Press, 2013).

[87] Reinhold Niebuhr to Ursula Niebuhr, 3 November 1931, Box 58, RNP.

[88] Ibid.

lack of sensitivity of scholars to the world around them."[89] Niebuhr was in a radical mood, rejecting the pretensions of the academy and thinking about the impending collapse of capitalism.

Given his animosity toward most of UTS's faculty, Niebuhr turned to the students, cultivating close relationships with radicals. He singled out a few outstanding young socialists. This group included James Dombrowski, who was Niebuhr's walking partner. On one evening in the fall of 1931, Niebuhr went looking for Dombrowski to "see whether Jim would take a walk with me."[90] When he arrived at Dombrowski's room, he found a number of students and visitors engaged in discussion over tea. He joined their discussion.[91] Niebuhr also regularly supped with his favorite students.[92] King Gordon remembered the community they built in a letter to Ursula Niebuhr: "Jim's [James Dombrowski] passing brought back so many memories—you, Reinie, Myles, Zilla, Franz, K.—and it was something more than nostalgia for the struggle and faith and hope continue."[93] Niebuhr provoked admiration from the students. Franz Daniel's sister reported that he "adored" Niebuhr.[94]

Niebuhr was developing the ideas in *Moral Man and Immoral Society* at a time when young Socialists including Myles Horton, Franz Daniel, James Dombrowski, and other notable students were in his classes. Discussions of the material that would become *Moral Man* made up much of their academic life. King Gordon recalled that "what we were getting in Niebuhr's Christian Ethics course, in his sermons, in the dialogue in the Common Room and in weekly open-house evenings in his apartment on Claremont Avenue, was the unedited material out of which *Moral Man and Immoral Society* was being fashioned."[95] Whether or not they were able to understand and fully appreciate the tensions that emanated from Niebuhr's thought remains an open question. They extracted from Niebuhr's work what they found compelling and disregarded what they did not. In Niebuhr

[89] Ibid.

[90] Reinhold Niebuhr to Ursula Niebuhr, 18 October 1931, Box 58, RNP.

[91] Ibid.

[92] Ibid.

[93] J. King Gordon to Ursula Niebuhr, 1983, Box 48, RNP.

[94] Berthe Daniel to Grossmama, 26–31 December 1929, Box 13, Folder 6, FDC.

[95] J. King Gordon, "Reinhold Niebuhr: The Portrait of a Christian Realist," Unpublished Paper, June 1971, Box 48, RNP, 10.

they had found a paradoxical source of encouragement and dispiritedness. They were certain enough of Niebuhr to ask him to lead their faction in the Socialist Party. Niebuhr declined, of course.[96]

While Niebuhr had his doubts about the future of civilization—bourgeois or socialist—his students were less restrained by pessimism, even if they grew cynical about the piety and practices of their Christian teachers. Their ideas turned on a certainty about the finality of capitalism's looming end, which they had gleaned, in part, from Niebuhr's lectures and from their participation in socialist education programs. Their radical fire for social justice was a crusading spirit passed on from Norman Thomas. Their hope in the Soviet experiment, which they saw as a troubled potential ally against economic and social disintegration, derived from Harry Ward's own escalating appreciation of the Soviet Union's economy.[97] Ward, who had his roots in English Methodism's revival culture and the class conflicts present between lay preachers and more educated and officious clergymen, was closest to Dombrowski, who traveled to the Soviet Union as part of a European tour in 1932.[98]

Niebuhr's attraction to Marxism has been denied or overqualified by historians and by his former students, who were ready to protect the prophet-of-realism's reputation against the stigma of Marxism that intensified during the Cold War. For Niebuhr's student King Gordon, this debate turned on the connotations that Marxism had accumulated. Writing in the 1970s, Gordon argued, "it would be quite wrong to describe Niebuhr as a Marxist in the accepted sense of commitment to a dogmatic interpretation of socio-political structure and to the inevitable revolutionary process through which the structure will be destroyed and replaced by another."[99] In this analysis, Gordon effectively precludes Niebuhr's democratic socialist orientation developed, in part, from Marxian insights. As if to firm up his argument, Gordon concludes: "moreover, he had an active following in the churches, many of whom were readers of *Radical Religion* and members

---

[96]Reinhold Niebuhr to Ursula Niebuhr, 15 July 1933, Box 58, RNP.

[97]David Nelson Duke, *In the Trenches with Jesus and Marx: Harry F. Ward and the Struggle for Social Justice* (University of Alabama Press, 2003), 152.

[98]Duke, *In the Trenches*, 9, 149–150.; Adams, *An American Heretic*, 46–48.

[99]J. King Gordon, review of *Reinhold Niebuhr: A Political Account*, by Paul Merkley, Unpublished, February 1976, Box 48, RNP, 5–6.

of the Fellowship of Socialist Christians."[100] Niebuhr viewed Christianity and a certain type of Marxism as two manifestations of the same social phenomenon. Gordon refused to acknowledge the complexities of Marxism and place his teacher and friend within this heterogeneous intellectual tradition. Niebuhr was no communist—but as a democratic socialist, he owed much of his analysis in the 1930s to a Marxian intellectual mood.

Niebuhr's Marxism was of a variegated variety. As he shifted his historical or political focus, his attention to Marxism shifted. He occasionally took a long view of the struggle—a not fully developed idea of a bourgeois future akin to Arno Mayer's sophisticated Marxist reading of the seemingly implacable staying power of the European "old regime."[101] Niebuhr thought that fascism might be the tool through which the bourgeoisie held onto their power, but regarded this as ultimately impermanent given fascism's inability to cure the "two basic defects of capitalism, inequality of consumption and international anarchy."[102] Yet, the fear of fascism in the United States did occupy Niebuhr's thoughts. It would, in turn, be easy for his students who organized in the South to see and experience the basic outline of an American fascism. Niebuhr thought that the United States would be particularly prone to fascism. He argued that the lack of an American "old regime" made for particularly dangerous bourgeoisie arrivistes.[103] In envying the supposedly steady hand of the European aristocracy's noblesse oblige as a social palliative, Niebuhr revealed himself to be a very unorthodox Marxist. His categories were roughly Marxist, even if his views were of an analytical "Marxism from above," or, rather, Marxism viewed sideways—from a distance. He saw "the revolution" as an open question full of tensions and potential terrors. Niebuhr took a moral and political position, and yet, despite his socialist activities, it was qualified and never found concrete expression within the world that he was so keen to observe and lament. His socialist politics were tinged with a fatalistic appraisal of humanity: "I feel in a very misanthropic mood for some reason or other and morbidly contemplate on the evils of the human race and

[100] Ibid.

[101] Arno Mayer, *The Persistence of the Old Regime: Europe to the Great War* (Pantheon, 1981), 4; Niebuhr, "After Capitalism—What?" 203–204. This source can also be found in the Box 56, RNP.

[102] Niebuhr, "After Capitalism—What?" 203–204.

[103] Reinhold Niebuhr, "Catastrophe or Social Control? The Alternatives for America," *Harper's Magazine*, June 1932, 117.

wishing among other things that our past had been brighter and not so full of the proof of the pettiness of human nature."[104] His dim view of human nature prevented him from committing the error of his students: accepting rank-and-file utopianism. He was not only skeptical of the historical power of the proletariat to burst the dam of accumulating human horrors forever; he also rejected the very idea of such "absolutes."[105]

Niebuhr argued—utilizing his understanding of Marxist theory—that capitalism was dying.[106] Niebuhr was not wrong. The sort of capitalism that he and his students had known was to die; first through the inauguration of the New Deal and then through a period of red-hot production and expansion of the state's powers associated with the Second World War. In 1933, Reinhold Niebuhr's introduction to an essay in *The World Tomorrow* reflected the sentiment of many radicals caught up in the desperation of the Great Depression. "The following analysis of American social and political conditions," he told readers, "is written on the assumption that capitalism is dying and with the conviction that it ought to die." For Niebuhr, capitalism was dying as a result of its own contradictions. He argued that capitalism could not "support the necessities of an industrial system that requires mass production for its maintenance..." Nor, he explained, could it "make the wealth created by modern technology available to all who participate in the productive process on terms of justice." Niebuhr speculated that capitalism could "perish in another world war" or that it might fall like a house of cards, as the system of credit, stretched to its limits, collapsed. Niebuhr was sure that "capitalism will not reform itself from within." Thus, his rejection of liberalism took on a revolutionary character between 1933 and 1934, a rejection his students seized on when they began to formulate a

---

[104] Reinhold Niebuhr to Ursula Niebuhr, 15 July 1933, Box 58, RNP.

[105] Reinhold Niebuhr, "Let Liberal Churches Stop Fooling Themselves!" *The Christian Century*, 25 March 1931, 683.

[106] For works that wrestle with Niebuhr's Marxist commitments, see Larry Rasmussen, "A Few Facets of Niebuhr's Thought," in *Reinhold Niebuhr: Theologian of Public Life* (Minneapolis: Fortress Press, 1991), 35–35; Ronald H. Stone, *Professor Reinhold Niebuhr: Mentor to the Twentieth Century* (John Knox Press, 1992), 88–89; and Charles McDaniel, *God & Money: The Moral Challenge of Capitalism* (Rowman & Littlefield, 2007), 191–192. McDaniel effectively sets out the debate on Niebuhr's commitment to Marxism in this section: "That Niebuhr warmed to the economic theories of Karl Marx early in the 1930s is unquestioned; however, the extent to which he courted Marxist ideas is the subject of much debate." Paul Merkley, *Reinhold Niebuhr: A Political Account* (McGill-Queen's Press, 1975).

radical caucus within the SP, the Revolutionary Policy Committee. Drawing directly from a Marxian historical analysis, Niebuhr concluded, "there is nothing in history to support the thesis that a dominant class ever yields its position or privileges in society because its rule has been convicted of ineptness or injustices." For Niebuhr, class conflict shaped social life. In a world wrought with class interest, reform proved elusive.[107]

As such, Niebuhr condemned reformers, referring to them as "those who still regard [reform] as possible." He continued by arguing that they were "rationalists and moralists who have only a slight understanding of the stubborn inertia and blindness of collective egoism." He regarded global liberalism—efforts to salvage the social system undertaken by those who considered themselves to be rational and moral—to be a "spent force." In this vein, he regarded Roosevelt's efforts to be impossible and the efforts of those liberals to the left of Roosevelt as "equally futile," "a diluted socialism coated with liberalism [undertaken] in the hope that his aversion to bitter pills will thus be circumvented." From Niebuhr's position liberal reform to save capitalism was an absurdity. Niebuhr saw the policies advocated by Roosevelt and the progressive Democrats and Republicans as well-intentioned but ultimately ineffective. Niebuhr admired their intentions and basic humaneness, which he saw as a vital component of the new society and something that would have to be contested rather than develop automatically.[108]

Niebuhr was also concerned about the possibility of the "common ruin of the contending classes" and argued that much depended upon "the intelligence of [the] dominant group," which he saw as determining the future. Niebuhr feared that the "dominant group" would not yield power, but would "defend its entrenched positions so uncompromisingly that an orderly retreat becomes impossible and a disorderly rout envelops the whole of society in chaos."[109] Niebuhr's major critique of the progressive alternative, including his favorite intellectual to pillory, John Dewey, was that it tended to have an "optimistic estimate of human nature."[110] Niebuhr held little hope that liberals would be able to adequately defend against

---

[107] Reinhold Niebuhr, "After Capitalism—What?" *The World Tomorrow*, 1 March 1933, 203–204.

[108] Ibid.

[109] Karl Marx and Friedrich Engels, *Communist Manifesto* (Rand School of Social Sciences, 1919), 12; Reinhold Niebuhr, "After Capitalism—What?" 203–204.

[110] Niebuhr, "After Capitalism—What?" 203–204.

fascism, which he came to view as "a practical certainty in every Western nature."[111]

A non-doctrinaire Marxism—which included an emphasis on the socially constitutive function of the class struggle—was a dominant element in Niebuhr's thought. It was, however, always in tension with other ideas that disrupted it and ensured that it remained non-doctrinaire. Niebuhr's ideas were shaped by the historical moment in which he operated, but also by a fatalistic view of humanity. Niebuhr, then, vacillated. He held that capitalism had failed; it was dying. Its replacement was inevitable—dictated by history. His students took up this prognosis. Yet for Niebuhr, the idea that it would be replaced with a more just system was less inevitable and very much open to the vagaries of human behavior. Niebuhr's radical students broke with him on this point. Niebuhr had an angst-filled vision of the future. His students maintained a much greater certainty about a fixed collective future that would unfold out of the crises of the 1930s. The Depression, Niebuhr, and the Socialist Party forged the young socialists' politics around a set of radical concerns. They took his ideas, mixed them with the views of their other mentors, including those of Norman Thomas, and produced their own program for the present and vision for the future.

Thomas and Niebuhr in Dialogue

While recognizing the necessity of exorcizing "the sentimentalists, the romanticists, the believers in panacea," Norman Thomas thought that Niebuhr's pessimism went too far. "The net impression of the book [*Moral Man and Immoral Society*] upon me," Thomas explained, "was a degree of defeatism which I not believe the author intends."[112] Thomas, who lacked Niebuhr's predilection for doom, envisaged a more certain path forward for the socialist movement, which was, in his view, capable of avoiding Niebuhr's predicted fanaticism. As Thomas saw it, socialism was the responsible representative of the Western democratic tradition in the face of a reactionary bourgeoisie and powerful fascist movements. Thomas was less interested in Marxist abstractions than Niebuhr. Thomas preferred to ruminate on the "genuine working class solidarity and idealism which inspired the unsophisticated Knights of Labor movement, and later,

---

[111] Ibid.

[112] Thomas, review of *Moral Man and Immoral Society*, 265.

incarnate in the great Gene Debs, raised the American Railway Union to such power."[113]

Radical young intellectuals were caught between Niebuhr and Thomas. Niebuhr had convinced them that capitalism was doomed and that fascism was rising to replace it. They also embraced Thomas's optimism about "genuine working class solidarity and idealism" and gravitated toward the labor movement as a space to experience and foster their idyllic view of the working class. In addition to demonstrating what came of efforts to organize the professional class, the history of the Revolutionary Policy Committee reveals these tensions within the radical left during the 1930s.

If convinced by Niebuhr's certainty that capitalism was in the midst of its final crisis, his socialist radical students were unmoved by Niebuhr's sharpest critiques of and his warnings about the radical project, which were often wrapped up in a contradictory attitude. The attitude is best captured in the final lines of Niebuhr's *Moral Man and Immoral Society* published in 1932:

> Yet there is beauty in our tragedy. We are, at least, rid of some of our illusions. We can no longer buy the highest satisfactions of the individual life at the expense of social injustice. [...] In the task of that redemption the most effective agents will be men who have substituted some new illusions for the abandoned ones. The most important of these illusions is that the collective life of mankind can achieve perfect justice. It is a very valuable illusion for the moment; for justice cannot be approximated if the hope of its perfect realization does not generate a sublime madness in the soul. Nothing but such madness will do battle with the malignant power and 'spiritual wickedness in high places.' The illusion is dangerous because it encourages terrible fanaticisms. It must therefore be brought under the control of reason. One can only hope that reason will not destroy it before its work is done.[114]

The agents of social change had grasped hold of new illusions, which Niebuhr held to be essential components in a social shift toward a fractured and incomplete form of justice, that were also deeply problematic. Niebuhr saw the inherent dangers present in the new illusions. Fanaticism could be taken too far and used to justify excesses that went against the grain of a humane and democratic society. He was concerned with the implica-

---

[113]Ibid.

[114]Niebuhr, *Moral Man and Immoral Society*, 277.

tions of a utopian vision of the world in which "perfect justice" was seen as attainable. For Niebuhr the new illusions were those of a political left committed to "justice through revolution."[115] He saw this as a morally defensible position.[116] The tensions between the necessity of "new illusions" and the dangers they presented were at the core of Niebuhr's intervention. They were impossible to resolve intellectually. They had to be worked out through the historical process. Niebuhr was committed to finding a way to limit the power of the "new illusions," a power that in Niebuhr's words originated in "the world depression and the consequent misery and insecurity of millions of workers in every land, and finally the dramatic success of the Russian Revolution, all these factors have made the despised political philosophy of rebellious helots, the great promise and the great peril of the political life of the Western world."[117] Niebuhr's understanding of the potential peril inherent in a mass movement driven by sincere belief kept him from, in the words of Norman Thomas, "completely accepting a Leninistic version of Marx."[118]

Thus, the moment they found themselves in, the early 1930s, seemed to offer little hope of a proletarian uprising. For Thomas, then, the organization of the middle-class professional, the educated thoughtful man who might shape policy, was also a vital tool in building a socialist future. Thomas was particularly concerned with Niebuhr's ahistorical, "oversimplification" of the "American proletariat."[119] Niebuhr's acceptance of the "revolutionary role" of the proletariat, Thomas admitted, might be prescient. For Thomas, however, writing before the surge of labor organizing and revolt, this argument lacked a vitality of fact. Raymond Williams once wrote that Marxism in the 1930s was limited by its certitude, trapped in the horizons of its historical moment. This—"the very thing which at the time must have seemed to guarantee its sense of reality"—limited its appeal beyond the decade.[120] Many thinkers, including Niebuhr, proved to be wrong

---

[115] Niebuhr dedicated a chapter in *Moral Man and Immoral Society* to those who held these "new illusions." The chapter is titled, "Justice Through Revolution."

[116] Niebuhr, *Moral Man and Immoral Society*, 170.

[117] Ibid., 169.

[118] Norman Thomas, review of *Moral Man and Immoral Society*, by Reinhold Niebuhr, *The World Tomorrow*, 14 December 1932, 267.

[119] Ibid., 267.

[120] Raymond Williams, *Culture and Society, 1780–1950* (Penguin Books, 1963), 262.

about the swiftness of capitalism's decay and pending transformation into a wholly new economic system. Yet they clung to this view until it became apparent that they had misjudged capitalism's trajectory. Niebuhr was on the edges of this phenomenon. Thomas was, in this sense, more cautious than Niebuhr, more concerned with building a base and not so lost in the ecstatic hopes of a proletarian revolution. Thomas saw no widespread acceptance among the proletariat of its supposed role in the forging of a new society and saw both racial consciousness on the part of "white" workers and the imposition of middle-class ideology onto workers for whom the possibilities of upward mobility had largely closed with the settlement of the frontier.[121] To bolster his case, Thomas cited previous incarnations of working-class energy that had been more radical in content. Movements had to be built. The forces of history could not be trusted with such an important task. Thomas was to see an up-swell of working-class action, and the men that he and Niebuhr mentored would be among the throng, a militant minority trying, often in vain, to shape its political direction.

Where Niebuhr failed to inspire, the students turned to Norman Thomas, who championed the notion that well-intentioned radicals could work for a just society without becoming ensnared in Niebuhr's pessimism. Thomas argued that substantial gains were possible. Students could also look to the Socialist Party's educational strategy, and draw from deeper Socialist traditions. These sources of intellectual support led away from Niebuhr's warnings about the problems inherent in human nature and the limits of education as a means to social change. Thomas put a more hopeful gloss on the struggle's potential to achieve serious social change and avoid the lure of perfectionism identified by Niebuhr: "One may admit practically everything [Niebuhr] says about human society and yet stoutly maintain that it does not in sum total prove that man is incapable of working toward immense betterment of society without a faith in impossible perfection or that the faith in perfection as a possibility necessarily leads to bitter fanaticism."[122] Thomas also, while agreeing with Niebuhr to a degree, held to the favored socialist strategy of social change through persuasion via education and propaganda: "I agree with [Niebuhr] that education has its limitations as a means of redemption. He has not proved that education cannot help men to visualize and to realize a degree of progress which it

---

[121] Norman Thomas, review of *Moral Man and Immoral Society*, 267.

[122] Thomas, review of *Moral Man and Immoral Society*, 265.

does lie within the power of humanity to achieve."[123] On this point the students were in basic agreement with Thomas and held fast to the Socialist shibboleth of education as a primary means to social revolution, or at least as an important method to ensure that a democratic social revolution could be undertaken. In this way, they refused to accept Niebuhr's pessimistic view of human nature, as it ran contrary to socialism's period of revival and tremendous growth of confidence. Socialists believed that the workers were awakening to the veracity of socialism and were increasingly ready to "[march] abreast of the other great movements of the world toward the rising sun of the cooperative commonwealth."[124]

In the late 1920s and early 1930s, a cohort of young and ambitious radicals began to coalesce around UTS and the Socialist Party's institutions in New York City. They were concerned with reviving socialism in the United States and were part of an effort undertaken by an older generation of socialists to cultivate a new leadership from among the professional middle class. The networks in which the radicals moved were not large, but they covered expansive political territory both metaphorically and in geographic terms. Their inspirations were not only eminent Americans, though they developed relationships with the established figures of the democratic left in the United States, which included, most prominently, Norman Thomas, Roger Baldwin, a founder of the American Civil Liberties Union, and a coterie of other intellectuals, labor leaders, and socialites, but also political leaders, émigrés, and refugees from Europe. Integration in these networks prepared the way for their careers, which they linked to the struggle for socialism in the United States and the world. Looking out at a world in disorder, they dreamed of a new, humane order and set to work to accomplish this task. It is not surprising that some studied religion and found a secular world in their studies. Their political consciousness was shaped by the unemployment crisis of 1928, the Great Depression, the success of socialism abroad and at home, the growing threat of fascism in Europe, and by the Marxism they encountered in New York City during a time when it seemed like the old explanatory frameworks were on the verge of collapse. For them, Marxism explained what had happened and what was to happen next. The political and economic chaos of their time bolstered their

---

[123] Ibid.

[124] Harry Laidler, "Marxian Socialism and Labor History," *The New Leader*, 25 February 1928, 3. This line comes from a quote Laidler used in his essay. He attributes the quote to the "brilliant young leaders of the Socialist movement."

youthful assurance and pushed them toward radical solutions. What followed was a hopeful period of institution building in the form of schools and labor unions. They were also driven by personal ambitions. These ambitions and their disagreements with the actions and policies advocated by the SP during the economic crisis led to the formation of a radical caucus within the Socialist Party, the Revolutionary Policy Committee.

CHAPTER 4

The Revolutionary Policy Committee

The Revolutionary Policy Committee (RPC) was a left-wing caucus within the Socialist Party of America. Its members included James Dombrowski and Franz Daniel, former students at Union Theological Seminary and members of the Morningside Heights Branch. The RPC had a short institutional life. The bulk of its activity took place between February 1934 and January 1935 when the group began to fragment. Its members adopted radical language in response to the destruction of robust socialist movements in Europe and facing a theoretical abyss left by a rapidly "decaying" capitalism.[1] In 1934, socialist Vienna lay in ruins and the residents of the George Washington Hof, a housing block constructed by Vienna's municipal socialists, faced intimidation by soldiers, who, under orders from the fascist chancellor, paraded through their courtyard armed with machine guns.[2] European fascists destroyed socialist organizations. Socialists and labor leaders were imprisoned, or fled into exile. The fall of socialist Vienna, in addition to the destruction of the Social Democratic Party of Germany, devastated socialists throughout the world, as Vienna was a city that housed what William Feigenbaum, a prominent New York Socialist, called, "the

---

[1] Gerd-Rainer Horn, *European Socialists Respond to Fascism: Ideology, Activist, and Contingency in the 1930s* (Oxford University Press, 1996), 8.

[2] "War Scenes in Vienna," *Manchester Guardian*, 16 February 1934.

© The Author(s) 2019
J. Altman, *Socialism before Sanders*,
https://Doi.org/10.1007/978-3-030-17176-6_4

53

most advanced working class in the world."[3] The RPC reacted to this trau-
matic loss by further emphasizing its revolutionary rhetoric and fixating on
the fascist threat to socialists.

Yet, the RPC retained the major commitments of the historic SP.
Democracy, education, and work in the labor movement remained at the
center of the lives of some of the RPC's most active members, and the
RPC took pains to stress its "educational role." Thus, there was a contradiction at the very heart of the RPC's program and actions. It had
democratic-oriented elements in that it saw persuasion and open discussion as the key mechanisms for advancing its ideas. This commitment to
debate and democracy overlapped with an attraction and rhetorical commitment to revolutionary methods such as armed resistance. The RPC
tried to solve this contradiction by placing emphasis on democratic workers' councils, institutions that, they argued, would also be the basis of armed
struggle against capitalists. This approach blended Reinhold Niebuhr's and
Norman Thomas's ideas explored in an earlier chapter. Because the RPC
never elaborated on *how* or *when* workers' councils would become sites
of armed struggle against capitalism, the tension between democracy and
armed struggle remained unresolved. With little concrete strategizing, revolutionary appeals were, for the most part, rhetorical.

The RPC was an experiment to find a new socialism, designed to answer
questions raised by the defeat of the social democrats in Germany and
the Austro-Marxists in Vienna. The RPC's members searched for answers
to what looked, at the time, to be an impending and inevitable struggle between workers and capitalism. The RPC's members were search-
ing for, what they called, "correct methods," the appropriate theoretical
answers necessary to solve the unemployment crisis and defeat fascism.[4]
They believed they would find answers as they wrestled with "the problem
of planning policies and tactics in the working class struggle that can attract
the masses fighting for their day-to-day existence."[5] Theory could be found
in praxis, they argued, and this emphasis on the "immediate struggles" of

---

[3]William Feigenbaum, "They Built a City for the Future: And So the Brave Vienna
Socialists Are Hunted Like Wild Beasts," *The New Leader*, 17 February 1934, 10.

[4]"The Editors' Reply," *Revolutionary Socialist Review* 1, no. 2 (February 1935), 11.

[5]Ibid.

workers made them relevant to workers whom they would educate to the cause of "revolutionary socialism."[6]

Some members of the SP accused the RPC of being communist infiltrators because of their revolutionary ideas. The RPC tried to convince others that they were good, loyal socialists. "The attempt to work out a clear revolutionary ideology within the party for the membership who have accepted Socialism," wrote several of the RPC's top leaders, "is not inconsistent with nor in contradiction to the day-to-day struggle to win the masses to Socialism. In our opinion, it is one of the complements to such activity."[7] The RPC's members were caught between a messianic view of the future and pragmatism, between their fear of fascism and hope for the Soviet Union, and their reluctance to embrace what they saw as a destructive, devious, and undemocratic Communist Party (CP). Their methods remained those of the SP even as they defended the socialism of the Soviet Union. The RPC, then, was not an external aberration "infecting" the Socialist Party— a contagion metaphor used by some of the RPC's opponents. Rather, it was a manifestation of the complexities of the 1930s born from within the SP and always reluctant to part with the most basic principles and methods of democratic socialism. They were revolutionaries of necessity, not conviction.

The RPC's historical importance was greater than its relatively small size. Its members, the self-labeled "RPCers," undertook practical work out of proportion to their numbers and helped to build up successful socialist institutions and expand the labor movement. Highlander Folk School and the Southern Tenant Farmers' Union benefited from the presence of RPCers, as did the Amalgamated Clothing Workers of America (ACWA). A number of the RPC's members went on to achieve much greater acclaim. Irving Brown became the American Federation of Labor-Congress of Industrial Organization's director for international affairs and was awarded the Presidential Medal of Freedom by Ronald Reagan.[8] George Streator became the first African-American reporter at *The New York Times*. Roy Reuther organized political action for one of the most powerful and politically active

[6] Ibid.
[7] Ibid.
[8] Seth Lipsky, "Irving Brown: All Along the Line," *Wall Street Journal*, 17 February 1989, A14.

trade unions in the world, the United Auto Workers (UAW).[9] When the AFL and CIO merged in 1955, Franz Daniel, a solid CIO man since the 1930s, became its new assistant director for organizing.[10] In the late 1940s during Operation Dixie, Daniel was director of the CIO's organizing efforts in South Carolina and North Carolina.[11] Alice Hanson, later Alice Cook, became a prominent professor of labor history at Cornell University, and has a building on campus named in her honor.[12] Cook and her RPC comrade Newman Jeffrey also assisted with the reconstruction of the German labor movement during the US occupation of Germany.[13] Merlin Bishop became the UAW's educational director.[14] John Green, a short time after joining the RPC, became president of the Industrial Union of Marine and Shipbuilding Workers of America (IUMSWA).[15] Paul Porter, who held a number of posts as part of the US effort to reconstruct postwar Europe, was listed as an endorser of the April 1934 version of the RPC's appeal. His name was removed from the second edition of the RPC's "An Appeal to the Member of the Socialist Party" published in March 1934, suggesting that there were already tensions over the group's program.[16] Nonetheless,

[9] Kevin Boyle, *The UAW and the Heyday of American Liberalism, 1945–1968* (Ithaca: Cornell University Press, 1995), 53.

[10] John Daniel, *Rogue River Journal: A Winter Alone* (Washington, DC: Shoemaker & Hoard, 2005), 101.

[11] Timothy J. Minchin, *What Do We Need a Union For? The TWUA in the South, 1945–1955* (University of North Carolina Press, 1997), 28.

[12] See Alice Cook, *A Lifetime of Labor: The Autobiography of Alice H. Cook* (Feminist Press, 1998). Cornell named one of its student residences after Cook.

[13] Carolyn Woods Eisenberg, *Drawing the Line: The American Decision to Divide Germany, 1944–1949* (Cambridge University Press, 1996), 156; Cook, *A Lifetime of Labor*, 100.

[14] Mary M. Stolberg, *Bridging the River of Hatred: The Pioneering Efforts of Detroit Police Commissioner George Edwards* (Wayne State University Press, 1998), 51.

[15] David Palmer, *Organizing the Shipyards: Union Strategy in Three Northeast Ports, 1933–1945* (Cornell University Press, 1998), 58.

[16] The Revolutionary Policy Committee, "An Appeal to the Membership of the Socialist Party," March 1934, Box 5, Printed Ephemera Collection on the Socialist Party (PECSP), Tamiment Library and Robert F. Wagner Labor Archives, New York University, New York; The Revolutionary Policy Committee, "An Appeal to the Membership of the Socialist Party," April 1934, Box 5, PECSP.

the group attracted some of the very best people the socialist movement had to offer.[17]

In the 1930s, the Socialist Party had split into two main factions, the Old Guard and the Militants. Descriptions of the factional landscape of the SP during the 1930s took on almost anthropomorphic airs. "On the right stood the Old Guard," wrote Irving Howe, "hard and unyielding."[18] Howe's other adjectives for the Old Guard included serious, shrewd, conventional, excessively moderate, and grouchy.[19] After the death of Morris Hillquit in 1933, James Oneal, Algernon Lee, and Louis Waldman led the Old Guard. They advocated working within prescribed legal boundaries and benefited from their connections to garment unions and fraternal societies, which reinforced their commitments to parliamentarism and anticommunism.[20] Garment unions and fraternal societies, significant institutions in the socialist movement, had been sites of struggle between socialists and communists prior to the 1930s.[21] The major opposition to the Old Guard in the SP came from the Militant faction, a loose grouping that had initially included the RPC's important leaders and counted on a sympathetic hearing from Norman Thomas.[22] In contrast to the Old Guard, the Militants were associated with "revolutionary" ideology, youthfulness, and advocacy for extra-parliamentary action in extreme circumstances.[23]

---

[17] Palmer, *Organizing the Shipyards*, 75; The Revolutionary Policy Committee, "An Appeal to the Membership of the Socialist Party," April 1934, Box 5, PECSP. In November 1934, the RPC's Executive Committee consisted of J.B. Matthews, Francis Henson, Irving Brown, William Chamberlain, David Felix, Howard Kester, W.W. Norris, Roy Reuther, Ruth Shallcross, Leo Sitke, and George Streator. See "What Is the Revolutionary Policy Committee?" *The Revolutionary Socialist Review* 1, no. 1 (November 1934): see cover page.

[18] Irving Howe, *Socialism and America* (Harcourt Brace Jovanovich, 1986), 54. Howe's colorful characterization of the Old Guard is worth more than a glance for its evocative style. His writing gives literary life to the SP.

[19] Ibid., 54–55.

[20] Warren, *An Alternative Vision*, 17. Importantly, much of the Old Guard was firmly committed to electoral independence, which distinguished it from allied elements of a more dispersed socialist movement. See, for instance, the Old Guard's reaction to EPIC in Warren, *An Alternative Vision*, 76.

[21] Jennifer Luff, *Commonsense Anticommunism: Labor and Civil Liberties Between the World Wars* (University of North Carolina Press, 2012), 130.

[22] Raymond F. Gregory, *Norman Thomas: The Great Dissenter* (Algora, 2008), 138.

[23] Howe, *Socialism and America*, 56–57; Warren, *An Alternative Vision*, 17.

THE RPC'S ORIGINS: THE MILITANT FACTION

The RPC developed out of the SP's Militant faction. Franz Daniel, the main voice of the RPC in Philadelphia; J. B. Matthews, one of the RPC's initial organizers; and Francis Henson, another RPC leader, endorsed the Militant program in 1932.[24] The RPC began to coalesce out of efforts taken by Militants in early 1933 to create a monthly socialist magazine tasked with the purpose of fostering an "effective revolutionary movement."[25] Both J. B. Matthews and Alice Hanson—prominent future members of the RPC—were listed as members of the proposed editorial board alongside many well-known members of the Militant faction, including Reinhold Niebuhr.

The RPC's involvement with the Militant faction, and its unwillingness to break with the SP demonstrate the degree to which it was primarily a manifestation of the extremes of the 1930s within the SP, rather than a subversive outside force. In fact, the claims that future RPCers put forward when they identified with the Militant faction in 1932 were not dissimilar from the RPC's later program. They wanted to make class struggle central to the SP's organizing efforts, develop and apply Marxist theory to the ongoing crisis of the 1930s, signal that the SP considered the Soviet Union's collectivization as "progress," and generally embrace a "revolutionary goal and method."[26] The RPC added much colorful revolutionary sloganeering to this formulation, and yet hardly changed its basic content.

After its formation, the RPC continually aligned itself with the Militant faction and others on left of the SP. Ruth Shallcross, the point-person for RPC organizing, was careful to convey the RPC's loyalty to the SP when she wrote Powers Hapgood, an important member of the SP's governing body and a well-respected labor organizer. The RPC hoped to recruit Hapgood. The RPC, Shallcross wrote, "is in no way a splitting process... We care only about crystallizing left policy and gaining discussion for a new program within the party."[27] Shallcross argued that the RPC would "unite"

[24]Franz Daniel, "The Militant Program for Socialism," *The New Leader*, 14 May 1932, 9; Francis Henson, "Shibboleths and Reformists," *The New Leader*, 6 February 1932, 11; and Bell, *Marxian Socialism in the United States*, 159.

[25]"Memorandum on a Monthly Socialist Magazine," March 1933, Box 5, Powers Hapgood Papers, Lilly Library Manuscript Collections, Indiana University.

[26]Henson, "Shibboleths and Reformists," 11.

[27]Ruth Shallcross to Powers Hapgood, 27 February 1934, Box 5, PHP.

with the Militant faction at the SP's 1934 convention. The RPC coordinated with allies within the SP on pragmatic issues such as elections. When considering elections to the SP's National Executive Committee in 1934, David Felix, a Philadelphia lawyer and RPC member, strategized with Powers Hapgood, a leftist SP member. Hapgood was considering a move to Philadelphia. Felix explained why it might be better if Hapgood remained in Indiana until the election was over, "If you are still in Indianapolis at the time of the Indianapolis convention, you can run on the N.E.C from Indiana, and Franz [Daniel] can run from Pennsylvania, whereas if you were here, it would mean you running from Pennsylvania and Franz would not be able to run." If Hapgood moved before the state conventions voted their representatives onto the NEC, the left could lose one of its seats. "Of course, after the convention," Felix added, "if you should move to Pennsylvania, it would make no difference and we would have more of our men on the N.E.C."[28] The RPC was strategic in its orientation and worked with non-RPC leftists in the SP to advance the general interests, as it saw them, of the Socialist Party.

CONSTRUCTIONS OF THE RPC

The diversity of the RPC, the real contributions of its members, and their personal trajectories are simplified in the historical literature. Most mentions of the RPC are brief and emphasize the group's connections to Jay Lovestone. Lovestone was the one-time CP leader who was turned out of the CP on Stalin's order for presuming that communists in the United States had to conform to the particularism of the American experience.[29] The RPC is depicted at its worst as "entryism"—a process by which a small cadre infiltrates and disrupts or attempts to take over another organization—and at its best as filled with "adventurists," the classic charge made the Old Guard faction within the SP at people they perceived, sometimes correctly, to be romantic revolutionaries who did not understand the implications

[28] David Felix to Powers Hapgood, 27 February 1934, Box 5, PHP.
[29] Alexander, *The Right Opposition*, 22–28.

of their own actions. Reinhold Niebuhr, associated with the SP's Militant faction, also leveled this charge at the RPC.[30]

Historians have overstated the influence of Lovestone on the RPC. Daniel Bell argues that the RPC was "a weird mélange of revolutionary romanticists and secret Lovestoneite agents."[31] Ted Morgan, a biographer of Jay Lovestone, confirms Irving Brown was Lovestone's man in the RPC, which seems to have been general knowledge among the SP's Militant faction and its allies.[32] Beyond Brown's presence and apparently unsuccessful efforts to engage with some of the RPC's other members, including Zilla Hawes, who showed equal interest in the ideas of Reinhold Niebuhr and Norman Thomas, Morgan offers little more to confirm the idea that the RPC was under Lovestoneite control.[33] Hawes did at one point voice interest in Lovestone's Communist Party Opposition (CPO), a breakaway group thrown out of the CP by Stalin, though it appears she did not pursue this interest.[34] Responding to Hawes' remark about the CPO, Ruth Shallcross told her, "Should you join Lovestone's group he would tell you to work in the S.P. and do the thing we all are trying to do anyway so you had better stay and fight with us!"[35] The assessment that Lovestone had *a* man in the RPC is not enough evidence to confirm claims of Love-

[30]Reinhold Niebuhr, "A Criticism of the R.P.C. Program," *Revolutionary Socialist Review* 1, no. 2 (February 1935), 8.

[31]Daniel Bell, *Marxian Socialism in the United States* (Cornell University Press, 1996), 165.

[32]Alexander, *The Right Opposition*, 109–110.

[33]Zilla Hawes to Myles Horton, 16 April 1931, Box 15, Folder 30, HREC; Zilla Hawes to Old Tarpot [Myles Horton], 24 September 1931, Box 15, Folder 30, HREC.

[34]Ruth Shallcross to Zilla Hawes, 26 February 1934, Box 68, Folder 15, HREC. It was not odd for socialists to engage with other leftists, including Lovestone, who spoke to a meeting of the SP's National Executive Committee in late 1934. Jay Lovestone presented a plan for a united front to the NEC, which its members rejected. Norman Thomas responded acerbically to Lovestone's admission that his Communist Opposition had been instructed to vote for CP candidates in the mid-term election that took place a month previously. "Your policy," Thomas told Lovestone, "is to march with Socialists on May Day and vote for Communists on Election Day." See Norman Thomas quoted in William M. Feigenbaum, "N.E.C. Appoints Committee for Nation-wide Survey," *The New Leader*, 8 December 1934, 3.

[35]Ruth Shallcross to Jim [Dombrowski] and Zilla [Hawes], 26 February 1934, Box 68, Folder 15, HREC.

stoneite control.[36] Constance Myers argues that the Socialist Party's turn away from the orthodox Marxism of the Old Guard was the result of this supposed Lovestoneite entryism.[37] She goes so far as to argue that the RPC represented an effort to turn the SP toward "bolshevism."[38] While there is evidence that members of the RPC admired an idealized vision of the Soviet Union, they made a distinction between the general "progress" of the Soviet Union and the tactics and programs of the CP and the CPO.[39]

Reincorporating the RPC into the history of the SP, establishing its context, and examining how its ideas informed action adds richness to the history of American socialism in the 1930s. Moving past the dominance of factionalism in the histories of the SP is a first step in the project of reclaiming a more expansive history of socialism in the 1930s and understanding the motivations of socialists in this turbulent decade. Myers and Bell, for instance, rely on denunciations voiced by the RPC's factional rivals in the Old Guard for much of their characterizations of the group. While some of these critiques of the RPC were accurate, they prevent an understanding of the events and ideas that gave shape to the RPC. A close reading of the sources suggests a more complex understanding is necessary when we consider that both of the SP's successful organizing efforts in the 1930s, Highlander Folk School and the Southern Tenant Farmers' Union, were aided by people who had been involved with the RPC. In addition, historians have missed that many of the RPC's leading members were students of Reinhold Niebuhr and not followers of Jay Lovestone.[40] This suggests a multifaceted understanding of socialist radicalism is required.

Robert Alexander's work on the international CPO offers a more complex reading of the RPC in terms of its membership and role within the SP. Alexander argues for a flexible interpretation of the RPC, which included members who were attracted to both the Lovestoneites and to the Stalinist

---

[36]Ted Morgan, *A Covert Life: Jay Lovestone, Communist, Anti-Communist, and Spymaster* (Random House, 1999), 113.

[37]Constance Ashton Myers, *The Prophet's Army: Trotskyists in America, 1928–1941* (Greenwood Press, 1977), 109.

[38]Myers, 109.

[39]"RPC and the Communists," *The Revolutionary Socialist Review* 1, no. 1 (November 1934), 9.

[40]Four members of Highlander's initial staff had studied with or knew Niebuhr. Two of the four were public members of the RPC. In addition, Myles Horton and Zilla Hawes had studied with Muste at Brookwood.

CP—one of whom apparently consulted with both groups, much to Love-stone's chagrin. Alexander established that Irving Brown's presence within the RPC elicited a general consensus among the SP's leadership (and within the RPC's own ranks) that Brown was Lovestoneite.[41]

Robert Bussel, writing about the life of Powers Hapgood, who was sympathetic to the RPC, had a more accurate view of the group. Fore-shadowing the course of many socialists toward an increasingly pragmatic approach to social change, Bussel writes, "Among workers, Hapgood had begun to display ideological flexibility, but within SP circles his rhetoric grew more strident, as if to assure both himself and his fellow Socialists that his revolutionary credentials remained intact." "Hapgood," continues Bussel, "allied himself with the Revolutionary Policy Committee, a small but vocal group within the Socialist Party that was agitating for a more mil-itant party platform."[42] The RPC developed out of the Militant faction, though its members thought of themselves as distinctive, revolutionary, authentic Marxists, and were interested in workers' councils and not par-liamentary democracy. Both groups repudiated social democracy, as repre-sented by the Old Guard, though the RPC took its rhetorical break with the electoral politics further than the Militants. The Militants were willing to employ extra-legal methods in a crisis situation. The RPC's members spoke of a more immediate transformation from capitalism and the elec-toral system that they associated with it.[43] Bussel's analysis of the RPC is correct: "Fearful of being outflanked by the Communist Party, the RPC, in April 1934 issued 'An Appeal to the Socialist Party,' a fiery manifesto declaring that there was 'no longer a middle road' in American politics. If socialists were to be relevant, the RPC argued, they would have to consider disavowing electoral politics and embrace direct action in order to ensure success in the antifascist struggle."[44] Hapgood accepted this position.

Other scholars have downplayed individuals' associations with the RPC. Downplaying the RPC's importance removes its members from their

---

[41] Robert Jackson Alexander, *The Right Opposition: The Lovestoneites and the Interna-tional Communist Opposition of the 1930's* (Greenwood Press, 1981), 110. The RPC officially denied that Brown was under Lovestone's discipline, however. See "Party Loy-alty," *Revolutionary Socialist Review* 1, no. 2 (February 1935), 2.

[42] Bussel, *From Harvard to the Ranks of Labor*, 132.

[43] The Militant faction and many members of the RPC increasingly embraced anti-communism as the 1930s unfolded. McGreen, 113.

[44] Ibid., 132–133.

political and intellectual context and obscures the significant changes that they underwent throughout the 1930s. This was the case with James Dombrowski.[45] Despite the circumstances and experiences that led Dombrowski and his comrades to the RPC, association with the group remained an embarrassment. Frank Adams explained away James Dombrowski's attraction to the RPC as part of his preacher's mentality ready to denounce "out-of-touch elders" and separated this Dombrowski from the more staid, seasoned, and scholarly Dombrowski.[46] The RPC only appears embarrassing in retrospect, when analysis is removed from incredible uncertainty of the 1930s. Experimentation was an essential feature of the 1930s and was at the heart of the RPC's attractiveness for Dombrowski and his comrades.

Perhaps the best exploration of the RPC to date focuses on the work of its members in Philadelphia and the organization of the shipyard workers in particular. By imbedding RPC members in their local contexts, David Palmer captures their motivations and contributions. Palmer focuses on the content of the RPC's program, including its emphasis on racial equality and denunciation of the National Recovery Administration as essentially pro-capitalist.[47] He also understands the trajectory of the RPC's members from revolutionary ideology to reformism, an important indication of their experimental mentality. Palmer qualifies the RPC's views and places them in the context of rising industrial unionism, which the RPC's members supported and aided from their earliest manifestations. This work expands on Palmer's efforts to explicate the history of the RPC by further contextualizing the RPC's development and accomplishments and by avoiding the narrow conceptions of the organization as controlled by either the CP or by Lovestone's Communist Party (Opposition).[48]

FACTIONALISM AND THE RPC

February 1934 found New York in the depths of a bitter winter. Lake Ontario froze for the first time in sixty years. The Civil Works

[45] Adams, *An American Heretic*, 80.

[46] Ibid., 79–80.

[47] Colin Gordon, *New Deals: Business, Labor, and Politics in America, 1920–1935* (Cambridge University Press, 1994), 166–167.

[48] Palmer, *Organizing the Shipyards*, 26–27. David Palmer's work on the IUMSWA provides a superlative examination of the complex labor left that created victories for labor in the 1930s and 1940s.

Administration, an emergency public works program designed to combat unemployment and champion the dignity of labor, suspended its projects when the temperature plunged to record lows. The program had undoubtedly saved many lives that winter by ensuring that previously unemployed people had sufficient resources to survive the cold.[49] Mayor La Guardia expanded the city's offerings to its residents without home or sustenance. The brutal winter also halted commerce, as ships loaded with goods for European markets were stranded in fourteen-inch-thick ice on the Hudson River near Tarrytown. The record cold killed a handful of New Yorkers—and probably more who were missed by official counts or fell ill in the foul weather. The weather fit the bleak, seemingly arbitrary cruelness of life in the midst of the Depression.[50]

Cold and the continued callousness of the Depression were not the only bitter experiences in New York City during the hard winter of 1934. If the wind was howling outside Madison Square Garden on February 16, inside socialists, trade unionists, and communists were trying to out-howl each other. "5,000 Reds Battle with Socialists at Garden Rally," read a front-page report complete with pictures of the fighting in *The New York Times*.[51] The pandemonium began when "5,000 Communists who had made their way inside tried to 'capture' the meeting."[52] Communists met fierce resistance from their socialist interlocutors, who "hurled" one of the communist leaders off the stage during the struggle. In an effort to aid their fallen leader, communists in the balconies assailed the socialists below with a barrage of chairs.[53]

The communists, in pamphlets distributed before their attempted subversion in the Garden, "denounced both the Mayor [La Guardia] and Mr. [Matthew] Woll [an AFL official] as Fascists engaged in fostering fascism

---

[49] Bonnie Fox Schwartz, *The Civil Works Administration, 1933–1934: The Business of Emergency Employment in the New Deal* (Princeton University Press, 1984), 70–71.

[50] "10 Below Zero Due in New Cold Wave," *New York Times*, 9 February 1934, 1; David Stout, "But What About February 9, 1934...," *New York Times*, 6 February 1996.

[51] "5,000 Reds Battle with Socialists at Garden Rally," *New York Times*, 17 February 1934, 1.

[52] Ibid.; "Reds Denounced for Garden Raid," *New York Times*, 18 February 1934, 32.

[53] "5,000 Reds Battle with Socialists at Garden Rally," 1; "The Meeting at the Garden," *The New Leader*, 24 February 1934, 1.

in the United States."[54] The pamphlets also decried the social-democratic leaders of Austria.[55] La Guardia and Woll had been scheduled to speak to the gathering, but stayed away when it was clear that the communists intended to disrupt the event.[56] This was wise, as the communists who assailed the rostrum sang, "We'll hang Matthew Woll [from] a sour apple tree" and shouted, "Fascist LaGuardia."[57] The CP also called for rank-and-file socialists and communists to unite, though their action in the Garden ensured that such an alliance remained unlikely.[58] A CP pamphlet distributed at the Garden rally told socialists and workers that their "leaders [had] united with American Fascists."[59] A socialist commentator remarked, "The meeting was forced to defend itself against the atrocities of the communists who came in the guise of friends. This was [their] conception of the united front."[60] The only speaker who was heard over the riotous shouting and fighting was Frank Crosswaith, a leading black socialist, "who compared the Communists to pigs 'who will always remain pigs because it is in the nature of Communists to be pigs.'"[61]

Socialists, as Crosswaith intimated, were particularly furious with their long-time enemies and rivals, the communists, for they had not disrupted an ordinary meeting. They had stormed a meeting held to protest the fascist attack on Austrian democracy and the murder of socialist comrades who rose up in defense of their republic and working-class institutions. The communists mischaracterized working-class anti-fascism in Austria, and publicly denounced Austrian socialist leaders. Clarence Hathaway, the CP leader who was hurled from the rostrum had, at a communist-organized meeting in Bronx the day before, told the crowd, "The treachery of the

---

[54] "5,000 Reds Battle with Socialists at Garden Rally," 1.

[55] "The Meeting at the Garden," 10.

[56] Norman Thomas referred to Matthew Woll as a "right wing, non-Socialist labor leader." Despite disagreements with Woll, Thomas believed that right-wing laborites had proven themselves reliable allies in the struggle against fascism. Norman Thomas, "What the Communists Did," *The New Leader*, 24 February 1934, 12; "The Meeting at the Garden," 1, 10.

[57] "5,000 Reds Battle with Socialists at Garden Rally," 1.

[58] George I. Steinhardt, "The Communists Succeed in Uniting the Socialists," *The New Leader*, 24 February 1934, 5.

[59] "The Meeting at the Garden," 1.

[60] Steinhardt, "The Communists Succeed in Uniting the Socialists," 5.

[61] "5,000 Reds Battle with Socialists at Garden Rally," 1.

Social Democratic leadership has stood out in paving the way for the liqui-dating of the revolutionary Austrian working class."[62] This was the context in which the socialist and trade union organizers of the Garden gathering issued a statement that expressed their indignation at the CP's intrusion and denunciation of Austrian social democracy:

> [The communists'] conduct is all the more revolting in that men, women and children were lying dead in Austria, killed in defense of the ideals for which this meeting was called. We declare that the Communist psychology and conduct as manifested at this meeting do not differ from Fascist psychology and conduct, and that communism has become a pariah among the workers and all fighters for democracy and liberty.[63]

Norman Thomas was unequivocal in his ill regard for the communists' actions at the Garden. He argued that the communists sought to "dis-credit the cause of our Austrian comrades throughout an America all too ill-informed about Austria."[64] Thomas thought that the communists had intentionally sabotaged any chance of a united front against fascism. Thomas added that they had done "*the very thing that helped pave the way for Hitler in Germany* [italics in original]."[65] Experienced testimony against the CP's disruption came from Martin Plaettl, who had been the president of a German trade union before fleeing a Germany now domi-nated by Hitler, and who had experienced the Communist International's "Third Period." Plaettl, told journalists, "It was precisely such spectacles as they staged here today that led to the triumph of Hitlerism in Ger-many."[66] The CP espoused "Third Period" analysis, which held that rev-olution would engulf and destroy capitalism as its contradictions became increasingly impossible to rectify. Fascism was a manifestation of the dying gasps of the bourgeoisie attempting to maintain their power.[67] Socialists were more afraid of the rise of fascism than was the Third Period CP, which

---

[62] "The Meeting at the Garden," 10.

[63] "5,000 Reds Battle with Socialists at Garden Rally," 1.

[64] Thomas, "What the Communists Did," 12.

[65] Ibid.

[66] "5,000 Reds Battle with Socialists at Garden Rally," 1; "The Meeting at the Garden," 1.

[67] Fraser M. Ottanelli, *The Communist Party of the United States: From the Depression to World War II* (Rutgers University Press, 1991), 18–20.

officially regarded fascism as a mere apparition that heralded capitalism's final doom.[68]

Fear of fascism and a desire to avoid the failures of European comrades who had been unable to stop fascism were central to the RPC's mentality. Its members were caught between Niebuhr's apocalyptic view of the future, which, they argued, might necessitate revolutionary upheaval, and Norman Thomas's practical affirmation of the major source of class struggle in American history, the labor movement. These did not seem to be mutually exclusive options until the RPC's members were confronted with the actual demands and limitations of the labor movement. The tension between armed revolution and the labor movement shaped the RPC through its short history, with many of its prominent members eventually choosing the labor movement over revolution. The RPC was a dynamic group that desperately tried to find a way out of the twin crises of the 1930s, economic depression and fascism. Though the RPC did lose some members to the CP and the CPO, its most vocal adherents responded to crises *by remaining within the socialist movement.*

The RPC stressed education as a means to social change, even as its members adopted revolutionary rhetoric. If the RPC did embrace "armed insurrection" in theory, its emphasis remained on education and practical work in the labor movement. "We believe," wrote the editors of the RSR, "[the SP] wants to know what revolutionary socialism means." "We believe," they continued, "[the SP] is not shocked to be told that there must be an armed overthrow of the capitalist state machinery by the working class."[69] This statement was followed by an immediate affirmation of the group's educational role. "Our major task is," wrote the editors, "to assist in this educational effort."[70]

By the summer of 1934, the RPC was the subject to attacks from the Old Guard and from communists as well. James Oneal, *The New Leader's* editor, delighted in printing the names of two former RPC members who had resigned from the Socialist Party and joined communist organizations. One had joined the CP and the other had joined Jay Lovestone's Communist Party (Opposition). Oneal was delighted because the two

---

[68]James Weinstein, *Ambiguous Legacy: The Left in American Politics* (New Viewpoints, 1975), 38–39.

[69]"Party Loyalty," *Revolutionary Socialist Review* 1, no. 2 (February 1935), 2.

[70]Ibid., 3.

defections proved, to him, that the RPC was a communist organization. The defections confirmed his view that RPC's members had never really been socialists, in Oneal's definition. Their goal was and had always been the subversion of the SP.[71] In reference to the RPC, he reported that socialists had driven "Communism out of the front door in 1919; it enters through the window in 1934!"[72] If Oneal was certain about what was and was not "socialism" and "communism," others had doubts.

Oneal's criticisms of the RPC echoed his earlier problems with the Militant faction.[73] Oneal regarded the Militants and RPC members' marriage of Christianity and Marxism to be an absurdity. In reality, Oneal overemphasized the RPC's Christian component because so many of its prominent members came out of UTS, and, as such, he assumed that they were Christians. Francis Henson, Oneal reported, "finds a united front between Marx and Jesus possible. All this is carried into the Revolutionary Policy Committee."[74] "All that is required to round it out," he added, "is the addition of Moses and Mohammed."[75] Oneal regarded these groups as "entirely alien to a working-class movement." This was not true in a strict sense, though culturally Oneal was correct to associate the most vocal members of the RPC with something other than the working class.[76] He savaged them, raising the specter of faddism, by quoting Georgi Plekhanov on anarchists: "Alas, gentlemen, you will try everything. You will become Buddhists, Druids, Sars, Chaldeans, Occultists, Magi, Theosophists, or Anarchists, whichever you prefer—and yet you will remain what you are now—beings without faith or principle, bags emptied by history."[77] Francis Henson had asked Oneal for his thoughts on the RPC's new publication. This was

[71]"Two Recruits," *The New Leader*, 30 June 1934, 11; James Oneal, "To Comrade Thomas," *The New Leader*, 23 June 1934, 3.

[72]James Oneal, "United Front Maneuvers," *The New Leader*, 15 September 1934, 2.

[73]The Militant faction also rejected social-democratic "reformism." Their controversial "Declaration of Principles," adopted by the SP at its 1934 convention and supported by the RPC's delegates, called for called or a clear break with social democracy in favor of an ill-defined revolutionary socialism. The Declaration included a call to seize state power in a crisis situation, a rejection of bourgeois democracy, an explicit attack on the Old Gurad social democrats.

[74]James Oneal, "The R.P.C. Magazine," *The New Leader*, 24 November 1934, 5.

[75]Ibid.

[76]Ibid.

[77]Ibid.

Oneal's response. He was not interested in dialogue with the RPC. He did not wish to instruct. He desired to obliterate the RPC. It was an odd choice for a man who claimed he wanted to avoid a return "to the sterile sectarianism that began in 1919."[78]

Oneal misjudged the impulses that led to the RPC. The socialists who came out of UTS and joined the RPC had pursued religious education and come away without much religious motivation, though their language still carried the mark of a seminary education. "But—some comrades ask—is not the [RPC] presumptuously setting itself up as a Mosaic law giver and interpreter of Truth? No, we have no Messiah complex," the editors of the RPC's publication responded to their critics.[79] Their Christianity was reduced to religious analogy. Their mentor Niebuhr, who saw Marxism as akin to Christianity, argued that they had merely changed religions, exchanging the teachings of Christ for those of Marx. His students disputed this point. Francis Henson regarded Marxism as a science and class struggle as akin to a disease, which manifests itself in society.[80] It was, in his view, no religion. Further, Henson rejected "organized Christianity" and accepted the "irreconcilability… of Marxism and Christianity," though he was quick to point out, "this does not mean that, as a Marxist, I have given up contacts with religious groups." The fight against fascism mandated work among middle-class groups, including Christians. "I consider it more important than ever in the struggle against fascism," wrote Henson, "to try to win over religious people, who are essentially middle class, to the cause of the working class."[81] The RPCers, then, were socialists who believed that circumstances necessitated cooperation and action.

The Old Guard, Oneal included, viewed the RPC and the Militant faction from which they sprung as intruders impinging on their socialist tradition. Old Guard critics viewed their left-wing interlocutors as products of a new "impetuous" energy, which entered the SP as a host of young people joined. The Old Guard also saw the RPC as an indication of a looming split between the SP's diverging factions—reminiscent of the intense factionalism that they had experienced in the late 1910s after the success of

---

[78] Ibid.

[79] "Party Loyalty," *Revolutionary Socialist Review* 1, no. 2 (February 1935), 3.

[80] Francis A. Henson, "The Marxist Position," in *Informal Report of a Seminar on Religion*, 30 May 1935, Box 69, RNP.

[81] Francis Henson to James Oneal, *Revolutionary Socialist Review* 1, no. 2 (February 1935), 47.

the Bolshevik Revolution, the same frame of reference that the Old Guard had used to attack the Militant faction. James Oneal told *The New Leader's* readers that the RPC reminded him of the United Communist Party, one of the ephemeral communist sects that formed in the aftermath of the Bolshevik victory in Russia. And he regarded the RPC's view that workers' councils were the proper means to carry forward working-class insurrection as communism. "We can thank the R.P.C. for this candor," wrote a characteristically acerbic Oneal, "for there are some party members who assert that it is not a Communist organization within the Party."[82] The RPC was, he said, an open invitation for police spies. The Old Guard, with much experience of repression and internal disruption, mediated the experience of the 1930s through their memories of past repression and factional struggles.

Prominent Militants misremembered the RPC's roots within the Militant faction and repeated claims that the group was communistic. H. L. Mitchell, a socialist and officer of the Southern Tenant Farmers' Union, who sided with the Militant caucus in the SP's fraught faction fighting, remembered that "those who were in the Revolutionary Policy Committee believed that the socialist world could not be brought into being except by violent revolution."[83] This was too narrow a view to apply to the entire RPC and many of its members considered circumstance an important determining factor in deciding tactics. "They were communists," Mitchell said, "but without the Russian dressing."[84] Mitchell also believed that the RPC was operating under the control of Jay Lovestone.[85] The RPC did have some Communist Opposition sympathizers within its ranks, including, for a short time, Zilla Hawes. Yet at the 1934 convention, the majority of the RPC's delegates voted with the Militants, Mitchell's faction, on important points.[86] Lovestone, for his part, was disappointed with the RPC's failure to push a revolutionary agenda at that convention.[87]

---

[82] Ibid.

[83] Mitchell, *Mean Things Happening in This Land*, 47.

[84] Ibid.

[85] Ibid.

[86] Zilla Hawes to Myles Horton, James Dombrowski, and HFS, June [1934], Box 15, Folder 31, HREC; A.M., "A Socialist on the Convention," *Workers Age*, 15 June 1934, 5.

[87] Jay Lovestone, "Leftward Wings in the S.P.," *Workers Age*, 15 June 1934, 1, 3; A.M., "A Socialist on the Convention," *Workers Age*, 15 June 1934, 5.

Editorials in Lovestone's *Workers Age* confirm that the RPC was not under his control. Chastising the RPC's members for not operating as effectively as they should have done, a pseudonymous SP member wrote in *Workers Age*, "If the members of the RPC continue this vacillating line [*Workers Age* argued that the RPC moved too readily from revolutionary rhetoric to compromise] they will rapidly and well deservedly find themselves an isolated and uninfluential group."[88] The Lovestoneites also criticized Franz Daniel for having secured his position on the NEC through a compromise with the Militant faction.[89] At the same time, they singled out two RPC delegates to the convention who held the line on revolutionary tactics, thus suggesting emerging divisions within the RPC and indicating the relative weakness of Lovestoneite representation among the RPC's membership.

COMMUNISTS AND THE RPC

Even the RPC, the group within the Socialist Party of America most committed to the principle of building alliances with other groups out of necessity, abandoned united-front action with the CP over the Garden debacle. This action revealed the RPC's antipathy toward the CP's tactics. An RPC member reported that their Austrian event in Philadelphia was undisturbed because they threatened the CP's representatives with violence. "We warned them what would happen to them," David Felix wrote to Powers Hapgood, "[if they disrupted the event] and they had a healthy respect for us in this town."[90] The RPC's J. B. Matthews resigned as chairman of the American League Against War and Fascism, which was a united-front organization, over the Garden affair.[91] Matthews had been charged with communist subversion by some of his comrades in the SP and threatened with expulsion. "They can't say he is C.P. now," Ruth Shallcross wrote to

[88] A.M., "A Socialist on the Convention," *Workers Age*, 15 June 1934, 5.

[89] A.J. Muste, "Has the Socialist Party Gone Revolutionary?" *Labor Action*, 15 June 1934, 5.

[90] David Felix to Powers Hapgood, 27 February 1934, Box 5, PHP.

[91] Ruth Shallcross to Zilla Hawes, 26 February 1934, 68:15, HREC files; Ottanelli, *The Communist Party of the United States*, 56–57; and Randi Storch, *Red Chicago: American Communism at Its Grassroots, 1928–35* (Urbana-Champaign: University of Illinois Press, 2007), 209.

her fellow member of the RPC Zilla Hawes.[92] Francis Henson, an active Christian socialist and a leader in the RPC, also resigned from the League over the Madison Square Garden attack.[93]

The events at the Garden briefly united the SP, whose members, despite rhetorical differentiation, nonetheless continued to have much in common. The traditional socialist emphasis on education, the labor movement, and political action animated all segments of the SP. What separated the RPC from the CP was the former's revulsion to communist methods and "tactics." The RPC's response to the Madison Square Garden fight was evidence of this mentality. The RPC represented a segment of the SP that embraced revolutionary rhetoric, saw the Soviet Union as a socialist society to be defended, and yet its members rejected the disruptive behavior of the CP. Powers Hapgood, who was sympathetic to the RPC, expressed this sentiment to a friend after the Garden debacle. "It's natural for you to take the word of the DW [Daily Worker]," wrote Hapgood, "before you will that of the NL [New Leader] about the Madison Square Garden affair. My reason for accepting the NL... version of the affair is because they have never justified lying to me and the communists have on many occasions."[94] Hapgood did not trust the *Daily Worker* or the CP. He regarded their embellishments as harmful to the movement's legitimacy, as lies alienated workers. This was self-defeating, Hapgood argued. Hapgood's experiences with "sincere miners" who knew firsthand of the *Daily Worker's* "lies" affirmed his skepticism.[95]

The distrust was mutual, as European history shaped responses to crisis in the United States. "In principle," wrote Hapgood's interlocutor, "Powers, there isn't any difference between hitting Hathaway over the head with a chair and murdering Liebknecht. The difference is not in principle but in power available."[96] Karl Liebknecht, along with Rosa Luxemburg, was murdered in the aftermath of an abortive 1918 uprising in Germany. The communists blamed social-democratic leaders for their murders. Hapgood's debate partner extended the Germany analysis further and critiqued

---

[92] Ruth Shallcross to Zilla Hawes, 26 February 1934, 68:15, HREC files.

[93] "All Leaders Quit the Anti-Fascist League," *The New Leader*, 31 March 1934, 3; "Socialist Christians Announce Program," *The New Leader*, 31 March 1934, 3.

[94] Powers Hapgood to Raymond, 10 March 1934, Box 5, PHP.

[95] Ibid.

[96] Raymond to Powers Hapgood, 2 March 1934, Box 5, PHP.

the socialists proposed united front against fascism: "In principle there is no difference between a united front with Hindenburg against [Ernst] Thälmann, the dock worker, and a united front with Woll against Hathaway [the communist leader assailed in the Garden], the machinist. The theory and practice of Social Democracy in America will help pave the way for Fascism just as it did in Germany."[97] Debates devolved into accusations about who was really doing the work of the capitalists and undermining socialism. For some, the choices that confronted an uncertain world in 1934 were stark: "Every hour Communism is growing stronger and capitalism weaker... The realist sees clearly that the only choice is between Fascism and Communism."[98] Socialists such as Hapgood and the RPCers disagreed.

While sympathetic with revolutionary ideology, Hapgood was not convinced that the CP had a tactical solution to the crisis or a successful strategy for organizing opposition to reaction. "As far as revolutionary ideology is concerned, I doubt if I have any political difference with communism," wrote Powers Hapgood as he outlined the reasons why the CP's tactics were destructive.[99] "The results of CP tactics on the united front is fatal and splits the workers," he argued, "They say they do not advance as a condition of the united front that the SP shall not criticize the CP and ask why the SP demands as a condition that the CP will quit its crazy tactics. We don't demand that the CP not criticize. I would be the last to ask it." "We do ask," he added, "that deliberate lies not be told, however."[100] Hapgood found Lovestone's group more honest in its analysis, citing Lovestone's *Workers Age* as an example of "decent criticism."[101]

Moscow's centralized control of national parties was a further reason for the RPCers and their allies to be skeptical about the CP's effectiveness. Hapgood drew on an example from the labor movement to support his claim that centralized control made the CP ineffective. "Poor old Bill Foster," wrote Hapgood, "writing and speaking about the folly of dual unionism and then because the CI [Communist International] says that the CP of this country should start dual unions he and the CP generally become the laughing stock of trade unionists by starting unions that have

[97] Ibid.
[98] Ibid.
[99] Powers Hapgood to Raymond, 10 March 1934, Box 5, PHP.
[100] Ibid.
[101] Ibid.

never gotten to first base."[102] The RPC also rejected dual unionism—i.e. forming radical, inclusive unions under the banner of the CP's Trade Union Unity League to compete with and oppose the AFL's affiliates.[103] Hapgood's rejection of the CP's obsequiousness also cooled his attitude toward the Lovestonites. "Theoretically," concluded Hapgood, "I think the Lovestoneites are sound. The only thing I can't understand about them is their belief that they can reform the CI [Communist International], which has been captured by a machine of which Lewis's machine in the UMW is a very small counterpart."[104] Hapgood's rejection of the CPO was based on its adherence to tactics that he could not accept as compatible with socialism. The means by which a revolutionary program was conducted mattered to Hapgood.

In an attempt to resolve this issue, the RPC clarified that it was different from the CP in four ways. The RPC did not adhere to the CP's "theory of social fascism." The CP regarded socialists and social democrats as the primary enemies of the working class who served to throw the rank and file "back into the arms of reaction."[105] The RPC also supported genuine united fronts, though not "united fronts from below," which it held to be disruptive and hostile. Communists advocated for "united fronts from below," efforts to unite rank-and-file workers from across leftwing organizations, while at the same time denouncing the leaders of socialist and social-democratic groups. Instead of promoting dual unionism, the RPC supported the AFL and "genuine independent unions" as vehicles for working-class mobilization and action.[106] Finally, the RPC rejected "the mechanical domination of the American [Communist] Party by the

---

[102] Ibid.

[103] Affiliates of the Trade Union Unity League did form, in some areas, a core of new industrial unions that would affiliate with the CIO. See Walter Galenson, *The CIO Challenge to the AFL: A History of the American Labor Movement, 1935–1941* (Harvard University Press, 1960), 255–256, 497–498; and Ronald L. Filippelli and Mark D. McColloch, *Cold War in the Working Class: The Rise and Decline of the United Electrical Workers* (SUNY Press, 1995), 21–23. The CIO itself was accused of dual unionism by the AFL's leadership. See Melvyn Dubofsky and Warren R. Van Tine, *John L. Lewis: A Biography* (University of Illinois Press, 1986), 164.

[104] Powers Hapgood to Raymond, 10 March 1934, Box 5, PHP.

[105] "RPC and the Communists," *The Revolutionary Socialist Review* 1, no. 1 (November 1934), 7.

[106] "Why the RSR?" *The Revolutionary Socialist Review* 1, no. 1 (November 1934), 5.

Russian Party."[107] The RPC also rejected the "mechanical domination" of both Trotsky and Stalin.[108] The RPC, or at least those of its members with a hand in drafting the November edition of *The Revolutionary Socialist Review*, did claim to embrace "democratic centralism."[109] Democratic centralism was a disciplinary device used by the CP to impose the majority's will on dissenters, who were expected to adhere to and carry out decisions adopted by the majority. Disagreements between the RPC's members and public resignations suggest that the RPC's members never reached or adhered to an internal consensus. They were unable or unwilling to practice "democratic centralism" because they lacked central control and cohesion.

For good measure, the RPCers extended their exercise in differentiation to the Lovestoneites. They saw Lovestone and his followers as too eager to rejoin the official CP. They also regarded the CPO's vision of the "Communist International [as] the logical political home of revolutionary workers" to be counterproductive. Most of the organized workers in the world, the RPC argued, found the Labor and Socialist International (LSI) to be a more satisfactory home because of its large membership. Socialist organizations, they argued, had revolutionary potential. Social-democratic policies, after all, looked much less appealing as a response to fascism when compared with revolutionary ideologies and appeals to violence in the face of repression. The RPC's members wanted to reform the LSI not leave it—and urged its members and leaders to follow their revolutionary program.[110] Using a similar argument, the RPCers dismissed the Trotskyites' call for a new international. The RPC planned to educate the workers of the LSI in revolutionary socialism.[111] Revolutionary socialism remained at the core of their program, and yet their means of organizing for "revolutionary socialism" were not incompatible with the Socialist Party's emphasis on debate and education as means for social transformation. It operated in the open, its members did not use pseudonyms, its appeal and ideas

[107] "RPC and the Communists," 7.

[108] Ibid., 10.

[109] Ibid.

[110] "An Appeal to the Membership of the Socialist Party," February 1934, Box 5, PHP.

[111] Ibid., 9.

were public, and one of its main achievements as an organization was the publication of a magazine to spread its ideas.

THE END OF THE RPC

The RPC's unraveling was a product of internal tensions and outside pressure from the SP. In June 1934, after a hostile response from across the SP, the RPC changed its name. It became the Revolutionary Policy Publishing Association. The leaders of the group adopted this change to assure the SP that it was not "a party within the Party." Further, the RPC's leaders reported that as a publishing association, it had "no dues-paying or disciplined membership... It has no connection with political groups outside the Socialist Party. It is loyal to the Party and willing to accept discipline—short of being forced to repudiate its revolutionary socialist convictions."[112] This was part of a concerted effort to satisfy critics. It also indicated the degree to which the RPC was willing to bend in order to remain within the SP.

These reassurances did not prevent further hostility toward the RPC and its ideas. The SP's governing body, the National Executive Committee, issued a harsh public statement on the RPC in December 1934. The statement suggests that the SP's leaders saw the RPC as little more than a communist plot to subvert the party and endanger the movement. Drafted by James Oneal and officially adopted by the National Executive Committee in late 1934, the statement confirmed that the RPC's position on insurrectionary revolution did not conform to the socialist principles upheld by the Socialist Party of America. "We hold that such doctrines are not only in conflict with the position of the Socialist Party, but are subversive of its aims and purposes," the NEC declared.[113] The rebuke came on the heels of the RPC's publication of the first issue of *The Revolutionary Socialist Review*. The NEC repudiated the tactical efficacy of the RPC's position on revolution. "It leads," the NEC declared, "the workers into unnecessary dangers, exposes the Socialist movement to the intrigues of agents provocateurs, diverts the workers from the work of organization and education as the basic means of attaining power, and commits the Socialist Party to the use of methods that will delay, instead of hasten, the triumphs of

[112]"The Michigan Convention," *Revolutionary Socialist Review* 1, no. 2 (February 1935), 7.

[113]"Party's Resolution on the Revolutionary Policy Committee," *The New Leader*, 8 December 1934, 7.

Socialist ideals."[114] The repudiation was complete and lacked any room for public compromise: "We hold that such doctrines are not only in conflict with the position of the Socialist Party, but are subversive of its aims and purposes."[115]

Norman Thomas took a more equivocal approach to the RPC. He rejected the RPC's views and opined that the formation of the group was an ominous sign for the SP.[116] Thomas proposed the RPC be investigated.[117] There is a possibility that Thomas's shock was disingenuous. He showed little animosity toward members of the RPC at Highlander when they asked him for help with recruiting shortly after the RPC's formation, though well before the NEC's statement of opposition.[118] Thomas did not limit his contact with the RPC's members after the NEC's December 1934 statement. He appointed J. B. Matthews as a League for Industrial Democracy (LID) lecturer, though, under pressure from other socialists, he eventually agreed to stop Matthews speaking on behalf of LID.[119] Thomas sided with the RPC when a member of the Young People's Socialist League (YPSL), the youth branch of the SP, was excluded from becoming a member of the party. He voiced his disquiet to the RPC. "I like Draper's statement," Thomas wrote to Francis Henson about the exclusion, "He expressed the basis on which I think the Socialist Party should contain him as well as those who do not agree with him on certain questions." Qualifying his position, Thomas continued, "As you know, I emphatically am critical of your RPC

[114] Ibid.

[115] Ibid.

[116] William M. Feigenbaum, "N.E.C. Appoints Committee for Nation-wide Survey," *The New Leader*, 8 December 1934, 6; Norman Thomas, "Timely Topics: The United Front Situation," *The New Leader*, 8 December 1934, 8.

[117] Feigenbaum, "N.E.C. Appoints Committee for Nation-wide Survey," 6.

[118] James Dombrowski to Norman Thomas, 7 March 1934, Box 24, Folder 27, HREC; Norman Thomas to James Dombrowski, 15 March 1934, Box 24, Folder 27, HREC; and "Minutes of the Board of Directors of L.I.D.," 2 April 1934, Box 29, Folder 3, League for Industrial Democracy Records, Tamiment Library and Robert F. Wagner Labor Archive, New York University, New York. Thomas did politely decline an offer to visit Highlander during its "labor week" in the summer of 1934. See Norman Thomas to Myles Horton, 12 July 1934, Box 27, Folder 24, HREC.

[119] J. Dennis McGreen, "Norman Thomas and the Search for the All-Inclusive Socialist Party" (Dissertation, Rutgers University, 1976), 116–117, 183. It is very likely that Thomas was able to exercise a moderating influence on the RPC's members, or at least those who were genuinely loyal socialists.

program and some of the things done by your group or by members of it."[120] Norman Thomas's relationship to the RPC was one of critical support. Thomas wanted to keep the RPC's members in the SP and told them, "I support the right of men like Draper to come into the Party. I shall try to make that support effective."[121] Even though he hoped to moderate the views of the RPCers, who were active and important members of the SP, advocating "armed insurrection" was too much for Thomas.[122]

As a result of the NEC's action (and lobbying from Norman Thomas), many of the RPC's members involved in the labor movement lasted less than a year in the organization.[123] In December, shortly after the NEC had adopted its position, a large block of the RPC's members in Philadelphia resigned over an internal dispute and mounting pressure from within the SP against the RPC's positions. Those who resigned argued that they broke with the RPC over its controversial stance on insurrection published in November 1934. Disagreements over the content of the RPC's program, voiced by RPCers in Philadelphia who worked in the labor movement, had been the subject of internal debates in early 1934, giving some credence to the claim, their claim, that they left the RPC for this reason and not due to pressure from Thomas or others in the SP.[124] The NEC's statement, however, was the final determining factor in their flight. If it had been unease with the RPC's public pronouncements alone that had precipitated their flight, they would have left much earlier in 1934. Instead, at the end of that year, David Felix, John Green, Wesley Cook, Alice Hanson, Julius Huss, Elwin Riemensynder, Newman Jeffrey, Philip Van Gelder, and John Park Lee issued a collective letter of resignation to the RPC.[125] The RPC splintered. Three months later, the mercurial J. B. Matthews and Ruth Shallcross—who were then married—resigned or were forced to

---

[120]"RPC News," *Bulletin of the Revolutionary Policy Committee of the Socialist Party of the U.S.A.*, 25 November 1934, Box 6, Folder 21, PVGC, 5.

[121]Ibid.

[122]McGreen, "Norman Thomas and the Search for the All-Inclusive Socialist Party," 190.

[123]Ibid., 188–189, 193.

[124]Franz Daniel to Philip Van Gelder, 19 March 1934, Box 6, Folder 21, PVGP; Ruth Shallcross to Phil [Van Gelder] and others, 17 March 1934, Box 6, Folder 21, PVGP.

[125]"Nine Resign from R.P.C.," *The New Leader*, 15 December 1934, 8.

resign from the RPC.[126] Matthews and Shallcross embraced the "theory of social fascism" in *Partners in Plunder: The Cost of Business Dictatorship*, a book the pair published in January 1935. The RPC officially severed its ties with Matthews and Shallcross and denounced "the theory of social fascism."[127] By 1938, Matthews had reconfigured his beliefs again. He took a job working for the Dies Committee, a forerunner to the House Un-American Activities Committee.[128]

The factionalism stoked by the RPC had hurt the SP in Philadelphia, not helped it. Alice Cook came to think of the RPC as a communist-influenced caucus within the Socialist Party. She compared it to similar caucuses within the establish trade unions led by communists. "The Revolutionary Policy Committee, which aimed to attract left-wingers in the Socialist Party, was headed by T. J. Matthews [actually it was J. B. Matthews, and he was not the group's only leader], nominally a Socialist Party left-winger," Cook wrote decades later. "Since the majority of the Philadelphia Socialist Party was very right-wing, made up largely of Jewish immigrant workers in the garment unions," she continued, "the RPC focused on the Kensington Branch, where it succeeded in creating a severe schism, one that used up time and energy needed for acute social issues." Her break with the RPC was a manifestation of the tension between a commitment to socialist ideals and the RPC's emphasis on the need for "armed insurrection."[129]

The RPC evaporated under internal and external pressures. Cook's remembered reasons for leaving the RPC must be weighed against the pressures that were placed upon the RPC's members at the end of 1934 and the beginning of 1935. An SP local in Buffalo expelled its RPCers for advocating "Communist theories." Oneal personally presided over the expulsions.[130] Norman Thomas was busy persuading them to abandon their most controversial positions. Cook explained her reasons for leaving by citing local conditions, "I was for a year or so an outspoken RPC

[126]McGreen, "Norman Thomas and the Search for the All-Inclusive Socialist Party," 183–184.

[127]"Concerning Ruth Shallcross and J.B. Matthews," *Revolutionary Socialist Review* 1, no. 2 (February 1935), 48.

[128]Landon R.Y. Storrs, *The Second Red Scare and the Unmaking of the New Deal Left* (Princeton University Press, 2013), 55–56.

[129]Alice Hanson to Comrades, in *New International* 2, no. 1 (17 January 1935), 32–33.

[130]"Buffalo Local Backs Expulsion of Five," *The New Leader*, 26 January 1935, 6.

advocate, until I saw that our branch, despite my best persuasion, was losing members rather than gaining influence. I came to the conclusion that
I had been used in an endeavor that had anything but the welfare of the
Socialist Party as its goal."[131] By 1936, still committed socialists, Alice Hanson, Franz Daniel, George Streator, and David Felix were listed alongside
many of their Militant comrades as contributors to the *American Socialist
Monthly*, the SP's theoretical publication.[132]

The development and organization of the RPC owed much to the con-
comitant pressures of fascism and the economic crisis. Its members included
many of those students radicalized at Union Theological Seminary. The
perceived inability of social democrats to defend against fascism coupled
with the belief that capitalism was in a terminal crisis radicalized these
young socialists. More than an actor in the parody of leftwing factionalism, the RPC was a genuine effort to wrestle with the complexities of the
1930s. As such, it reveals much about the specific rationales used to justify
a radical turn and indicates how SP tradition served as a break on violent
activity—if not violent rhetoric. Education and work within the established
labor movement continued to characterize the RPC's activities, even as its
members wrote about armed struggle. While the RPC's rhetoric divided
the SP, the revolutionary outlet that it offered kept young radicals inside the
SP and allowed them to retain their connections to the social-democratic
branch of the labor movement. Despite all of the RPC's claims to represent a revolutionary alternative, it did not stray far from the SP's imperatives
of education, work within the mainstream labor movement, and electoral
action. If the RPC moved beyond these tactics it was primarily in word and
not deed. Even radical experiments undertaken by the RPC's members,
explored in detail in the next chapter, were designed to educate workers,
offer an example of the new socialist society, and support the labor movement.

---

[131] Cook, *A Lifetime of Labor*, 76.

[132] Socialist Party of America, "Among Our Contributors," *American Socialist
Monthly* 5, no. 5 (July 1936).

CHAPTER 5

Fruits of the Socialist Revival

The socialist revival of the 1930s offered tangible organizing successes. Soviet House and Highlander Folk School were each attempts to put socialist ideals into practice. They represented some of the revival's vibrancy and success at the local level and refute claims that the revival resulted in little more than renewed factionalism or at best an alternative vision never put into practice. Even utopian idealism imbued with Marxist certainty, serving as metaphorical spark, could produce practical benefits for human society. This idealism could and did give way to real organizing successes and adapted to American political life. The socialist vision did change. Socialists *did* adapt to the conditions in the United States.[1] First, however, they experimented. The existence of the productive socialist network that fostered Soviet House and Highlander challenges the image of the Socialist Party in the 1930s. It was not a complacent party, absorbed only in the petty internal struggles. Rather socialists experimented in the 1930s, striving to make the world they envisioned a reality. This, more than destructive factionalism, is the legacy of socialism in the 1930s.

[1] Daniel Bell, "The Problem of Ideological Rigidity," in *Failure of a Dream? Essays in the History of American Socialism*, ed. John H.M. Laslett and Seymour Martin Lipset (University of California Press, 1984), 6.

SOVIET HOUSE

Founded in 1933, Soviet House, a row house located in Philadelphia's Kensington neighborhood, was an important site of socialist experimentation.[2] North Fifth Street was home to Philadelphia's radical socialists.[3] It served as cooperative housing, a center for SP activity, and a hub for union organizing efforts in the region. The community lasted for seven years and underwent transformations as its members' politics and the labor movement changed through the 1930s.[4] Franz Daniel was among Soviet House's founding members. Daniel lived in the house, where Zilla Hawes visited him often. During their time in Philadelphia, Daniel and Hawes worked in the labor movement alongside their comrades at Soviet House——who made up the core of socialist labor activists in Philadelphia and across the river in Camden, New Jersey—aiding working people in their struggles to organize labor unions.[5]

The communality of Soviet House was tied to its members' socialist identifications and desire to live out their ideals. Alice Cook confessed in her memoir that the people who lived and worked out of Soviet House "became an intimate group." Clarifying, she continued, "What today might be called a commune."[6] Cook remembered the communal atmosphere in the context of the games that the group developed for leisure. The lively socialists of Soviet House would gather and create "rhymes about current events as we viewed them." Their songs carried acerbic political content. Cook remembered one rhyme that castigated George Meany, at the time a prominent labor leader in the region and future leader of AFL and then the merged AFL-CIO, for his perceived misunderstanding of the economic crisis and his advocacy of entente with American capitalism: "Eeny, Meany, meiny mo, / American capital, go, stop, go! / You can stuff your planning / Of investment and manning / If profits continue to grow."[7] Cook's

---

[2] Cook, *A Lifetime of Labor*, 79.

[3] "Memorial Service for Franz E. Daniel," 29 September 1976, Box 15, Folder 19, FDC, 9; Cook, *A Lifetime of Labor*, 76, 79–80.

[4] "Memorial Service for Franz E. Daniel," 29 September 1976, Box 15, Folder 19, FDC, 9.

[5] Cook, *A Lifetime of Labor*, 80.

[6] Ibid., 309.

[7] Ibid., 310. The Soviet House socialists would end up working for Meany in the AFL-CIO, though resentments never cooled. See Daniel, *Rogue River Journal*, 116.

experience at Soviet House was so meaningful that she and her husband decided to name their son Phillip Jeffrey after their "Soviet Housemates, Philip Van Gelder and Newman Jeffrey."[8]

A socialist ethos shaped Philadelphia's Soviet House. Alice Cook remembered that life at Soviet House was financed in a way that helped spread the economic burden among residents with differing income levels. Each member of the community contributed a percentage of their earnings to the household's finances: "Our whole method of living there was that each of us contributed one-quarter of what we earned each month to keep the house going. And since most of the inmates were on relief, that meant that their monthly contribution was $15." The purpose of Soviet House, wrote Cook, was to "live together, share poverty and intermittent work, as we combined our talents and resources to assist with community efforts to meet the depression and spread the Socialist word."[9] Cook also remembered that Soviet House, like its counterpart Highlander Folk School, functioned as an unofficial extension of the SP: "We took in waifs and strays and committed wanderers, some sent to us by Norman Thomas, who I think used us as a dumping ground for the impossibles and as a training ground for the possibles."[10] Soviet House was an alternative form of housing, an intentional community, and a vibrant center of labor activity.

Soviet House connected college-educated socialists to the labor movement, cooperation that foreshadowed the future trajectory of the socialist movement. Alice Cook recalled, "Out of that house moved much of the dedication, the useful promise of those of us who were young in the 1930s."[11] Cook also remembered that Franz Daniel "made the place a vibrant, intensive discussion, never sleepy, always hoping, always planning, always active center."[12] Eventually, Daniel and Philip Van Gelder were "loaned" by the SP to the Amalgamated Clothing Workers of America's organizing campaign in northeastern Pennsylvania, which reflected the SP's role as a proving ground for talented organizers, who would then gradu-

---

[8] Cook, *A Lifetime of Labor*, 312.

[9] Ibid., 79.

[10] "Memorial Service for Franz E. Daniel," 29 September 1976, Box 15, Folder 19, FDC.

[11] Ibid.

[12] Ibid.

ate into social-democratic unions.[13] Both men eventually worked for the ACWA in a more permanent capacity, as did Zilla Hawes.[14]

The courage and dedication of socialists helped to build the labor movement. Capturing the moment of experimentation and radical fervor, Cook characterized Soviet House as "a group with diversity, with dedication, often with foolishness, sometimes with courage."[15] Many of Soviet House's alumni went on to important positions within the labor movement and as such were politic enough to distance themselves from previous activities that might have opened them up to critique from opponents inside and outside the labor movement. Notable residents of Soviet House included Franz Daniel, Alice Cook, Paul Porter, Eleanor Nelson, Newman Jeffrey, Miriam "Gob" Seaman, Philip Van Gelder, Wesley Cook, and Michael Harris.[16] Zilla Hawes and Mildred McWilliams, later Mildred Jeffrey, visited frequently while courting their future husbands, Daniel and Jeffrey.[17] Other important figures in the burgeoning industrial union movement were neighbors or visitors to Soviet House. John Green—an SP member who emigrated from the shipyards of Clydeside in Scotland and became president of the Industrial Union of Marine and Shipbuilding Workers of America, which won its foundational strike in 1934—lived with his family in a row house directly behind Soviet House.[18] Emil Rieve, president of the American Federation of Full-Fashioned Hosiery Workers and later the Textile Workers Union of America, also regularly visited Soviet House, which hosted frequent discussions on socialist policy.[19] Soviet House welcomed

[13]"Party Progress," 12 August 1933, *The New Leader*, 9; Karen Pastorello, *A Power Among Them: Bessie Abramowitz Hillman and the Making of the Amalgamated Clothing Workers of America* (University of Illinois Press, 2008), 91–93; and Daniel, *Rogue River Journal*, 28.

[14]Joseph Schlossberg to Whom It May Concern, 1 August 1933, Box 1, Folder 1, PVGP.

[15]"Memorial Service for Franz E. Daniel," 29 September 1976, Box 15, Folder 19, FDC, 10.

[16]Cook, *A Lifetime of Labor*, 78–79, 83, 309, 310.

[17]Ibid., 80. Mildred Jefferies went on to play an important part in the UAW and in Michigan politics.

[18]Cook, *A Lifetime of Labor*, 83.

[19]Gail Radford, *Modern Housing for America: Policy Struggles in the New Deal Era* (University of Chicago Press, 2008), 112.

a number of socialists who traveled to Philadelphia in the 1930s.[20] Alice Cook, who had connections to the socialist movement in Germany, helped to see that two comrades, officers of the German Carpenters' Union, found refuge first at Soviet House and later at Highlander Folk School.[21] When the CIO was established, its roving organizers found sustenance at Soviet House, too. "And when the CIO moved in," Alice Cook said, "and was organized or was in the process of organizing many of the great figures of the CIO, Charlie Ervin, many others came to us, shared our rather simple meals."[22] Ervin was a close associate of Sidney Hillman, president of the Amalgamated Clothing Workers of America.[23]

The movement for industrial democracy benefited from socialist support, particularly in terms of the confident young leaders that Thomas and the SP had mentored. The Philadelphia taxi strike, the Schwedische Kugel Fabrik strike in Kensington, and the success of the Industrial Union of Marine and Shipbuilding Workers of America were victorious organizing efforts rooted in Soviet House's socialist community. Soviet House provided aid for each of these campaigns.[24] In 1934, Alice Cook worked to develop a local of the American Federation of Teachers to which she was elected secretary.[25] Van Gelder and John Green led a strike of over three thousand workers at the New York Shipbuilding Company in Camden, NJ, just across the Delaware River—patrolled by union pickets on boats during the strike—from Soviet House.[26]

When the recalcitrant employer of the city's taxicab drivers locked the union's members out of their jobs for expressing pro-union sentiments,

---

[20] Cook, *A Lifetime of Labor*, 80.

[21] Cook, *A Lifetime of Labor*, 309–310; "Memorial Service for Franz E. Daniel," 29 September 1976, Box 15, Folder 19, FDC, 10.

[22] "Memorial Service for Franz E. Daniel," 29 September 1976, Box 15, Folder 19, FDC, 9.

[23] Galenson, *The CIO Challenge to the AFL*, 295.

[24] "Memorial Service for Franz E. Daniel," 29 September 1976, Box 15, Folder 19, FDC, 9; Cook, *Lifetime of Labor*, 81; and David Palmer, *Organizing the Shipyards: Union Strategy in Three Northeast Ports, 1933–1945* (Cornell University Press, 1998), 26.

[25] "North Phila. Socialists in the Labor Movement," *The Kensington Socialist*, 28 March 1934, Box 6, Folder 21, PVGC.

[26] Philip Van Gelder, "Ship Yards Picketed by Land and Sea as Strikers Hold Ranks in Camden," *New Leader*, 7 April 1934, 1-L, 4-L.

nine local unions went on strike in support of the cabbies. Socialists were responsible for much of the organizing impetus behind this action. Paul Porter and Franz Daniel helped organize the 900 taxicab drivers in late 1933 and led them to a victory when the employer's lockout was transformed into a strike that resulted in a largely unionized fleet of cabs in Philadelphia.[27] The strike of Philadelphia Taxi Drivers' Union Local 156 attracted great support from the nine other locals of the International Brotherhood Teamsters (IBT), who then engaged in sympathy actions. These sympathy strikes had not been sanctioned by the IBT, which makes these efforts at labor unity in the city and the union's eventual victory all the more extraordinary.[28] The strike also affirmed among socialist radicals that Roosevelt's government and the NIRA were instruments of capitalism. The National Labor Board was used to entice some of the IBT locals back to work with the promise of higher wages via a friendly decision in a wage dispute.[29] This skepticism would soon be challenged. At the time he led the strike, Porter had replaced Franz Daniel as the SP's organizer in Philadelphia.[30] In establishing Porter's fitness for the important position of the SP's labor secretary, *The New Leader* testified to the scope of the Soviet House socialist's abilities to build a dynamic labor movement in Philadelphia.

Porter and his comrades were directly involved in Philadelphia's most important labor struggles.[31] Beyond the taxi strike, Soviet House's socialists were involved in the 1933 Philadelphia Storage Battery Co. (referred to colloquially as "Philco") strike, a strike that provided the initial spark for the United Electrical, Radio, and Machine Workers of America (UE) and initiated conflicts within the AFL's arcane system of trade union orga-

[27] Cook, *A Lifetime of Labor*, 80.

[28] "Workers' NRA Faith Shattered After Three-Day Strike in Phila.," *New Leader*, 30 December 1933, 1, 6.

[29] Ibid., 1. The New Deal had, however, played a decisive role in helping Industrial Union of Marine and Shipbuilding Workers of America win employer recognition. The increasing role that the New Deal state played in labor relations may explain why laborites in the RPC were so quick (in the span of a few years) to convert to Roosevelt's Democratic Party.

[30] "Socialist-Led Strike Won in Philadelphia," *The New Leader*, 23 December 1933, 3; "Paul Porter Appointed Party Labor Secretary," *The New Leader*, 29 September 1934, 4.

[31] "Paul Porter Appointed Party Labor Secretary," *The New Leader*, 29 September 1934, 4.

nization.[32] Taking advantage of the protections offered by the National Industrial Recovery Act and assisted by Rieve's Full-Fashioned Hosiery Workers, the Philco strike was an impressive victory for the growing industrial union movement.[33]

Soviet House's candidates for state and local office were less successful.[34] Part of a larger socialist slate, neither Franz Daniel, who ran for coroner, nor Philip Van Gelder, who sought the office of register of wills, won their elections in 1933.[35] Even if the party failed to win elections in Philadelphia, the socialists at Soviet House demonstrated the efficacy of linking socialist ideals with the practical struggles of working people.

The origins of the name Soviet House remain murky. In the 1970s, Alice Cook took pains to point out that the neighbors—and not the residents—had named Soviet House.[36] This may have been apocryphal, as the radical socialists at Highlander Folk School embraced the term "soviet" in the 1930s. Given that many of Soviet House's members belonged to the RPC, which supported the concept of the workers' council or soviet, it seems unlikely that its members would have found the term alien. In the context of the Cold War and given the ascent of Soviet House's former members into the ranks of labor's leadership and into government service, troubled associations with the term "soviet" made revision necessary. Cook, for instance, went into government service during WWII and later held high-profile posts at Cornell University, including the position of Ombudsperson.[37] Cook, though, was fairly candid. She acknowledged associations that the right had used to damage many socialists and progressive liberals, though she was also aware of the destructive potential of McCarthyism.[38] Cook recounts, for instance, a trip to Germany in 1933 as

---

[32] "Party Progress," *The New Leader*, 12 August 1933, 9; Filippelli and McColloch, *Cold War in the Working Class*, 18; and Cook, *Lifetime of Labor*, 83.

[33] Irving Bernstein, *The Turbulent Years: A History of the American Worker, 1933–1941* (Haymarket Books, 2010), 102–103.

[34] James Carey, a Philco worker who helped to lead the 1933 strike and eventual UE and CIO leader, would later come to Paul Porter's defense when Porter was attacked at part of the Second Red Scare. See Storrs, *The Second Red Scare*, 142. Carey attacked Highlander as pro-Communist in the early 1940s.

[35] "Party Progress," *The New Leader*, 12 August 1933, 9.

[36] Ibid.

[37] Arlene Kaplan Daniels, introduction to *A Lifetime of Labor*, viii.

[38] Cook, *Lifetime of Labor*, 73, 157–158, 191.

the "secretary-cum-interpreter" for Mary Van Kleeck— an alleged communist. Associations with Van Kleeck had been used as evidence of subversion in partisan attacks on other left-liberal activists.[39]

If Soviet House's name later provoked a sense of unease, the staff members at Highlander Folk School in 1934 were less restrained in their use of the term "soviet" to describe the democratic meeting that governed the community program and regulated behavior.[40] Highlander's staff and students organized a "workers' council" at their Allardt extension in June 1934. They defined a workers' council as "a self-constituted body composed of the students and staff [that] governs the life, activities, and discipline of the summer school."[41] For them, the workers' council, used interchangeably with "soviet," was a means by which they could practice and model direct democracy. It was an important component of their political and social project.[42] It also suggests that Highlander's staff viewed social experiments with optimism and confirms an intellectual linkage with the Soviet House experiment in Philadelphia.

HIGHLANDER FOLK SCHOOL

Many excellent histories of Highlander, those written by both professional historians and former staff members, have explored the school's origins and operations.[43] Yet, these histories have not fully examined the importance

---

[39]Storrs, *The Second Red*, 149. Cook's memoir was not published until the 1990s and she apparently escaped anti-progressive investigations that did not spare her former comrades. Cook, therefore, was not constrained by the Cold War's pernicious domestic reaction or by the personal traumas of having lived through an investigation. Her Soviet House comrade Paul Porter was not so lucky. Porter became a leading administrator of American aid to Europe, whose career as a government official was undermined by partisan maneuvering and unsubstantiated ad hominem attacks that resulted in his resignation from the Mutual Security Agency. See Storrs, *The Second Red*, 141–143; Adam Bernstein, "Paul R. Porter, 94; Economist, Consultant," *The Washington Post*, 26 April 2002.

[40]"The Daily Record," 13 August 1934, Box 2, Folder 4, HREC.

[41]Ibid.

[42]"Minutes of Staff Conference," 29–31 July 1934, Box 2, Folder 4, HREC; Ralph Tefferteller to James Dombrowski, [1934], Box 15, Folder 31, HREC.

[43]Glen's *No Ordinary School* remains the most authoritative and exhaustive account of Highlander's history, though Frank Adams's biography of James Dombrowski and James Lorence's biography of Don West are indispensable contributions that add much complexity to presentations of Highlander's history.

of Highlander's socialism and its role in determining the staff's early under-standing of their project, its communal aspects, and the broader transfor-mative yearnings present at Highlander. This lacuna has resulted in a dearth of analysis of Highlander's socialist-inspired commune and reinforces the assumption that Highlander *itself* was not explicitly or primarily a socialist project.[44] Neglect of Highlander's socialism and a failure to contextualize it also limits our understanding of the extent and nature of socialism's revival in the 1930s. Highlander's early years are difficult to interpret without a thorough examination of the school's socialist context, which informed the shape of its inherently political community.

In the realm of ideas and in its networks of support, Highlander was a socialist school. Highlander owed much of its early content to the belief that capitalism was waning and a revolutionary uprising loomed on the horizon. And, like Soviet House, its early history was bound up in the revival of the SP in the 1930s. Highlander was a product of this socialist reawakening. Its embrace of workers' councils as a method of democratic organization also reveals the appeal of the RPC's ideas. Further, devoted staff members ready to sacrifice for the cause of socialism made up the ranks at Highlander. Leading socialists endorsed Highlander's work, and the school found the socialist press ready to advertise its efforts and requests to the broader socialist movement. Norman Thomas and Reinhold Niebuhr took personal interest in the school's welfare and in the development of its staff. In addition to occupying pride of place at the top of Highlander's list of members on the advisory committee, both Thomas and Niebuhr were also keen to visit Highlander in 1933–1934.[45] Highlander's survival as an institution, then, was due, in part, to the socialist networks from which it drew support to find students, staff members, money, publicity, and, as discussed in previous chapters, its intellectual genesis.

Highlander's initial choices for a location included a site offered to the school through contacts in the socialist movement. Following on a general commitment to work in the South, Myles Horton and Don West decided to establish their school near Monteagle, Tennessee, in Grundy County. This Monteagle site and not at the initially proposed Allardt, Tennessee, location was conditional. Dr. Lilian Johnson, a local education activist who

[44] Glen, *No Ordinary School*, 44.

[45] James Dombrowski to Rupert Hampton, 13 March 1934, Box 15, Folder 31, HREC; "Public Speaking," 26 May 1933, Box 31, Folder 8, HREC.

wished to retire, offered Horton and West the use of her property for their new school on a trial basis. The Monteagle location had modern facilities, a big house, and, as such, offered Horton and West more of a start than the undeveloped Allardt location owned by Joe Kelley and Kate Bradford Stockton, socialist comrades with whom the Highlander staff were close.[46] Later, Horton contextualized the plan to build an additional school at Allardt in 1934 as the result of Dr. Johnson's initial unease with Highlander's radical program, though it was also conceived and eventually became an expansion of Highlander into a new area.[47]

Grundy County proved a problematic choice for socialists who wished to foster a proletarian awakening. The land was poor. The forests had been cut down, and the mines were played out.[48] Grundy County in the 1930s was an object lesson in what happens to extraction-driven economies when resources have been stripped away to benefit outside interests.[49] The community and the land on which they lived were both impoverished. Grundy led Tennessee, and ranked very near the top nationally, in the proportion of people on relief in the middle of the decade.[50] A highway running through the county provided its only real economic engine.[51] With a nonexistent economic base and reliance on unfriendly local and regional administrators for relief jobs, the local community's efforts to organize in the 1930s were vulnerable. They possessed little power to alter their circumstances.[52] The realities of the region also helped to reshape Highlander's expectations for the future and redirected its purpose. "We... found that our talk about brotherhood and democracy and shared experiences," recalled Horton, "was irrelevant to people in Grundy County in 1932. They were hungry. Their problems had to do with how to get some food in their bellies and how to get to a doctor."[53] Revolutionary rhetoric did not feed hungry people. There were times when the diet of staff at Highlander was lean.

[46]Horton, *The Long Haul*, 63; James Lorence, *A Hard Journey*, 35.

[47]Horton, *The Long Haul*, 66.

[48]Michael E. Price, "The New Deal in Tennessee: The Highlander Folk School and Worker Response in Grundy County," *Tennessee Historical Quarterly* 43 (1984), 100.

[49]Ibid., 102.

[50]Ibid.

[51]Ibid., 101.

[52]Horton, *The Long Haul*, 73.

[53]Ibid., 69.

Staff members were conscious of Highlander as a socialist project from its earliest beginnings. In 1931, Zilla Hawes, who would later join Highlander's staff, wrote to Myles Horton confirming her desire to work in the movement "as a socialist."[54] Both of Highlander's initial founders—West and Horton—were card-carrying socialists and, as Don West's biographer stressed, "Horton and West had made socialist organizing the central feature of [Highlander's] program."[55] After the close of Highlander's first term, *The New Leader*, the most prominent socialist paper in the country, lauded the school's good work and praised Highlander for its contributions to the furtherance of "the cooperative commonwealth."[56] Don West's plan for a chain of libraries dedicated to workers and located throughout Georgia was also praised in the pages of *The New Leader*: "The necessity for books is highly stressed and all individuals who wish to co-operate are invited to correspond with Don West, Georgia Workers Co-operative Library, Kennesaw, Georgia."[57] West's plan to establish libraries for workers in Georgia fit well with the socialist emphasis on an auto-didactic program for informing working people of the benefits of a socialist society.

Highlander was a recognized outpost of socialism. Highlander's staff organized a local of the SP for the area, though it remained small.[58] One of Highlander's students from the local community reported, "one just had to be around [Highlander's staff] and in the community for a short while until one became a socialist."[59] Don West, who was briefly the state organizer for Tennessee's branch of the SP, also published poetry in addition to appeals for support in the *New Leader*.[60] West's poem spoke of poverty in the South and the death-dealing toil that condemned workers to an early grave. A reviewer for the *New Leader*, S. A. DeWitt, described West as "a Socialist poet" and informed readers that the money raised from the sale of West's

---

[54] Zilla Hawes to Myles Horton, 27 September 1931, Box 15, Folder 30, HREC.

[55] Lorence, *A Hard Journey*, 34.

[56] "The Highlander Folk School," *New Leader*, 8 April 1933, 11.

[57] Ibid.

[58] Dorothy Thompson to Rupert Hampton, 17 April 1934, Box 15, Folder 31, HREC.

[59] Rupert Hampton to James Dombrowski, [March 1934], Box 15, Folder 31, HREC.

[60] Lorence, *A Hard Journey*, 26; Don West, "Factory Child", *New Leader*, 4 March 1933, 9; and Don West, "Highlander Folk School Appreciates New Leader," *New Leader*, 4 March 1933, 13.

book of poems would help to fund Highlander Folk School. DeWitt's review of his comrade's work was wholly positive.[61]

In 1933, Highlander helped to foster a branch of the YPSL. Staff put on a "socialist summer school," which was organized in cooperation with the SP.[62] The "Yipsels," as members of the YPSL were called, put out a weekly broadsheet titled *Nit Wit: Live and Learn*. *Nit Wit*, most of the paper was apparently cribbed from the *American Guardian*, a paper edited by Oklahoma socialist Oscar Ameringer. The students' selections provide clues about the intellectual atmosphere at Highlander. One short piece compared workers in "6932 B.C." to their modern counterparts in "1933 A.D." The workers of the precapitalist world each created a surplus, and, in the end, realizing their bounty when the products of their labors were shared, called out together in glee, "Whoopee! Let's eat, drink, love, snooze and make merry until we need more." By contrast, the modern workers, who had also created a surplus, were bound by capitalism to have this wealth expropriated from them. They cried, "Come on, everybody, let's starve, freeze, go naked and homeless together."[63] The Yipsels hit out at capitalism's inhumanity in poem after poem, saying after saying, and sketch after sketch. They denounced contemporary economic thinking: "We were taught to believe that capitalists create employment, and now we are learning that capitalists create unemployment. Oh well, experience is the best teacher."[64] They lambasted politicians, bureaucrats for forsaking the farmer and ridiculed the claim that overabundance was responsible for the economic crisis.[65] They argued instead that private property and the insufficient sharing of all of the goods produced by human labor were at the root of the crisis. "No monkey ever went hungry," one Yipsel included, "because there was a 'No Trespassing' sign on a coconut tree!"[66] Another wondered if a mouse had ever "starved to death in a hunk of cheese because the hunk was bigger than she could eat." "No," replied *Nit Wit*, "maybe

---

[61] S.A. DeWitt, "A Poem Out of the Deep Misery of The Blue Ridge Mountains; and an Open Letter to Upton Sinclair," *New Leader*, 4 March 1933, 9.

[62] "Socialist Summer Schools," *New Leader*, 22 April 1933, 11.

[63] "Then and Now," *Nit Wit: Live and Learn*, [1933], Box 85, Folder 2, HREC.

[64] *Nit Wit*, Vol. 1, No. 4, [1933], Box 85, Folder 2, HREC.

[65] Ibid.

[66] Ibid.

it was the fellow who doped out the term 'over-production' while dying of malnutrition."[67]

When it came time to recruit help for Highlander's ambitious second location, the staff used their socialist networks to find recruits. Recruitment for this project was particularly difficult because, as James Dombrowski explained, "the only remuneration we can promise them is the experience of working in a thoroughly interesting mountain community, good fellowship, and the participation in a significant social adventure."[68] Prospective workers were expected to contribute five dollars a week in expenses.[69] James Dombrowski wrote to Andrew Biemiller, who was then education director in the SP's Milwaukee stronghold and editor of the city's socialist newspaper, asking for help finding student workers willing to spend the summer building socialism. Biemiller was not optimistic about finding willing recruits who would pay their way to work on the school's new buildings and farm, but he offered to run a feature on Highlander and its recruitment efforts in his paper, *The Milwaukee Leader*.[70] Howard "Buck" Kester, another of Highlander's socialist comrades, also recommended students.[71] Dombrowski asked the League for Industrial Democracy (LID), a socialist organization for college students codirected by Norman Thomas and Harry Laidler, for help in identifying students for Highlander's summer session and building program. While several LID members were already going to Highlander, the organization could find no more who would be able to pay their way to Allardt and wanted to do "straight manual labor" with no remuneration.[72] When Highlander's staff wanted reliable recruits to help with an ambitious building project planned for the summer of 1934, they also asked Norman Thomas to provide suggestions, which he did.[73]

Highlander's relationship with Norman Thomas was particularly important to the school. Thomas offered to help the school financially and

---

[67] Ibid.

[68] James Dombrowski to Norman Thomas, 7 March 1934, Box 27, Folder 24, HREC.

[69] Ibid.

[70] Andrew J. Biemiller to James Dombrowski, 27 March 1934, Box 31, Folder 8, HREC.

[71] "Soviet Meeting: Allardt Staff," 2 April 1934, Box 31, Folder 8, HREC.

[72] "Anna Caples to James Dombrowski," 1 June 1934, Box 31, Folder 8, HREC.

[73] James Dombrowski to Norman Thomas, 7 March 1934, Box 27, Folder 24, HREC; Norman Thomas to James Dombrowski, 15 March 1934, Box 27, Folder 24, HREC.

through his various connections. He wrote Myles Horton in the autumn of 1933, "My promise stills holds good that as soon as I get that legacy which is coming some time I'll contribute to your school and your general work in the South. I do wish you all the luck in the world."[74] In response to a plea from Horton and West for books to populate their planned libraries for workers and "to conduct study classes in socialism," Thomas added a suggestion for immediate and practical support: "I do think that possibly through the L.I.D. some arrangement might be made to send out a loan library recalling books from time to time."[75] Thomas traveled Wilder, Tennessee, when the town's miners when out on strike to offer his support and to, at the behest of optimistic Highlander staff members, spread the gospel of the socialist movement.[76] Thomas's personal feelings for the younger socialists found expression in his regret at having missed them on a trip to Tennessee:

> I was awfully sorry not to see you and Myles. I was going to stop and see Myles at the sanitarium but by mistake Clarence [Senior] and I took the wrong fork in the road and got to Nashville without passing the sanitarium. How is he now? Give him my love. Let me know how the financial situation looks to you. How many students have you? Thanks for the good news about active work [for the party] in Tennessee.[77]

His regard for their work and his concern for the project's future were apparent.

Highlander's staff cultivated a socialist culture at the school. Highlander's leftwing rhetoric also included the occasional letter with the valedictions, "yours for the revolution," "yours for a real revolution," and the more tongue-in-cheek "yours for a functional revolution."[78] Capitalism

---

[74] Norman Thomas to Myles Horton, 19 September 1933, Box 27, Folder 21, HREC.

[75] Myles Horton to Norman Thomas, 24 April 1933, Box 27, Folder 24, HREC; Norman Thomas to Myles Horton, 19 September 1933, Box 27, Folder 21, HREC.

[76] John Thompson to Norman Thomas, 23 February 1933, Box 27, Folder 24, HREC.

[77] Norman Thomas to James Dombrowski, 15 March 1934, Box 27, Folder 24, HREC.

[78] "Special to the Daily Record," 29 August 1934, Box 31, Folder 8, HREC; Ralph Tefferteller to James Dombrowski, [1934], Box 15, Folder 31, HREC, 2; and Zilla Hawes to Old Hussey, 24 January 1934, Box 15, Folder 31, HREC.

was always due a good verbal flogging at Highlander.[79] Staff members referred to one another as "comrade." They were aware of various SP factions in the 1930s. Dombrowski reported back to his comrades after attending the convention proceedings of the United Textile Workers. He told them, "much of the Old Guard leadership has been reelected, and with such leadership the militant workers will have a hard fight."[80] The event had also given Dombrowski hope, as "a motion to approve the general strike in the event of war was lost by a narrow margin."[81] Staff members' letters were sometimes signed "commissar," indicating the young socialists' continuing fascination with the Soviet Union.[82] A hammer and sickle—perhaps sketched by Highlander staff member Mac Chisholm, the illustrator, puppeteer, and volunteer for the Spanish Civil War—artfully adorned the tops of the "Daily Records" written by Highlander comrades at Allardt.[83] Perhaps not every person was pleased with the hammer and sickle, but its presence and the debate about communism and socialism indicate that the early to mid-1930s was a period, at least for some of those on the left of the SP, during which experimentation and cross-party intermingling were permissible. This was particularly true in the South. Highlander was far away from the intense and bitter battles in Northern cities where relations between the SP and the CP became increasingly hostile.[84] For the socialists, who had lost to fascism their two most impressive political movements in Germany and Austria, the threat of rightwing reaction and all that it entailed remained greater than the CP.

Zilla Hawes connected the program of Highlander's two soviets, one at Monteagle and one at Allardt, to the larger, international struggle of the socialists against fascism and in doing so firmly rooted Highlander within a tradition that viewed immediate action as an essential component of the project of social transformation. "Our movement," Hawes opined, "must bear the kind of results the Austrian Socialists are showing in their

---

[79] "Greetings, Comrade," 7 September 1934, Box 31, Folder 8, HREC.

[80] "The Daily Record," 19 August 1934, Box 31, Folder 8, HREC.

[81] James Dombrowski to Al Lovejoy, 20 August 1934, Box 31, Folder 8, HREC.

[82] "Daily Record," 10 September 1934, Box 31, Folder 8, HREC.

[83] "Daily Record," 10 September 1934, Box 31, Folder 8, HREC; "Daily Record," 11 September 1934, Box 31, Folder 8, HREC.

[84] Raymond Gregory, *Norman Thomas: The Great Dissenter* (Algora, 2008), 134–135.

determined opposition to fascist forces."[85] Hawes was far too optimistic. Under artillery bombardment, for which the socialist militia had no answer, armed resistance to fascism collapsed a few days after she wrote her letter. The small arms of the socialist rebels could not fend off the artillery of Austrian army, which was turned on the socialist-constructed apartment blocks that were the last redoubts of Red Vienna.[86] Nonetheless, American socialists cheered the heroism of their fallen Austrian comrades. James Oneal, editor of *The New Leader*, called Austrian socialists' resistance, "the most heroic struggle since the first captives of antiquity revolted against their enslavers."[87] The Highlander's socialists held a similar view. They had finally found common ground with William Green, president of the AFL, who said, "The inhumane persecution of the Socialists and working people of Austria has excited the righteous indignation of all the working people in our country."[88]

Highlander received support from the older socialists who tried to keep the torch of socialism aloft in Tennessee. This was a reciprocal relationship. As Highlander was supported by the remnants of Tennessee's state branch of the SP, its staff members sought to revive the SP on the local and state level. In 1932, Zilla Hawes asked Myles Horton, "Has Debs left no imprint on the country to help you?"[89] Debs had actually left a small imprint in Tennessee, which helped Highlander's staff and was the basis of the second school at Allardt. The revival of Tennessee's socialists was limited. There were few old members and younger members were concentrated at Highlander. Their ideas also revealed one of the reasons why the SP floundered after its brief revival: Roosevelt's New Deal held a palpable attraction for socialists. The Tennessee socialists were organized enough to draft four resolutions and send them to President Roosevelt. It is not clear who was responsible for drafting the document. It was signed "State Executive Committee of Socialist Party of Tennessee," and a further signature indicated that it was prepared by the state secretary, J. K. Stockton, a

[85] Zilla Hawes to Old Madame, 13 February 1934, Box 15, Folder 31, HREC.

[86] David Clay Large, *Between Two Fires: Europe's Path in the 1930s* (New York: W. W. Norton, 1991), 87.

[87] James Oneal, "Austrian Rising Greatest Labor Epic Since Days of the Paris Commune," *The New Leader*, 24 February 1934, 5.

[88] "Green Flays Butchery in Austria," 24 February 1934, *The New Leader*, 3.

[89] Zilla Hawes to Myles Horton, 20 November 1932, Box 15, Folder 30, HREC.

friend of Highlander's staff members. In the document, Tennessee's socialists demanded that President Roosevelt recognize the Soviet Union. Their
argument for this recognition acknowledged the diplomatic, economic, and
intellectual benefits of such a move. They urged Roosevelt to "abrogate
the Platt Amendment" and affirm a bond of friendship and solidarity with
the Cuban people. Further, they indicated that they thought the National
Industrial Recovery Act was a good beginning and that the government
planning of and control over "the three great elements of production, distribution and consumption" would yield great benefits for working people.
They championed the Tennessee Valley Authority as an indication of what
the government could accomplish in the lives of its people, and they held it
to be a stupendous example of the efficacy of "government ownership, control and operation." They urged President Roosevelt to "carry this through
to the ultimate social good and a comprehending grateful humanity will
crown the names of Roosevelt and Norris [a senator from Nebraska who
was instrumental in passing the Tennessee Valley Authority Act in 1933,
resisting the objections of private energy suppliers] with laurels of perpet-
ual peace."[90] The older variants, older than the RPC's aggressive strain,
of socialism that remained in rural regions were quickly swept up by New
Deal achievement. Most of the SP would join them.

Though immediately more sympathetic to the New Deal than his
younger comrades, J. K. Stockton, shared Highlander's affinity for intentional community and social transformation. He was, at least briefly, an
adherent of the Revolutionary Policy Committee.[91] Stockton had plans
with the local SP and Highlander's staff to open a children's summer
camp at Allardt, Tennessee, after a successful "Southern summer school for
Socialist workers" was held at Highlander's Monteagle location in 1933.[92]
In December 1933, Stockton's land became the site of Highlander's second
unit when the socialist summer camp project morphed into a Highlander
extension.[93] Stockton and the Highlander's plan never completely materi-
alized. Stockton hoped to turn over 1000 acres of land into a cooperative

[90]State Executive Committee of Socialist Party of Tennessee to the President of the
United States, 28 October 1933, Box 68, Folder 15, HREC.

[91]J.K.S. Stockton to Myles Horton, 1 July 1934, Box 27, Folder 3, HREC.

[92]"Party Notes," *New Leader*, 18 November 1933, 7; "Begin Socialist Drive in the
South," *New Leader*, 25 November 1933, 6.

[93]James Dombrowski to Al and Dot, 18 March 1934, Box 31, Folder 8, HREC;
"Begin Socialist Drive in the South," *New Leader*, 25 November 1933, 6.

with its own productive industries to provide employment and sustenance for a community hard hit by the economic crisis. It was a beautiful dream, a vision of Highlander's community magnified to incorporate a much larger community.[94] The Highlander project at Allardt captured Stockton's hopes and dreams on a smaller scale, which explains why J. K. and Kate Bradford Stockton were generous patrons of school and friends to its staff.[95]

Committed socialists at Highlander and their allies throughout the state were not able to turn their incredible energy into a successful, full-fledged resurgence of socialism's fortunes in Tennessee. Yet they were successful in developing education, political action, and labor organization, all key components of the socialist program, and they did attract some attention for the party.[96] The SP's few committed representatives in Tennessee during the revival quickly became involved in labor work, which eroded the amount of time they could spend on party work.[97] This was true of Howard Kester, who provided vital support for the Wilder strike and later for the Southern Tenant Farmers' Union. It was the same for Horton and West, who also provided support for the Wilder strike.[98] In the spring of 1933, the *New Leader* published Don West's heartrending report from the coalfields of Wilder, Tennessee. Barney Graham, union leader of a ten-month miners' strike in Wilder, was assassinated on April 30, 1933. Graham and his family—who had become friendly with Highlander's Horton and West, as well as socialists Howard and Alice Kester—were nearly destitute and he had gone out in the evening to find food and medicine for his sick wife. Men in the pay of the Fentress Coal and Coke Company shot Graham ten times and crushed his skull as he lay dying in the street outside the company's

[94] Joe Kelly Stockton, "Fentress County Cooperative," [1933], Box 31, Folder 8, HREC.

[95] J.K. Stockton to Myles Horton, 22 March 1933, Box 27, Folder 3, HREC; K.B. Stockton and J.K. Stockton to Myles Horton, 8 April 1934, Box 27, Folder 3, HREC.

[96] See Price, "The New Deal in Tennessee," 99–120; H. Glyn Thomas, "Highlander Folk School: The Depression Years," *Tennessee Historical Quarterly*, 23 (1964), 358–371.

[97] Most of Tennessee's committed socialist activists had come to Tennessee from other areas and were involved with the labor or another social cause. The paucity of organizers outside of a few major centers of support meant that little time could be dedicated to the rebuilding of the party's apparatus in states where it had been decimated by anti-socialism and then by a decade of neglect. There was simply too much work and too few people to do it.

[98] Grubbs, *Cry from the Cotton*, 75–76.

store.[99] Two of Graham's murderers faced trial. They were acquitted.[100] The Fentress Coal and Coke Company operated with impunity. Before the New Deal reforms in labor relations that sanctioned union representation and collective bargaining, only the collective force of the organized and implacable workers could hold the unmitigated power of the coal companies in check. The outbreak of strikes and the coal company's actions provoked violence that would bring the National Guard—which did not operate as a neutral arbitrator. The Wilder strike was typical of this pattern of pre-NIRA and pre-Wagner labor relations. The socialists, including Norman Thomas who visited Wilder at Highlander's request, had failed the striking miners not because they were wrong, weak, or too ideological.[101] The strike failed because workers and their socialist supporters lacked the resources and power of the coal company and its allies in local and state government. The coal company's use of violence broke the strike. Blacklisted miners eventually found some relief from federal agencies.[102] Labor organizing came to occupy much of the staff's time. The socialists were unable to resist the pull of working-class struggles.

Highlander's relationship with some of the SP's individual members, including its supporters, became tense when two of the school's staff members and Franz Daniel, its close collaborator, endorsed the radical program of the RPC.[103] Highlander staff's public approval of the RPC stained its relationship with Kirby Page, a prominent Christian socialist, reformer, and pacifist, who resigned from Highlander's advisory board over the supposedly revolutionary content of Highlander's program.[104] His disagree-

---

[99]Accounts of Graham's death are remarkably consistent with only a few minor variations. He was undoubtedly targeted by Fentress Coal because he was the indefatigable leader of the strike, and his murder was meant as a message to the other miners out on strike; "The Ballad of Barney Graham," *Southern Exposure*, 5, no. 1 (1976).

[100]Frank Adams, *Unearthing Seeds of Fire: The Idea of Highlander* (John F. Blair, 1975), 191.

[101]Norman Thomas to Myles Horton, 7 February 1933, Box 27, Folder 24, HREC; Myles Horton to Norman Thomas, 20 February 1933, Box 27, Folder 24, HREC; and John Thompson to Norman Thomas, 23 February 1933, Box 27, Folder 24, HREC.

[102]Lorence, *A Hard Journey*, 32–33.

[103]Ruth Shallcross to James Dombrowski, 14 February 1934, Box 68, Folder 15, HREC. This parting of the ways mirrored the larger split in the socialist movement between the party's gradualist, social-democratic elements and the militants who employed revolutionary rhetoric.

[104]Zilla Hawes to Myles Horton, [Winter 1933–1934], Box 15, Folder 30, HREC.

ment with the RPC was public, though not his break with Highlander. Page attacked the RPC for leading "the workers into unnecessary dangers, [exposing] the Socialist movement to the intrigues of agents provocateurs, [diverting] the workers from the work of organization and education as the basic means of obtaining power, and [committing] the Socialist Party to the use of methods that will delay, instead of hastening—the triumph of Socialist ideals."[105] In turn, the RPC critiqued Page's "reformism."[106] Page's break with Highlander was unnecessary and was primarily about language and not substance; the school's staff never abandoned or displaced the work of organizing and education. These two socialist strategies remained central to Highlander's identity and mission throughout its existence. In a short time, many of the RPC's members would agree with Page's general conclusion that "such doctrines [armed insurrection and dictatorship of the proletariat] are not only in conflict with the position of the Socialist Party, but are subversive of its aims and purposes."[107] They embraced social democracy. By this time, however, they were firmly under the spell of the New Deal coalition and the SP was becoming irrelevant.

The socialists at Highlander differed from some of their party elders, though not Stockton, on an important point of socialist theory, the path to socialism. The comrades at Highlander believed that they could create a model of the new society. Some socialists put much less emphasis on individual or collective agency as the catalyst to create a socialist society, preferring to rely on historical abstractions. They favored waiting for history to unfold (i.e. the contradictions of capitalism would do the work for them) and give birth to a new world, or, they argued, that socialists could hardly be expected to usher in a new social order in a single locale.[108] "Of course Socialists in control of a single city cannot establish Socialism there while the rest of the state and the nation remains capitalist," wrote James Maurer, the

---

[105] Kirby Page, "Property: A Consideration of the Tactics of Violence and Dictatorship Raised by Communists Throughout the World," *New Leader*, 24 August 1935, 5.

[106] Revolutionary Policy Committee, "Tendencies within the Socialist Party: An Outline," 22 May 1934, Box 6, Folder 21, PVGP. The document named Page as the representative of "reformism."

[107] Page, "Property: A Consideration of the Tactics of Violence and Dictatorship Raised by Communists Throughout the World," 5.

[108] Mark Pittenger, *American Socialists and Evolutionary Thought, 1870–1920* (University of Wisconsin Press, 1993), 159.

SP's vice-presidential candidate in 1932.[109] The social-democratic vision of what was to be done was limited. "They cannot do much more than give a clean, honest, efficient, humane administration, free from graft," explained Maurer, "thereby proving that workers are not all hands and no brains, as exploiters of labor would have the world believe. To do that is worth while."[110] Highlander, then, at the outset represented a rebellion against the received wisdom of the social democrats, though Highlander's staff also advocated electoral action and helped local workers achieve limited success in that realm. They envisioned their work as truly transformational. They were bringing a new world into being.

No Perfect Place: Living Socialism at Highlander

Highlander's program included an effort to model socialism, to build a new society amidst the perceived collapse of capitalism. Highlander's intentional community was a direct consequence of the socialist ideology of its staff members, an ideology that, in the 1930s, had millenarian and utopian sentiments at its core. The staff's vision of their project was unambiguous. They were building a new world in opposition to the old. Highlander's efforts to create an alternative to capitalism can be properly characterized as an example of a socialist commune. The school's staff explicitly rejected the idea that their project was "utopian" and hoped that it would be more engaged with the world than the inward-looking utopian efforts they had studied.

Highlander, despite the efforts of its staff, was a utopian project. It was carefully planned in accordance with the staff's socialist principles and designed to represent the new way of living, the indisputable future. The staff's ideological assumptions shaped the material and cultural foundation of the school and provided a common organizing goal of building a socialist community in a deliberate way. This ultimately proved too demanding a task. Tensions between staff members arose as an idyllic utopian ideal came into conflict with the realities of running a commune, a school, and providing aid for the labor movement. Highlander's efforts to foster a living

---

[109] James Maurer, *It Can Be Done: The Autobiography of James Hudson Maurer* (The Rank School Press, 1938), 305.

[110] Ibid., 305.

socialism were further inhibited by logistical and economic difficulties and by the demands of the labor movement.

The socialists who created Highlander were keen to build a community engaged with broader struggles of working people and capable of stoking the boilers of working-class unrest. They did not want to build Highlander for its own self-aggrandizement or as a colony that would distance itself from the main currents of society. Rather, the school's staff wished to influence and transform society. The comrades at Highlander envisioned a political commune that would reach into the surrounding communities and, to paraphrase Zilla Hawes, spread a radical fire of socialism among the workers and peasants.[111] Myles Horton believed that "the tie-up with the conflict situations and participation in community life keeps our school from being a detached colony or Utopian venture [indecipherable] our effort to live out our ideals makes possible the development of a bit of proletarian culture as an essential part of our program of worker education."[112] While their efforts were not entirely successful, these ideas set Highlander apart from other communal projects that had no basis in an explicitly party-political or theoretical-revolutionary movement. The radical socialist politics of the Highlander project were central to its communal project.

Staff members' choice of governance confirms Highlander's status as a commune, developing out of the RPC in the 1930s. They chose to name their democratic mechanism of government a workers' council or "soviet." By explicitly calling the governing body of the community a "soviet," Highlander's staff demonstrated the radical left of the SP was more than rhetoric; they were undertaking an experiment. Historians have traced the origins of soviets, or workers' councils, to the Russian revolutions of 1905 and 1917 as well as the upheavals following WWI when, for a moment, it appeared that Europe might be engulfed in revolution.[113] "Soviets" did not have their origins in the Bolshevik faction of the Russian Social Democratic Labor Party. They were important enough for the Bolsheviks to incorporate—at least in name—into their new state.[114] If socialists from the United

[111]Zilla Hawes, "Recommendations," September 1934, Box 2, Folder 4, HREC.

[112]Highlander Staff, "Rules," 1934. Box 2, Folder 4, HREC.

[113]Albert S. Lindemann, *A History of European Socialism* (Yale University Press, 1984), 356.

[114]David Childs, *The Two Red Flags: European Social Democracy and Soviet Communism Since 1945* (Routledge, 2000), 2. Workers' councils had a life well beyond the emergent Soviet Union. See Loew, "The Politics of Austro-Marxism," 32–35.

States adopted the term to refer to their community's governing structure, it was because they valued the workers' council as a form of government with a base at what they saw as the very root of society.

Highlander's staff differentiated their communal efforts from the capitalist society that they had come to reject. "Comrade Schlee returned to the Soviet yesterday," one Highlander communard reported in the school's work schedule for the summer of 1934. "He was gone into the wilds of civilization for approximately seven working days. He came in with tall tales of the capitalist world in general."[115] The *Highlander Fling*, the school's newspaper, described the labor on Highlander's Allardt extension as a part of the construction of a socialist world that the Highlander community was creating. "Everyone from the chief architect to the least wheel-barrow pusher," read the *Fling*, "works without pay to transfer the dream of a new world into reality."[116] Highlander's staff conceptualized their project as a revolutionary program. They were building an alternative to the capitalist society that had failed to provide for so many. There was no mincing of words about the intent and import of their project.

Highlander's staff struggled to create an intentional community that remade people, social relationships, and education according to their understandings of socialist principles. Daily life became a didactic exercise. "Use actual things which occur here as illustrative material, in an objective way," a member of Highlander's staff told their comrades during a meeting. "To quote from Myles [Horton]," the staff member continued, "To make such discussions realistic we will have to use situations exactly as they are found in our own group." Highlander's commune was a model to work out the shape of the new world, which meant members of the Highlander community were test subjects. "This means that individuals must submerge their individualism and be willing to be used as illustrative material," the staff member said, continuing to quote Horton, "Personal problems are important but do not come into this particular discussion except as they grow out of the larger and more immediate problem of group control and working class leadership." The subordination of "individualism" was a part of the utopian program. The assertive, middle-class personalities of some staff members had to be restrained to solve the "problem of group control

[115]"Work Schedule," 12 July 1934, Box 31, Folder 8, HREC.
[116]"School's New Site," *Highlander Fling*, September 1934, Box 84, Folder 7, HREC.

and working class leadership." Criticism would, in theory, not be a personal attack on an individual. People were encouraged to think of themselves as separate and detached from their immediate past experiences and instantly capable of establishing rational perspective to further an experiment that had to be properly interrogated and improved. "If you are brought into the discussion," the staff member said, "it will be because a certain thing was done, not because you did a certain thing. In other words, what happened is the important thing, not who did it. All this required a high degree of objectivity and genuine interest in the labor cause."[117] By incorporating "objectivity" to foster the detachment of the personal problems from the problems of the community, Horton implied the two could be disentangled. This was not the case, as problems with the school's work regime indicated.

WORK AND CONTROL

Staff struggled to build and sustain their model for society. They wanted to encourage freedom and creativity, and yet they had to balance these ideals against the requirements of work necessary to sustain the commune and school. Highlander's answer was a rigid work regime (not always so rigidly enforced) and a system of hierarchy with managers responsible for each aspect of the community's existence. "We started out with classes, work, and leisure, and set up a council for the purpose of government," read one account of work's centrality at the school, "The work was included, not because of the educational program, but because it was necessary. The work had to be done, and not wishing nor being able to hire it done, we had to do it ourselves."[118] Contradictions inherent in the concept of the radically egalitarian society plagued work life, as staff attempted to solve the problem of management coercion in a putatively egalitarian society.

Highlander's staff was conscious of their work-coercion problem, which was exacerbated when Highlander's community decided that "guards" were needed to protect the school at night. Highlander's staff faced threats of violence in March 1934 when they argued for trade unions build on solidarity between black and white workers.[119] This raised questions of fairness.

---

[117]"Minutes," 16 July 1934, Box 2, Folder 4, HREC.
[118]Ibid.
[119]Glen, *Highlander*, 30.

The three people who raised issue with the work regime did not perform guard duty. There were at least some at the school (guards perhaps) who argued that guarding should provide an exemption from other required work.[120] People who did not perform guard duty were upset over the guards' privilege of sleeping in. "Everyone got to sleeping late because the guards did," the meeting minutes recounted, "and the work was slacked." This disintegration of the work standards at Highlander had consequences: "Work was cut down to bare essentials, only the work connected with protection, eating, sleep, and [maintaining] clothes was continued. This guarding and other incidents have given rise to several problems under the general heading of Management of Work."[121] Staff wrestled with the problem of work in an egalitarian society with few mechanisms for or personal inclinations to enforce hierarchical control.

The structure of the work hierarchy at Highlander was a necessary disciplinary mechanism to ensure that the community continued to function as designed and could serve as a school. "Supervisors" or "commissars" oversaw the day-to-day workings of the school, the kitchen, cleaning crew, and management of the school's grounds.[122] The workday began at Highlander's bulletin board, which listed each worker's responsibilities for the day and contained the details of each assignment. Highlander's staff decided, "Everyone is responsible for reading the bulletin board right after breakfast daily."[123] Though the structure and schedule of work at Highlander would change throughout its intentional community period, the imperative remained the same. Work had to be accomplished efficiently and effectively, as time and resources were limited. The winter schedule, for instance, reflected the seasonal imperatives of the school. Winter was a study-heavy time at Highlander. Only four hours a day (and only on days with "good weather") were set aside for work, which meant physical labor. An additional hour each day was added for staff meetings during the winter. The staff set 10:30 p.m. as "lights out."[124] The community's activities, then, were planned according to a strict schedule, which included time for

---

[120]"Minutes," 16 July 1934, Box 2, Folder 4, HREC.

[121]Ibid.

[122]"Rules," [1934] Box 2, Folder 4, HREC; "Minutes—Soviet Meeting," 1 January 1934, Box 2, Folder 4, HREC.

[123]"Rules," [1934], Box 2, Folder 4, HREC.

[124]"Minutes—Soviet Meeting," 1 January 1934, Box 2, Folder 4, HREC.

non-work activities, though some of this time was allocated for required community recreational activities. There was little room for differences in schedules among community members. The breakfast cook, who had to rise early to prepare the morning meal, was tasked with waking up the entire community at 6:30 a.m.[125] The housekeeper, who served as a sort of manager, dismissed the community from breakfast at 7:20. Classes were held between morning work and a community meal at noon. Staff quantified time spent at work and what they had achieved. They came together to make a wall chart that showed the "number of hours worked" and what tasks were performed during those hours of work.[126]

Despite the regimentation of work, there was resentment over work assignments. The staff was unable to reach a conclusion on the question of requiring all community members to perform "dirty jobs."[127] Highlander's staff also worried over the mandated hours of work. In addition to teaching, learning, and regular staff duties, community members had to perform other work for two hours each day, which did not include a period of "morning work" set aside for sweeping and other essential household tasks.[128] The problem of differing paces and motivations created difficulties for this two-hour regime. Staff debated the problem. Some people, they argued, worked much harder than others in the allotted two-hour period, "while others laugh and talk some of the time."[129]

Highlander's staff had not transcended the difficulties of work; rather, their effort to live intentionally had introduced a whole host of new problems pertaining to the control and character of work in a new society. They approached their communal work arrangements with knowledge of the difficulties associated with such an undertaking. In identifying "general problems," the staff asked, "Are people adverse to planning at all? Does it interfere too much with their own freedom?" [130] The implications of these questions suggest the serious limitations that staff encountered as they questioned the ambitiousness of their plan. Moving from more philosophical questions to "concrete and specific problems," the staff outlined

---

[125]"Rules," [1934], Box 2, Folder 4, HREC.

[126]"Minutes: Meeting of the Soviet," 20 January 1934, Box 2, Folder 4, HREC.

[127]"Minutes of Staff Conference," 29–31 July 1934, Box 2, Folder 4, HREC.

[128]Ibid.

[129]"Minutes," 16 July 1934, Box 2, Folder 4, HREC.

[130]Ibid.

the basic disputes that animated work life at Highlander. Some, such as the suggestion that "there be inspection during the work period," indicate the struggle over questions of oversight and management in an egalitarian intentional community.

The demands of the community necessitated clearly articulated work rules. Experience had taught the socialists at Highlander that without proper oversight, work was partially completed, neglected, or undertaken at a pace not acceptable to all members of the community. A set of rules developed by the Highlander's members in 1934 reveal the underlying problems that they had encountered. The specificity of the rules indicates the community had had problems with the quality of work, efficiency, and with workers' lack of motivation. Rules that governed radio use suggest that the community regarded the use of the radio during work and study times to be a barrier to productivity for workers and students. The radio was banned between 8:30 and 11:30 a.m. (when courses met during the winter), 1 and 5:00 p.m. (time reserved for physical labor or study if the weather necessitated indoor activities), and after 7:30 p.m. ("except on special occasions").[131] One of the rules stipulated that "changes in [the] schedule[s] of workers when needed, are to be made through supervisors."[132]

The problem of work-shy community members who altered their schedules was a serious concern for a community that considered itself a model for the future socialist society. In theory, people would work because they viewed the community and the work required to maintain it as a vital social duty. Experience dictated labor controls and mechanisms of oversight. The morning dish crew also had to be given specific rules to ensure that essential tasks were no longer neglected: "morning dish crew is to mop the kitchen; noon dish crew is to wash the dirty dish towels."[133] Oversight was also built into the work regime at Highlander. Supervisors were mandated to report to Rupert Hampton, Highlander's bookkeeper and administrator, with "suggestions and recommendations" to improve work at High-

[131] "Minutes—Soviet Meeting," 1 January 1934, Box 2, Folder 4, HREC.
[132] "Rules," [1934], Box 2, Folder 4, HREC.
[133] Ibid.

lander.[134] Nonroutine work had to be cleared through Hampton.[135] His own days were filled with hours of financial work.[136]

Highlander's staff debated an appropriate division of labor for their communal project. They were not convinced that any person could do any sort of work. Questions about skill, ability, and efficiency presented a real challenge to Highlander's egalitarianism. One staff member asked, for instance, "should carpenters mop?"[137] The staff was uncertain about how work should be delegated to the community's members, though, in the end, they decided not to limit jobs based on skill level. There were also questions of stamina and variety. Workers, it was assumed, may not want to or be able to perform the same tasks day after day. Conspicuously absent was a discussion about the gendered division of labor, although their conclusion that anyone could do any work must have been at least a tentative answer. Day-to-day practice, explored in the next chapter, suggests that staff had difficulty reaching this ideal.

Horton's assessment of the work problem stressed a lack of discipline and planning rather than any sense that staff or students had shirked their tasks.[138] "Members of the staff had been asked to blow a whistle ten minutes before class time," Horton recalled, "so that the students could get cleaned up and ready for 10 o'clock classes."[139] Staff had not done this because they were "so absorbed in the staff meeting."[140] Some students stopped for class while others continued to work or had to change their dirty work clothes before they could start class. Some students told Horton they wanted to keep working because "they had wanted to complete their work before they stopped."[141] Horton pointed out that "all the staff members and students that I have mentioned were genuinely interested in the school." He blamed the failure on the fact that "a definitive plan was

[134] Ibid.

[135] Ibid.

[136] "Staff Meeting," 9 January 1934, Box 2, Folder 4, HREC.

[137] Ibid.

[138] Myles Horton, "Myles Horton's Criticism," [Summer 1934], Box 2, Folder 4, HREC.

[139] Ibid.

[140] Ibid.

[141] Ibid.

lacking."[142] "Later," Horton said, "when a plan was made and explained the program ran more smoothly." Horton's program, then, called for careful planning and continued enforcement of the plans staff had developed. Horton, however, later admitted that the school's work regime had problems beyond a lack of effectively planning: "manual labor periods should be definitely planned and an effort made to get reasonable tempo and efficiency."[143] The pace and quality of the work mattered and were more difficult to account for in the school's plans.

Highlander's staff made various efforts to address slack work. Rupert Hampton confirmed that lax work was a serious problem: "some sort of effort should be made to secure better work results from school sessions students."[144] An announcement to Highlander's Allardt branch enjoined "all members of the Soviet will be sure to make their own beds before starting the day's work, also take as much care of their clothes as possible under the present conditions."[145] Comrades had to constantly be reminded to complete basic tasks necessary for proper housekeeping. There was a clear, yet satirical, call issued to the school's shirkers in the July 31 work schedule:

> Comrades, we are quite sorry for not having awakened you earlier. We are rather fearful lest you become inflamed and fire us as chairman, etc, etc... However, after realizing that it is not fair to you to allow you to sleep so late, that you cannot possibly do the amount of work you desire, we suggest thereby, that you might enter upon a bit of Socialist Competition. Now this is a very gentle hint, and we don't want you to feel that it is coming from us. On the other hand, think about the matter a great deal and do some planning until you feel fairly certain that you thought the matter up yourselves, for we do not wish to curb your Initiative [emphasis in the original].[146]

Key staff members were aware of tensions revolving around the school's fairly rigorously planned daily schedule, but were flexible enough to approach a situation in a way that would gently encourage, through humor,

[142] Ibid.

[143] Ibid.

[144] Rupert Hampton, "Criticisms," [Summer 1934], Box 2, Folder 4, HREC.

[145] Highlander Folk School: Allardt Division, Household Department, "Report to Secretary," 13 January 1934, Box 2, Folder 4, HREC.

[146] "Work Schedule," 31 July 1934, Box 2, Folder 4, HREC.

a return to form. Highlander also lacked qualified people to do all the work that needed to be done. Hawes reported, "And who will be our labor foreman while Delmas helps Pa Horton put in the Monteagle garden?" "The answer is," a frustrated Hawes added, "a student worker with a wife."[147]

At Highlander's Allardt branch, democratic action was a troublesome subject for a school balancing work demands and slim financial resources. The hot organizing issue of the summer of 1934 was coffee. Hot water was in short supply because it had to be heated and hauled from the kitchen. As such, coffee was a precious luxury, requiring significant additional labor, for a thirsty and tired construction crew. The "commissar" at Allardt asked the staff to limit their coffee intake to one brew each day. In response, the community of workers held a vote. The pro-coffee faction won, and coffee was served three times each day. The revolution was percolating. Negotiation was constant, and this contestation made the community less efficient. The coffee example is but one of many instances of small-scale conflict over labor and the provisioning of resources at Highlander during its most communal moment.[148]

Staff took extensive efforts to resolve problems of scheduling and resources and make the community work—both metaphorically and literally.[149] That Highlander never reached work equilibrium demonstrates that its efforts to build an intentional community, its work in the labor movement, and the ambitious plans for expansion were too much to sustain. Staff added clean up time to the schedule, adjusted course length, and revamped the entire schedule.[150] Even some of the published schedules were incomplete and did not include time spent tutoring or daily-required chores. Thus, an eight-to-six schedule published with the minutes of a staff meeting in the summer of 1934 does not represent the school's full schedule, which included morning duties and frequent evening events, which added to the general sense that the community was overburdened.[151] When one staff member proposed a four-month session for the winter of 1934–1935,

[147]Zilla Hawes to Old Madame, 13 February 1934, Box 15, Folder 31, HREC.

[148]"Work Schedule," 19 July 1934, Box 31, Folder 8, HREC; "Work Schedule," 20 July 1934, Box 31, Folder 8, HREC; "Work Schedule," 24 July 1934, Box 31, Folder 8, HREC; and "Work Schedule," 25 July 1934, Box 31, Folder 8, HREC.

[149]"Minutes of Staff Conference," 29–31 July 1934, Box 2, Folder 4, HREC.

[150]Ibid.

[151]Ibid.

another staff member asked, "will four months be too much of a strain, when we are all so tired out after 6 weeks?"[152] The ceaseless plans for expansion added more work. Staff collectively wondered, "are we going to build while school [is] on?" They answered, "possibly[,] possibly we could build a shop at Allardt, and have four hours [of] work daily for students, rain or shine. If we had the shop, on rainy days, the work could be there."[153] Staff eventually concluded that it would undermine the educational mission of Highlander to increase the workload. Students were not prepared for the level of courses taught by Highlander staff, which required additional time with teachers and added to an already burdened schedule.[154]

As Highlander's teachers took on multiple duties to keep the community operational, the worry mounted. Rupert Hampton noted the strain placed upon teachers, who had taken on the roles of managers, administrators, manual laborers, and much else: "students [should] relieve teachers from routine work thus giving [teachers] more time for creative work."[155] He wanted "more sabbatical absences on the part of staff members."[156] He acknowledged that "this of course is being done in rather an unscheduled way, and it should be more worked out over a longer period."[157] This was a reference to absences caused by labor strife in the surrounding region, Horton's absence, and the health requirements of other staff members. These were hardly restful sabbaticals. The flunkey system adopted by Highlander's staff to organize student labor added managerial duties to the teachers' workloads. Zilla Hawes reported, "I've been meaning to drop you a line for a long time, but it takes so much of my time planning what the flunkeys should (and can) do, and then doing it after them."[158] The staff's "flunkey" system ensured that minor, essential chores were completed. In theory, this system would have removed some of the day-to-day burden off of staff members. The flunkeys were responsible for a litany of small and

---

[152] Ibid.

[153] Ibid.

[154] Ibid.

[155] "The Daily Record," 13 August 1934, Box 2, Folder 4, HREC.

[156] Rupert Hampton, "Criticisms," [Summer 1934], Box 2, Folder 4, HREC.

[157] Ibid.

[158] Zilla Hawes to Old Hussey, 24 January 1934, Box 15, Folder 31, HREC.

large tasks that ranged from maintaining a supply of wood and water to cleaning rooms and washing dishes and clothes.[159]

Despite efforts at differentiation from an early variant of socialist utopianism, Highlander's challenges with work make it not entirely distinctive from its communal precursors. American socialists and reformers had a long history of establishing alternative communities in an effort to both provide for people in difficult times and to build a different and more egalitarian system of social relations. Jim Maurer, the Reading socialist, labor leader, state legislator, and eventual vice-presidential candidate for the SP, recalled that during the late 1890s a colony, established by the local labor-exchange movement, had failed because people were less than committed to the agricultural work that the venture entailed. "Most of the colonists managed to arrive late in the fall after all the farm work had been done," wrote Maurer, "the whole outfit stayed through the winter and ate up everything on the farm, but with the arrival of spring—and work—nine-tenths of the loafers cleared out and that was the end of the colony."[160] Highlander was more fortunate in that it *could* choose its recruits, yet choice (which was limited in Highlander's earliest years) did not always forestall conflict and staff wanted a strict screening process to vet potential students because willingness to labor proved a problem for Highlander as well.

GRIEVANCES, STANDARDS, AND THE OUTSIDE COMMUNITY

The effort to model socialism embroiled Highlander's students and staff in daily struggles to balance individual freedom with communalism, and egalitarianism with more efficient forms of hierarchy. These tensions were evident in the day-to-day operations and relationships within the community, as well as the interactions between Highlander and the surrounding community.

If stress, personal conflicts, and close quarters all exacerbated tensions, the open and democratic nature of Highlander helped to prevent these tensions from being sublimated. While acknowledging the difficulties of their cooperative venture, in 1932 Hawes argued that honesty and openness in socialist communities would allow "cooperative living" to be undertaken

---

[159]Highlander Folk School: Allardt Division, Household Department, "Report to Secretary," 13 January 1934, Box 2, Folder 4, HREC.

[160]Maurer, *It Can Be Done*, 114–115.

successfully.[161] Describing the events at Highlander's Allardt branch in the summer of 1934, Ralph Tefferteller told Dombrowski, "I had Pat with me all day in the quarry, and he was more or less airing his grievances to me concerning the incidents of Sunday last."[162] Tefferteller went on to describe the way in which the community dealt with grievances. "He had brooded over the situation all day, so that by the time we reached the house he was ready to put the matter before the Soviet," he wrote, adding, "I was able to handle the situation somewhat effectively, I think." "However," Tefferteller concluded, "he may have a personal quarrel with you subject to your return. He apologized to the group after a little lecture from the chairman. He put the matter so that one received the impression that he could not very well have been here—being called home for some reason."[163] This openness had its limit. Sex was discussed euphemistically.

The prevailing bohemianism, a feature of Highlander's particular brand of radical socialism, of 1934's summer school hurt Highlander's relationship with the community. Wardrobe choices that were risqué when compared to local culture set Highlander's staff apart from the community they wished organize. The staff decided that they would have to institute a dress code. "[The] dress situation makes problems worse," they decided at a staff meeting, "the next time, clothes (more than shorts and bandolas) should be worn for meals and at all times except during work and play."[164] They conceded, "the prevailing summer school fashions in clothes [have] made it difficult for some of the people of the community who are loyal to defend the school. This is unfair to them. Another year, we should plan to have the student body take care of this problem."[165] It was not only students whose dress preferences were too immodest for locals. An image from 1934 shows Highlander's staff and miners in attendance at the school. Myles Horton is shirtless. Zilla Hawes and two other women are sitting with shoulders and part of their torsos exposed and wearing mid-thigh length bottoms. The image provides a stark contrast. Most of the other men, presumably miners,

[161] Zilla Hawes to Myles Horton, 20 November 1932, Box 15, Folder 30, HREC.

[162] Ralph Tefferteller to James Dombrowski, [1934], Box 15, Folder 31, HREC.

[163] Ibid.

[164] "Minutes of Staff Conference," 29–31 July 1934, Box 2, Folder 4, HREC.

[165] Ibid.

are in shirts and overalls and the other women visible in the photograph are dressed in much longer dresses and have their shoulders covered.[166]

Dorothy Thompson was instinctively repulsed by the behavior of her comrades during the early period of Highlander's intentional community. She never fully elaborated on every aspect of this behavior; however, it included "drinking, the dress situation during the summer school, and other things in this category which students have complained to me about."[167] Thompson may have referred to indiscretions of a sexual nature. Thompson went on to say, "I have heard two different members of the staff, and perhaps others, say, 'there is no such thing as morality', and at times I have felt that this was the dominant sentiment of the group."[168] Thompson went on to explain that these staff members might be correct about morality. She stated that she did not care if this were a purely personal question. The problems of community, however, made this personal belief a public concern. She identified the insouciance of these staff members as a major limitation on the school's success: "there are certain moral standards which are generally accepted, and deviation from these standards—which you may have a perfect right to make personally—often discount all your other ideals of social morality, and ruin everything you have tried to do."[169]

Relations with the community were strained, and not helped by the school's bohemian image and efforts to build a new society. Socialists also had a haughty disposition, assuming that they were correct and that the workers they set out to organize should behave in a specific way. Horton told staff, "avoid all paternalism and action that might be interpreted as a feeling of superiority."[170] Horton cautioned his comrades against saying or writing about members of the local mountain community and Highlander students in a derogatory manner: "In discussing members of the community or students before visitors, or in writing about them, do so in such a way that there could be no possible objection."[171] Horton also wanted the

---

[166]"Workshop for Coal Miners from Wilder," [1934], PH 4260, Box 2, Folder 69, HREC.

[167]Dorothy Thompson, "Criticism of Highlander Folk School," September 1934, Box 2, Folder 4, HREC.

[168]Ibid.

[169]Ibid.

[170]Myles Horton, "Myles Horton's Criticism," [1934], Box 2, Folder 4, HREC.

[171]Ibid.

community to have input when staff wrote articles about them: "in case of writing, let the people being written about read the article before it is sent in for publication. This will eliminate misunderstanding and also help to interest people in the school."[172] Horton made no effort to explain how this potential censorship or self-censorship fit into Highlander's commitment to democracy and emphasis on the individual's ability to dissent from the larger group. Intentional community coupled with the development of a very public project required contradiction. Students might create problems with the local community, too. Horton thought that students "should be given the benefit of what had been learned at previous sessions in regard to group life. The effect of such things as dressing in a certain way and its effects on the community should be specifically mentioned."[173]

Staff and their ability or inability to structure the schedule of the school created disorder, though not everyone saw this as problematic. Keeping the school's staff focused on important school-related issues proved difficult. Efforts to stay organized and maintain a system of governance broke down when sessions were underway. The school's staff failed to appointment chairmen for its meetings. "During the last week of school Jim asked who had been acting as chairman of the staff meetings. We answered that there had been no chairman."[174] Without a chairman meetings devolved into discussions that did not necessarily deal with the most pressing matters confronting the staff, though there were hints of resistance to the imposition of hierarchy and procedure. On the bottom of the soviet meeting minutes from Allardt a non-secretary typed, "THERE WAS NO CHAIRMAN, THERE WAS NO SECRETARY, THERE WAS NO ORDER."[175] "Time," Myles Horton told his colleagues, "should not be used for general discussion but for the discussion of ideas and problems formulated before hand by the one in whose department the subject falls."[176] Horton was further frustrated by staff's inability to stay to the prescribed daily schedule, "classes should begin and end on time, except when it is necessary to run over for a special purpose."[177] The school needed a whistle, he argued, in

[172] Ibid.
[173] Ibid.
[174] Horton, "Myles Horton's Criticism," [1934], Box 2, Folder 4, HREC.
[175] "Soviet Meeting," 2 April 1934, Box 31, Folder 8, HREC, 2.
[176] Horton, "Myles Horton's Criticism," [1934], Box 2, Folder 4, HREC.
[177] Ibid.

order to ensure the smooth administration of the daily schedule. Students and staff had to know when to move to the next activity.[178] Apparently, teachers had also changed the schedule of courses without informing all of the school's students, poor planning indeed.[179] Quiet time remains an issue of concern. Horton wanted at least "two hours of absolute quiet when people can rest or study."[180] Staff also believed that school's rules did not necessarily apply to them. Horton again reminded them that they "should make an effort to abide by the library rules and all other regulations which apply to them. Failure to do so may save time for one, but makes double work on someone else."[181]

The staff's ability to maintain a functioning democratic council was tenuous. By the end of April 1934, there had been no financial report for three weeks. Having convened a "Kangaroo Court," the school's students were in revolt.[182] The work schedule was breaking down and "the quality of work" was a serious concern. The staff decided to adopt a system based on units of labor rather than hours of labor.[183] The lack of a clear hierarchy and the necessity (or the desire) to explain trivial decisions limited productivity, fostered dissent, and contributed to the confusion that generally shaped decision making at Highlander. In one incident, James Dombrowski attempted to justify his decision about whitewashing a chimney by referencing the "dialectical method": "Near the close of the meal the Skipper [Dombrowski's nickname] rendered his decision concerning whitewashing the chimney. He tried to explain that he used the dialectical method in reaching this momentous decision, but the result was partial confusion for himself and total confusion for the group."[184] Dombrowski decided not to have the chimney whitewashed, which was met by the not entirely facetious response, "is there going to be any revolt? We encourage all revolts and revolutions."[185]

[178] Ibid.
[179] Ibid.
[180] Ibid.
[181] Ibid.
[182] "Minutes of Meeting," 22 April 1934, Box 2, Folder 4, HREC.
[183] Ibid.
[184] "The Daily Reminder," 8 August 1934, Box 2, Folder 4, HREC.
[185] Ibid.

Arguments among staff over the project also created difficulties and led to confusion inside the Highlander community. Horton advised that the staff always make an effort "to clarify its position on all problems relating to our purpose."[186] In a democratic socialist community, an effort to create or impose a central view had to be approached with caution. If the school was to have "consensus of opinion" to clarify the school's views and mission to both the school's supporters and the groups it wished to organize, as Horton wanted, it could not force its views on dissenters. The drive for a consensus and its presentation to the public, Horton said, "should not be allowed to force dissenting members of the staff in line."[187] This was perhaps too difficult a position for the staff, though it would certainly have simplified life at Highlander. Policy, Horton argued, had to be separated from the views of Highlander's individual staff members: "staff members should be allowed to differ from other members of the group and feel free to act accordingly. In important problems this personal difference of opinion should be made clear so that outsiders and supporters will not confuse individual opinion with the general policy of the school."[188] Problems with the staff directly shaped community relations. Horton advocated for the moderation of staff's behavior and attitudes.

Conclusion

Highlander encountered more difficulty than Soviet House in maintaining its community because Highlander's primary mission included the operation of a school. Furthermore, rather than serving a specific function for the members of the community, Highlander staff tried to create a model for the new society, which placed a drain on resources and energy. Schools require additional resources. Schools that have vital secondary functions—providing housing for students and staff and, in Highlander's case, modeling a socialist society for students—face even greater economic burdens. There were few sources of revenue for a school targeting working-class people in an area of high and endemic unemployment. Highlander produced no commodity that could be sold to bring in money to the community. Highlander wanted to be separate and non-reliant on capitalism and markets.

[186]Horton, "Myles Horton's Criticism," [1934], Box 2, Folder 4, HREC.
[187]Ibid.
[188]Ibid.

Staff members were never able to sustain their community without participation in the system of economic exchange that they repudiated. They had to buy materials for the school and buy goods to sustain the staff. The expenses were continual, a fact exacerbated by the inability of Highlander to pay its staff salaries, which meant that everyone dipped into a central fund for necessary items.

Soviet House in Philadelphia was successful in its effort at communal living because it was centered around an alternative housing arrangement based on socialist principles; each member contributed what they could toward the house's economic operations. Soviet House provided value to its members, who brought in money from outside employment. It was markedly nonutopian in its design and plans. Its primary function was limited to housing while its secondary function, serving as a hub for labor organizing, developed around its primary function. As long as enough members of the community found outside employment, the experiment worked both for its own members, the SP, the leadership prospects that Norman Thomas sent the community, and ultimately for the labor and social movements that employed or used these young professionals as organizers. Soviet House could serve its multiple and self-reinforcing functions as long as there was enough money to sustain the community and as long as limited demands of Soviet House did not interfere with the community's organizing activities in the labor movement—an ongoing problem for the cash-strapped Highlander. The Soviet House comrades gained efficiencies by pooling their resources, which helped to meet basic needs. Soviet House could, then, exist amidst an upswing in labor organizing. Highlander was different.

The intensity of commitment required by Highlander's commune could not be maintained in the face of demanding organizing taking place throughout the South, including Highlander's efforts to support textile workers in and around Knoxville and Chattanooga.[189] The urgency of the struggle in the Southern Highlands dictated that trade union work supersede efforts to build a socialist community on the Cumberland Plateau. Staff members viewed the labor movement as central to their vision of socialism. The urgency of the struggles of working people was a component of the decline of the expansive communal efforts at Highlander after 1935. The contradictions, practical and economic difficulties, and the sub-

---

[189]Glen, *Highlander*, 29, 31, 34.

tle ideological differences between the community's members meant that efforts to remake society root and branch would be relatively short-lived as an experiment to create a socialist model of the future society. The coming of that "future society" also seemed less certain as the 1930s unfolded and socialists' certainty of capitalism's collapse eroded.

CHAPTER 6

Their Party, Their Power: Socialist Women in the 1930s

It was the end of May 1932 when a thunderous clamor for order echoed across Milwaukee's municipal auditorium, a temporary convention floor for the Socialist Party. In a fury, B. Charney Vladeck, an officer of the *Jewish Daily Forward* and close associate of Norman Thomas, slammed his gavel into the lectern again and again in a vain attempt to reestablish order. Vladeck hammered away for so long that his gavel, rather unceremoniously, broke into pieces. The crowd of socialist delegates had been whipped into frenzy by a discussion of Prohibition and the Socialist Party's adoption of "a wet plank" by a vote of 76 to 68, or later, after division—a parliamentary tool used to clarify close votes—was called, by 81 to 71. Norman Thomas and other leaders who knew that the issue split the party along regional and cultural lines had suppressed open discussion of Prohibition.[1] With years of tension bubbling up, the "dries" were livid while the "wets" burst into such a jovial chorus that an onlooker might have concluded that they had been imbibing spirits all day. Order suffered as the group struggled to come to terms with the vote's outcome and find a compromise solution. When none could be had, one observer described the scene as "the most violent political explosion of the stormy convention."[2] To quiet the fervor emanating from

[1] Bernard K. Johnpoll, *Pacifist's Progress: Norman Thomas and the Decline of American Socialism* (Chicago: Quadrangle Books, 1970), 52–53.

[2] "Socialists Favor," *The Lewiston Daily Sun*, 24 May 1932.

© The Author(s) 2019
J. Altman, *Socialism before Sanders*,
https://doi.org/10.1007/978-3-030-17176-6_6

the crowd, thirty-five-year old Sarah Limbach of Pittsburgh, vice chairman of the convention, rose to the podium and restored order. Limbach's efforts to steer the uproarious convention in a more productive direction represent a larger endeavor on the part of socialist women to make the party their own during the 1930s. As Limbach's intervention demonstrations, women were anything but secondary during this mercurial period.[3]

The history of women and socialism in the United States, particularly during the Debs era, has received the attention of excellent historians.[4] Writing of the 1910s and 1920s, Sally Miller argued, "[Socialists] who saw women's liberation as a distinct part of the class struggle often did not transcend traditional role assignments and family structure."[5] In the 1930s, women chafed against these "traditional role assignments." Emphasizing the importance of the Women's National Committee in the Socialist Party in her final chapter and requiem, Mary Jo Buhle concluded that women's position in the Socialist Party in the 1930s was marginal at best: "Women who clung to the shrunken Socialist Party [in the 1920s and 1930s] did no better as a group. Male prerogatives, once challenged, now ruled undisputed. Half-hearted attempts to reorganize a women's committee suffered repeated defeat. A correspondent to the national office lamented in 1929, 'It is very plain that our present plan of enlisting women Socialists... is a

---

[3] Socialist Party, "The March of Socialism, 1928–1932," *Journal of the Seventeenth National Convention* (Chicago: Italian Labor Publishing Co., 1932), 33.

[4] See Sally M. Miller, *Flawed Liberation: Socialism and Feminism* (Westport, CT: Greenwood Press, 1981); Mari Jo Buhle, *Women and American Socialism, 1870–1920* (University of Illinois Press, 1983); Sally M. Miller, "Socialism and Women," in Laslett and Lipset, *Failure of a Dream?: Essays in the History of American Socialism* (University of California Press, 1984), 244–268. There are a number of works that focus on social-democratic and progressive women's organizing efforts during the 1930s, as well as biographical studies of important female labor leaders. See Landon Storrs's work on the social-democratic coalition (though communist women, too, participated in social-democratic coalitions during the Popular Front) that coalesced in support of the New Deal and included socialists and former socialists. Landon Storrs's *Civilizing Capitalism: The National Consumers' League, Women's Activism, and Labor Standards in the New Deal Era* (Chapel Hill: University of North Carolina Press, 2000) has examined a broader group of women in the 1930s, including socialist women, most notably Florence Kelley. Annelise Orleck's *Common Sense and a Little Fire: Women and Working-Class Politics in the United States, 1900–1965* (The University of North Carolina Press, 1995) explores the organizing work and achievements of Rose Schneiderman, Pauline Newman, and Clara Lemlich.

[5] Sally M. Miller, "Women in the Party Bureaucracy: Subservient Functionaries," in *Flawed Liberation*, 28.

failure. There are a few women who take pleasure in working in the party locals.'"[6] According to Buhle women neither formed coherent women's groups nor had much success working at the local level. This analysis omits the revival that socialists experienced in the early to mid-1930s. A view of the SP that incorporates important leaders like Sarah Limbach, Ethel Davis, Maud McCreery, and Lilith Wilson as well as rank-and-file socialists Zilla Hawes and Gretchen Garrison allows for a complicated and more complete analysis of women's role in a revived SP. Explicating the roles that women took on in the SP, as well as socialist women's daily interactions with men, also demarcates the limits of women's achievements within the SP.

Women within the party lauded the achievements of their sisters in the interwar period including the business achievements of some of its own such as Frances Violet Thomas, the wife of SP leader Norman Thomas, even while the media continued to portray her as a knitting wife and bystander. The SP's official publications praised career women who had achieved success and shown "power and ability" as "workers, executives and investors."[7] Thomas, while sometimes portrayed in the media as a dignified, restrained, and sober wife, had been a social worker and volunteer at a tuberculosis clinic in New York City, and later ran a tearoom to support her family and her husband's campaigning.[8] She said, "I expect to put my children through college by means of this tearoom." The journalist commented that Thomas was "taking it for granted that being a Socialist candidate is not a lucrative business."[9] The tearoom investment was in addition to her already financially successful dog breeding business, which produced

[6]Mari Jo Buhle, *Women and American Socialism, 1870–1920* (University of Illinois Press, 1983), 323.

[7]Gretchen J. Garrison, "Help Wanted—Female," May 1934, Box 5, PECSP. It may sound strange to hear socialists lauding marketers, but the SPA was by no means anti-market in the 1930s. The SP promoted cooperatives during this period. These cooperatives were designed to function within a market structure. They would, so the argument went, help to democratize both production and consumption and help to control prices and make the economy use driven rather than profit driven.

[8]"Norman Thomas' Wife Dies in New York City," *Reading Eagle* (Reading, PA), 1 August 1947; "Here's One Husband Who Dictates to His Wife," *Herald-Journal* (Spartanburg, SC), 6 September 1936.

[9]"Mrs. Norman Thomas Running a Tearoom," *The Norwalk Hour* (Norwalk, CT), 28 July 1932.

at least one champion cocker spaniel.[10] Thomas was every bit as much a "new woman" as her younger comrades. A misleading image in the *The Literary Digest* depicts Thomas knitting in a dark long-sleeved dress at party conventions juxtaposed with an image of her husband thunderously belting out the lyrics to the *Internationale*, while surrounded by young, bare-armed, short-haired women in the blue-shirt and red-tie uniform of the Young People's Socialist League.[11] Thomas's knitting obsession was picked up by media to portray her as an appendix to her husband rather than as an actor in her own right: "She is knitting, this wife of an agitator for peaceful revolution, but there is nothing about her that suggests the women of the French terror who knitted with gleaming eyes as the heads rolled. It is only by contrast that the thought comes at all... She rises from time to time to handle the telephone calls for her husband."[12] Another article featuring an image of Thomas knitting with a photograph of her husband inset the upper corner. The caption stated, "while her husband, Norman Thomas, was busy making plans with the national executive committee of the Socialist Party in New York city to campaign against Huey Long in Louisiana this October, Mrs. Thomas was content to stick on the sidelines and knit."[13] Thomas was no passive knitter of stockings but a tenacious and active woman who stepped beyond gender conventions. At the forefront of representations of Thomas was the knitting narrative with its connotations of domesticity. In these narratives, her life as savvy businesswoman and provider was secondary.

An ongoing debate about socialist women's organizational strategies demonstrates that women were actively engaged with the SP and reconsidering their role in it. While debate was afoot, women were still being channeled into auxiliaries and separate women's groups or clubs in large numbers. Ethel M. Davis, director of the Women's Department, extolled the virtues of the SP's women's groups, writing and distributing

[10]"Here's One Husband Who Dictates to His Wife," *Herald-Journal* (Spartanburg, SC), 6 September 1936; "Mrs. Norman Thomas Running a Tearoom," *The Norwalk Hour* (Norwalk, CT), 28 July 1932.

[11]"Socialist Rift: Norman Thomas Named for President as the Old Guard Bolts," [1936], *The Literary Digest*, Box 3, PECSP.

[12]Willis Thornton, "Norman Thomas Answers Questions Put to Candidates of Republicans," *Herald-Journal* (Spartanburg, SC), 6 June 1936.

[13]"Mrs. Thomas Minds Her Knitting," *The Milwaukee Journal* (Milwaukee, WI), 15 July 1935.

questionnaires for socialist women, distributing literature, urging women to vote and to organize around socialist campaigns, and writing to other women about their role "as wives and mothers."[14] "Wives and mothers" was a popular phrase in Davis's vocabulary—but she was also working beyond this paradigm. In a 1932 letter to the Vermont socialist Louise Wiener, Davis stressed the important role that women could and must play in elections. In order to raise the party's profile among the women of Wisconsin, Davis toured Milwaukee speaking to women in early October 1932 and praising both the importance of women's role in "public life" and the party's policy on economic redistribution. The immense industrial power of the United States, Davis argued, must serve need in the place of profit. "The Socialist Party," Davis said to a gathering of Wisconsin women, "advocates in the crisis provision for adequate and immediate relief, and adequate building program, better minimum wage laws, shorter hours and the abolition of child labor."[15] In Pennsylvania, where the SP was undergoing a large revival, Sarah Limbach, the state secretary from Pittsburgh, placed emphasis on organizing women's club and working to develop "an educational program to take care of the influx of new members."[16]

Upwardly mobile working-class women like Limbach were prominent in the SP's local and state-level organizations in Pennsylvania. Limbach, a resident of Pittsburgh's North Side neighborhood, was a Russian immigrant married to a second-generation German.[17] Her husband Emil was a skilled metal worker who eventually became a contractor. He had inherited a sheet metal shop from his father.[18] Socialism was blotted out of

[14] Ethel M. Davis to Mrs. G. Duff, October 19, 1932, SPAP, Reel 25; Ethel M. Davis to Louise Wiener, October 19, 1932. SPAP; Ethel M. Davis to Martha Croushore, October 19, 1932, SPAP; Ethel M. Davis to Mrs. Henry Wiegel, October 19, 1932, SPAP; and Ethel M. Davis to Caroline Goodman, October 18, 1932, SPAP.

[15] "Fix Machine Age, Women Urged by Socialist Leader," *The Milwaukee Journal* (Milwaukee, WI), 12 October 1932.

[16] "PA. Socialists Open Sessions Here Tonight: Young Men and Women to Hold State Conference Over the Weekend," *Reading Eagle* (Reading, PA), 1 July 1932.

[17] 1930 United States Census, s.v. "Sarah Limbach," Pittsburgh, Allegheny County, Pennsylvania; 1920 United States Census, s.v. "Sarah Limbach," Pittsburgh, Allegheny County, Pennsylvania; Obituary of Sarah Limbach, *Pittsburgh Post-Gazette*, 4 October 1989.

[18] 1930 United States Census, s.v. "Sarah Limbach," Pittsburgh, Allegheny County, Pennsylvania; 1920 United States Census, s.v. "Sarah Limbach," Pittsburgh, Allegheny County, Pennsylvania.

Limbach's past in an obituary that stressed her support for Franklin Roosevelt's 1940 and 1944 campaigns. Limbach was hailed as a community activist in Pittsburgh's North Side neighborhood. Advocacy for working people was mentioned in her obituary, but not Limbach's 1932 Congressional candidacy on the SP ticket, her 1936 run for auditor general of Pennsylvania, or the state-level office she held in the SP.[19] She was the executive secretary-treasurer of the Socialist Party of Pennsylvania.[20]

In the lead up to the 1930 mid-term elections, Limbach served on an election committee chaired by another woman, Jane W. Tait. The older Tait, who turned forty-six in 1930, was also from Pittsburgh and served as the secretary of the Socialist Party of Allegheny County in 1930.[21] Tait was the daughter of an English stonecutter who brought his family to the United States in 1887, when Jane was three. Like many of the working-class socialists, the Tait household valued education and the mobility that accompanied it. The children, even those old enough for work, were listed as "at school" by the census taker in 1900.[22] The value placed on education is reflected in the trajectory of Jane Tait's work life. By 1910, Tait was a teacher in a country school. Tait would have been well acquainted with working-class life but like many of her peers was part of an upwardly mobile group.[23] After her father died, Tait worked as a clerk in a grocery store to help support her mother.[24] It was around this time that she became involved with the SP. In 1912 she served as secretary of the convention of the Socialist Party in Pennsylvania.[25] Almost a decade later, Tait was also elected as a delegate to the 1921 Convention of the Socialist Party in

---

[19]"Roberts and Pinola Named," *Reading Eagle*, 28 April 1936; Obituary of Sarah Limbach, *Pittsburgh Post-Gazette*, 4 October 1989.

[20]"Socialist Hits Suffrage Bars," *The Pittsburgh Press*, 8 October 1930.

[21]1930 United States Census, s.v. "Jane W. Tait," Pittsburgh, Allegheny County, Pennsylvania.

[22]1900 United States Census, s.v. "John Tait," Pittsburgh, Allegheny County, Pennsylvania.

[23]Ibid.

[24]1920 United States Census, s.v. "Jane Tait," Pittsburgh, Allegheny County, Pennsylvania.

[25]"Refuse to Endorse Industrial Workers: State Socialists Stand by Trade Unions," *Reading Eagle*, 21 April 1912.

Detroit, Michigan.[26] Tait's and Limbach's roles in socialist electoral efforts are a window into the roles that socialist women across the United States played in the SP's electoral efforts in the 1930s.

Women canvassed for the party in the lead-up to elections. In a 1932 letter to the Vermont socialist Louise Wiener, Ethel Davis stressed the expanded role that women could and must play in elections. In Milwaukee, women pored over the voter rolls in order to identify and then visit socialists and likely socialist voters. Davis encouraged this strategy across Wisconsin and the nation.[27] According to Davis, women were an essential constituency to cultivate because they, only enfranchised in national elections after 1920, were less likely to vote than men.[28] Thus, turning out socialist women could substantially boost the SP's share of the vote. She hoped that this effort would bring an additional 10,000 votes for SP candidates in the election in Milwaukee alone.[29]

Further, the SP in Milwaukee developed a dual structure for its ward-level organizing. The dual structure meant that each ward had a woman and a man serving as co-chairs to coordinate activities in their wards. Though women's and men's groups coordinated, their organizations remained separate and women worked with other women within the women's division. The goal was to send women to households in order to talk to the wives and daughters of socialist men.[30] This strategy helped socialists win twelve council seats and the mayoralty in 1932: "Milwaukee's Socialist mayor, Daniel Hoan, was reelected in 1932 with 63 percent of the vote,

[26]"Minutes of the National Convention, Socialist Party," in *The Socialist World* [Chicago], v. 2, no. 6/7 (June–July 1921), 24.

[27]Ethel M. Davis to Mrs. Dorothy Thompson, 18 October 1932. SPAP; Ethel M. Davis to Ella Griffin, 18 October 1932, SPAP.

[28]Kristi Andersen calls into question Davis's assumption that women were not going to polls along with their husbands, though Andersen generally agrees that women's voter turnout was lower than men's during the 1920s. See Kristi Andersen, *After Suffrage: Women in Partisan and Electoral Politics Before the New Deal* (University of Chicago Press, 1996), 51–53; Margret Mary Finnegan agrees that women were not voting in large numbers during the 1930s. See footnote 74 in Margaret Mary Finnegan, *Selling Suffrage: Consumer Culture & Votes for Women* (Columbia University Press, 1999), 202.

[29]Ethel M. Davis to Louise Wiener, 19 October 1932, SPAP.

[30]Ethel M. Davis to Louise Wiener, 19 October 1932, SPAP; Ethel M. Davis to Pansy Waldron, 19 October 1932, SPAP; Maud McCreery to Ethel M. Davis, 20 October 1932, SPAP; Ethel M. Davis to Frances Atkinson, 20 October 1932, SPAP; Ethel Davis to Mrs. John Thompson, 18 October 1932, SPAP.

his strongest showing ever. The Milwaukee Socialists also captured twelve of twenty-seven council seats, and nine of the twenty posts on the county board."[31] The scope of their victory statewide was impressive too: "The Wisconsin Socialists greatly increased their representation in the state legislature, and won the mayoralty in Racine for the first time."[32] Mrs. John Thompson had been very active organizing women's participation in the election in Racine.[33]

The dual electoral effort was more complicated on the ground than it seemed from the party's official plans. Women in the 27th ward refused to go into the women's division and told the women in charge of the electoral efforts in Milwaukee that they "were working with the men in the 27th ward."[34] According to the leaders of the women's division, this revolt was largely symbolic, as their program was designed to get women and men to work together—though the dual structure was not quite as "together" as some women wanted.[35] In reality, the revolt was more than symbolic. Some women wanted the political and participatory equality that came from working in one group.

The battle within the party over the dual strategy was troubling for many. Undemocratic tactics were employed to stifle the women of the 27th ward. Ethel Davis chastised Maud McCreery, secretary of the women's division, for abusing her power by stripping the chairwoman of the 27th ward of her powers.[36] McCreery was primarily concerned with losing control over her authority. In her letters to Ethel Davis, she indicated that the admiration of Milwaukee's women socialists was important for her own sense of self: "I really believe that most of these women love me, and that [is] the thing that makes it possible for me to go on in the face of many of my obstacles."[37] McCreery took steps to firm up her position with Davis: "I hope that you and I will not be merely 'ships that pass in the night,' but that our work

---

[31] Seymour Martin Lipset and Gary Marks, *It Didn't Happen Here: Why Socialism Failed in the United States* (New York: W. W. Norton, 2000), 205.

[32] Ibid. Lipset and Marks do not mention the role that women played in organizing for this victory.

[33] Ethel Davis to Mrs. John Thompson, 18 October 1932, SPAP.

[34] Maud McCreery to Ethel M. Davis, 20 October 1932, SPAP.

[35] Ibid.

[36] Ibid.

[37] Ibid.

in the same cause will make our paths cross again. Being Irish, I have very strong and warm feelings for persons who get 'inside' me. You certainly did and have built a little niche all for yourself in my memory, heart, or wherever places like that are in our physical being."[38] The incident demonstrates that women debated how to best engage in party activities. Ethel Davis took the position that how women engaged was not as important as their willingness to engage. The younger Davis was likely less connected to the party's labor roots and had did not have the direct experience of the women who had been in the SP during the 1910s. She was also less wedded to past forms of organization.[39] She advocated joint efforts. Davis told women that some local organizations had abandoned the auxiliary model, which organized men and women into separate groups. More importantly, Davis told them that that was a fine way to organize. In locals that abandoned the auxiliary model, men and women participated as equals, as least putatively.[40] McCreery may have been hostile to the erosion of the idea of auxiliaries because she had long worked with women who led analogous auxiliaries in the labor movement. A photograph from 1936 shows McCreery with her students in Milwaukee at a Monday night class. The four women pictured with McCreery each represented a different women's auxiliary.[41] She taught the auxiliary leaders about "parliamentary procedure, public speaking, and labor problems as they affect housewives."[42] In many unions during the 1930s, including those with which the Socialist Party worked, women's auxiliaries grew during the 1930s.[43]

Beyond electoral activities or serving in auxiliaries, women in the party raised funds for the SP's candidates. Before the New Deal, it was not beyond the realm of possibility that the SP would experience a revival akin to its 1912 challenge to two-party hegemony and its local successes dating from roughly the same period.[44] The SP had strongholds that survived

---

[38] Ibid.

[39] Buhle, *Women and American Socialism*, 318–320, 323.

[40] Ethel M. Davis to Mrs. G. Duff, 19 October 1932, SPAP.

[41] "Labor Classes for Trades Union Women Open," *The Milwaukee Journal* (Milwaukee, WI), 29 September 1936.

[42] Ibid.

[43] Dorothy Sue Cobble, *The Other Women's Movement: Workplace Justice and Social Rights in Modern America* (Princeton University Press, 2011), 23.

[44] For more information on the heyday of American socialism see Richard W. Judd's *Socialist Cities: Municipal Politics and the Grass Roots of American Socialism*, Irving

into or grew in the 1930s: Milwaukee, Wisconsin; Reading, Pennsylvania; and Bridgeport, Connecticut.[45] It was important to raise funds for candidates who might actually win elections. Gretchen Garrison, a socialist activist, advised her follow socialists that "women can be especially valuable in money raising activities: parties, lectures, raffles."[46] Exaltations in the party's official publications followed successful activities pursued by female socialists at the local level. Funds were raised through the sale of literature. Meta Riseman handled the party's literature distribution—and pointed out printing errors to the publisher—in Detroit. She sold party literature to raise funds and propagandize for the party's candidates.[47] Another woman, Anna Steese Richardson, distributed several hundred copies of socialist literature, including one hundred copies of the SP's leaflet designed for women, "She Changed her Mind."[48] In the buildup to the 1932 election, women's efforts to raise funds for the party were essential. The SP was trying to run a modern, nation-wide campaign and meet the demand for Thomas as a speaker in 1932. The campaign needed money for a plane and literature to mount such a campaign. Most of the contributions came in small amounts from rank-and-file socialists.[49]

Women took vital political roles in the party's structure and propaganda. Ethel Davis was resident at the SP's headquarters in Chicago. She was head of the women's department and was involved in the student organizing efforts, two positions central to the party's efforts to reorganize in the 1930s. Women at the state level were taking on leadership roles too. They served as general organizers. Betty Naysmith organized fellow socialists at

Howe's *Socialism and America*, any one of James Weinstein's *The Decline of Socialism in America: 1912–1925*, and Paul Buhle's *Marxism in America*.

[45]William C. Pratt, "Women Socialists, Male Comrades: The Reading Experience," in *Flawed Liberation: Socialism and Feminism*, ed. Sally M. Miller (Westport: Greenwood Press, 1981), 146; Cecelia Bucki, *Bridgeport's Socialist New Deal, 1915–36* (Urbana: University of Illinois Press, 2001), 199. In addition to all of the major centers of socialism in the United States, there were many Socialists and sympathizers scattered throughout states that had only a dozen or so years earlier had relatively significant Socialist movements. Tennessee was one such state. Memphis had core of members and other committed Socialists were scattered across rural Tennessee.

[46]Gretchen J. Garrison, "Help Wanted—Female," May 1934, Box 5, PECSP.

[47]Meta Riseman to the Literature Technicians, 18 October 1932, SPAP.

[48]National Headquarters to Anna Steese Richardson, 24 October 1932, SPAP.

[49]Ethel M. Davis to Pansy Waldron, 19 October 1932. SPAP; J.H. Bangs to the National Office of the Socialist Party, 20 October 1932, SPAP.

Brookwood Labor College.[50] Dorothy Anderson had taken up politics in Louisiana. She was curious how to respond to detractors who wondered how socialists planned to pay for their proposed programs.[51] Mary Donovan, national secretary of Sacco and Vanzetti's defense in 1928 and wife of Powers Hapgood, was busy speaking on the campaign trail, memorializing Eugene Debs in Terre Haute, and organizing women, including black women, at the behest of Ethel Davis.[52] In 1932, Sarah Limbach led Pennsylvania socialists marching in Reading at the beginning of the state convention.[53] Lilith Wilson, a Representative in the Pennsylvania State Assembly and a member of the National Executive Committee of the Socialist Party, was one of two keynote speakers.[54]

Women also served a symbolic role in the SP's representational materials. In a cartoon from 1932 a young woman represented social ownership. "Miss Social Ownership" stands next to a tin barrel labeled "Socialist Party" that voters were supposed to place their ballots. In her arms she holds a shopping basket full of groceries representing the plenty that would come with social ownership. The artists associated young women with the very best promises that socialism had to offer Americans struggling through the Great Depression. In the cartoon, men represent the plutocrats, political grafters, and criminals that have little to offer workers and were the principle targets of socialist reforms.[55]

Women helped to reestablish SP locals throughout the country. Marguerite Thomas helped to organize a local in Crothersville, Indiana.[56] Helen Biemiller was safeguarding the gains that the SP had made from the problems caused by atheist socialists who might alienate potential recruits

---

[50] Betty Naysmith to Clarence Senior, 15 October 1932, SPAP.

[51] Dorothy Anderson to Heywood Broun, 18 October 1932, SPAP.

[52] Ethel Davis to P.K. Reinholt, 18 October 1932. SPAP; Ethel M. Davis to Mary Donovan, 18 October 1932, SPAP.

[53] "PA. Socialists Open Sessions Here Tonight: Young Men and Women to Hold State Conference Over the Weekend," *Reading Eagle*, 1 July 1932.

[54] "Death Takes Lilith Wilson: First Women Legislator From Berks Country Dies at Home," *Reading Eagle*, 8 July 1937; "PA. Socialists Open Sessions Here Tonight: Young Men and Women to Hold State Conference Over the Weekend," *Reading Eagle*, 1 July 1932.

[55] "Which Can Will You Throw Your Vote In?," October 1932, SPAP.

[56] Executive Secretary of the SP to Marguerite Thomas, 25 October 1932, SPAP.

from the party.[57] When Grace Johnson from Harrison, New York, joined the party, Ethel Davis sent her a of women's activities and instructed her to organize events from the list before the election in 1932. Davis used the example of Milwaukee's women and their electoral efforts to push Trimbath to organize. Davis asked, "How much can you increase the vote?"[58] Before November 1932 all of the party's efforts, including bringing new recruits into the organization, were tied to voting. This was true of its efforts to build a student organization as well.

Young women were essential in establishing "Norman Thomas for President" clubs on college campuses. They were also vital in the effort to bolster support for socialism on campuses and helping to build what some envisioned as the groundwork for a new student movement. While the Thomas was not winning polls on campuses in 1932, he was doing relatively well at some schools. At City College Detroit, Thomas (360 votes) finished behind Hoover (403) but ahead of Roosevelt (346) and the CP's candidate, William Z. Foster (43).[59] At Vassar, students gave Thomas 208 votes in the straw poll, which put the SP candidate head of Roosevelt (135), but well behind Hoover (563). Thomas actually won the straw poll among faculty at Vassar with 38 votes to Hoover's 24 and Roosevelt's 19.[60] Students at the University of Minnesota carried off a similar result: Hoover first, Thomas second, and Roosevelt third.[61] At John Hopkins, Thomas came in third, but Ethel Davis remarked that Hopkins was an outlier—at most of the universities Thomas finished second to Hoover.[62] The straw poll at DePaux University in Greencastle, Indiana conformed to the norm as identified by Davis, but was conducted differently than on other campuses. The results of first year students were separated from the others "because it was thought that their votes would be more influenced by parents." Among the older students, Hoover won with 328 votes. Thomas finished second with 179 votes. Roosevelt finished third with 116 votes. Hoover fared slightly

---

[57]Unknown to Helen Biemiller, 25 October 1932, SPAP.

[58]Ethel Davis to Miss Grace Johnson, 24 October 1932, SPAP.

[59]Walter P. Reuther to Paul H. Ritterskamp, 20 October 1932, SPAP.

[60]Alice Dodge to Paul Ritterskamp, October 1932, SPAP.

[61]Ethel M. Davis to Neils Nielsen, 24 October 1932, SPAP.

[62]Ethel M. Davis to Joel Seidman, 24 October 24 1932, SPAP.

better with the first year students with 181 votes. Thomas still finished second with 75 votes, and Roosevelt was again in third with 56 votes.[63]

Female leaders were essential to organizing efforts on college campuses from the Lake Erie College, University of Oklahoma, Lindenwood College in Missouri, Arkansas University at Fayetteville, and a number of other colleges throughout the South that were tapped to organize students for the election.[64] Frank Crosswaith, an African-American socialist and candidate for Congress from Harlem for 1932, identified Leonora Lane from Wilberforce University, an African-American college in Ohio, as an organizer of a Thomas for President club.[65] Crosswaith also identified Elinor Coleman as a potential organizer for socialists on the campus of New Orleans University.[66] Greta Mather reported faculty efforts to prevent the formation of a Thomas for President club at Stanford University for her brother.[67] Eleanor B. Semple, a student at Lake Erie College in Ohio, organized a Thomas for President club on her campus. She helped to organize the Thomas campaign at Lake Erie College and participated in the mock election, as most college students could not vote in 1932, to raise energy for the Socialist Party on campuses.[68] Semple wanted buttons to raise Thomas's profile on at Lake Erie's campus.[69] Ethel Davis sent her organizing instructions and literature to distribute.[70] Dorothy Alday at Albion College in Michigan carried out a similar organizing program and dutifully sent the proceeds of literature sales back to the SP. Alday wanted free literature for people who might be attracted to the socialist cause but unable to pay for materials, which suggests that college socialists were looking beyond the confines of the campus green. Davis facilitated Alday's request by sending a sheaf of literature free of charge.[71] Alday and Davis concurred that the Depression

---

[63] Albert H. Lenkau to Paul H. Ritterskamp, 26 October 1932, SPAP.

[64] Fern Babcock to Paul H. Ritterskemp, 23 October 1932, SPAP.

[65] Paul Ritterskamp to Miss Leonora Lane, 25 October 1932, SPAP.

[66] Paul Ritterskamp to Miss Elinor Coleman, 25 October 1932, SPAP.

[67] Ethel Davis to Greta Mather, 25 October 1932, SPAP.

[68] See Wendell W. Cultice, *Youth's Battle for the Ballot: A History of Voting Age in America* (New York: Greenwood Press, 1992).

[69] Eleanor B. Semple to Paul H. Ritterskemp, 24 October 1932, SPAP.

[70] Ethel M. Davis to Eleanor B. Semple, 24 October 1932, SPAP.

[71] Ethel M. Davis to Dorothy Alday, 24 October 1932, SPAP.

made organizing both essential and likely to succeed among the "towns-people" as well as on college campuses.[72]

In contrast with the college organizations, the Labor Committee for Thomas and Maurer (LCTM)—drawing strength from older Socialist Party constituencies—was a male-centered affair. The flurry of correspondence associated with the LCTM began, rather conspicuously given the juxtaposition of correspondence written by and to women, "Dear Sir and Brother." The SP continued to employ the language of a masculine construction of the industrial worker that so often defied the realities of working-class life.[73] The members of the LCTM were almost exclusively male. Irene Blaine of Philadelphia and Emma Shantz of Reading, Pennsylvania, were the exceptions.[74]

Socialist women ran for political offices at a higher rate than in any other party during the 1930s. They included Elizabeth Gilman of Maryland, who ran for a seat in the US House of Representatives in 1936. In Iowa, Laetitia Conrad ran for the US Senate. Two of the SP candidates in gubernatorial elections were women: Kate Stockton, a friend of Highlander Folk School, in Tennessee, and Ida Beloof in Kansas. Twenty-five women ran as socialists in 1936. Even by 1936, when the SP had undergone some serious internecine conflicts, its ability to field—or rather women's ability to operate within the SP as political equals—was unchallenged by the much larger Republican or Democratic parties. The dominant parties together fielded only fourteen female candidates. The Communist Party fielded only nine, outdoing the dominant parties but falling far behind the socialists. Women were on the ticket in the Socialist Party because they helped to make policy, led election efforts, and exercised power to a greater extent than in the other parties.[75]

While attempting to win elections, women were also shedding their husbands as identifiers. Of the letters to Davis from women across the United States, most, but not all, women put their own name after *Mrs.* and were occasionally dropping the formal *Mrs.* completely.[76] When "Miss"

---

[72]Ibid.

[73]See the high volume of correspondence from September to October 1932 in the SPAP, Reels 24–25.

[74]Secretary of the Labor Committee for Thomas and Maurer to Irene Blaine, 25 October 1932, SPAP; Secretary of the Labor Committee for Thomas and Maurer to Emma Shantz, 25 October 1932, SPAP.

[75]"85 Women Seeking Office This Year," *Reading Eagle*, 21 October 1936.

[76]Ethel M. Davis to Louise Wiener, 19 October 1932. SPAP; Ethel M. Davis to Pansy Waldron, 19 October 1932. SPAP; Ethel M. Davis to Martha Croushore, 19

was retained it was sometimes relegated to parentheses, as if to say that this might be helpful information but not a formal means of address.[77] Only rarely were women referred to by their husband's name.

The SP moved toward recognition of the problem of the wage gap between women and men in the 1930s. This was not a firm policy on wage equalization but it was a first step, which suggests that the party was moving away from the ideal of the working-class family headed by a male breadwinner. One party cartoon demonstrated this point. In the cartoon, two women complain about a male coworker who is paid double what they receive for the same work. Their boss—a chubby capitalist in pinstripe pants, a tie, and a vest—overhears them and fires the women for voicing their complaints about the wage gap. In the next frame, the women are seen leaving a socialist meeting. The implication was that the wage gap was not equitable, the SP was concerned with the gap, and this unfair treatment was a way to organize women and bring them to socialism.[78]

There were clear limits to the possibilities that women in the SP carved out for themselves in the 1930s.[79] Young men, while welcoming their female comrades into the political life of the party, continued in the expectation that women fulfill the role of supporters in addition to providing input in meetings. The younger generation of men carried their own strong prejudices about women. Socialist women had agency even if, as Sally Miller argues, "many revolutionary men were not able to cast off a deep contempt for women when they became socialists."[80] Zilla Hawes, a staff member at Highlander Folk School and a former member of YPSL in Pennsylvania, experienced similar vitriol directed at women.[81]

October 1932. SPAP; Ethel M. Davis to Mrs. Agatha Nagle, 19 October 1932. SPAP; Dorothy Halvorsen to Ethel M. Davis, 20 October 1932. SPAP; Ethel M. Davis to Frances Atkinson, 20 October 1932. SPAP; Ethel M. Davis to Ella Griffin, 18 October 1932. SPAP; Ethel M. Davis to Gretchen J. Garrison, 18 October 1932. SPAP; Ethel M. Davis to Caroline Goodman, 18 October 1932; Ethel M. Davis to Sarah Volovick, 18 October 1932, SPAP.

[77] Eleanor B. Semple to Paul H. Ritterskamp, 24 October 1932, SPAP.

[78] Garrison, "Help Wanted—Female," May 1934, Box 5, PECSP.

[79] This echoes Buhle's arguments about women and the SP in the time of Debs. See Buhle, *Women and Socialism*, 313.

[80] Miller, *Flawed Liberation*, xvii.

[81] Zilla Hawes Daniel, "The Plant, A little Café, and Lots of Coffee," in *Refuse to Stand Silently by*, ed. Eliot Wigginton (New York: Doubleday, 1991), 94.

CHAPTER 7

While the Men Played Revolution

In May 1931, Elizabeth "Zilla" Hawes was arrested during a rally, which she had helped to organize on behalf of the Socialist Party of America. Hawes had just finished delivering "a stirring address [that argued] against the right of one generation to bequeath money to the next."[1] Her denunciation of inheritance law attracted the attention of journalists because, a few days after her speech and arrest, Hawes inherited one thousand dollars. To put this amount in perspective, the median weekly wage for women working in department stores in ten cities in neighboring New Jersey was $17 for a six-day week.[2] Guided by the philosophy of "political as personal," Hawes decided to use the money in the fight against inherited wealth. "I'll accept the money," Hawes told a reporter, "but I'm going to spend it all in a fight against inheritances. This is a great opportunity to demonstrate my sincerity."[3] Hawes managed to combine a principled, radical position with a pragmatic solution to her "predicament," which was to use the money to further the movement for socialism. This episode indicates the idealism

---

[1] "Inheritance Opponent Given Test," *Los Angeles Times*, 25 May 1931, 7.

[2] Mary Loretta Sullivan, *Employment Conditions in Department Stores in 1932–1933: A Study in Selected Cities of Five States* (Washington, DC: U.S. Women's Bureau, 1936), 19.

[3] "Inheritance Opponent Given Test," 7.

© The Author(s) 2019
J. Altman, *Socialism before Sanders*,
https://doi.org/10.1007/978-3-030-17176-6_7

and commitment that young socialists brought to their movement. It also suggests that women played a prominent, public role in the life of the SP. Even as women became prominent leaders of the socialist movement, as the vignette above suggests, they faced animosity from their male comrades. In 1932, Hawes was pleased to get the approval of Tom Tippett, director of theater and music at Brookwood Labor College, because, she said, "he thinks women are generally useless."[4] Educated, intellectual men were dismissive of the role that women could play in the movement. This chapter, in addition to reclaiming the relevance of Zilla Hawes, examines male socialists' ambivalence toward socialist women and toward feminism.

The SP's membership was not universally committed to the liberation of women, even if the party's public pronouncements suggested otherwise. Instead, individual socialists were divided on what the "women question" meant, how it should be solved, and for what causes socialists should utilize their party's limited resources. At the extreme, as Tippett's comment in the last paragraph demonstrates, socialist men were openly dismissive of women's contributions and the very notion of equality.[5] While the Communist Party could enforce, or at least try to enforce, policies about gender relations, the Socialist Party could not do this without undermining its commitment to open debate. This was a problem because there was no consensus on women's status in society or in the SP.[6] Instead, socialists preferred to make appeals to education and self-reflection without an oppressive party apparatus to shape this process.

Socialist women in the 1930s regarded themselves as the party's chief architects and most skilled organizers. They believed that men and women possessed distinct inborn qualities. Women's qualities were uniformly positive, and men carried traits that could mean disaster for the efficacy of the socialist movement. This distinction was, in part, retaliation against male

---

[4]Zilla Hawes to Myles Horton, 20 November 1932, Box 15, Folder 30, HREC; Michael Denning, *The Cultural Front: The Laboring of American Culture in the Twentieth Century* (London: Verso, 2011), 71.

[5]The social and cultural meaning of gender was central to this debate within the Socialist Party. Both sides deployed gendered representations to make their arguments. For context, see Alice Kessler-Harris on the sexual division of labor and female domesticity in the 1930s, "Gender Ideology in Historical Reconstruction: A Case Study from the 1930s," *Gender & History* 1, no. 1 (1989), 34–35.

[6]*The Decline of American Socialism*, 62; Buhle, *Women and American Socialism*, 250–251.

comrades who publicly belittled women's abilities and contributions to the socialist movement.

Socialist men, in turn, held a variety of assumptions about women and, as a result, took varying opinions of women's ability. Some socialist men were openly hostile to and dismissive of women. Successful and articulate socialist women attracted the ire of these socialist men, who were in essence anti-feminists. Other men were patronizing and condescending, yet less aggressively hostile toward women. A third group offered women support and encouragement. This group saw women as an important constituency for the SP and an essential prerequisite for widespread socialist success. The strongest male supporters of women came from the social-democratic elements of the party, though these men were also often defenders of a Victorian conception of the family.[7] The more radical factions, though they included women, were less concerned with addressing the question of equality. The global upheavals of the 1930s, and the revolutionary potential these events supposedly engendered, took precedence.

Socialist women argued that women were superior organizers while men posed problems for the movement. Gertrude Weil Klein—a writer for *The New Leader*, staff person for the ACWA, and future member of the New York City Council—for instance, was quick to find evidence that women and men were equal in their ability to demonstrate solidarity and carry off a successful organizing campaign: "If there's one thing that was knocked into a cocked hat by our little strike in Lynbrook it is the notion that women are inferior to men in quickness of understanding, in loyalty and in spirit." Klein argued that women were perfectly capable of organizing unions in their workplaces. If young women who had "never heard anything about unions before" could wage a successful struggle for a union, it proved women were capable trade unions and socialists.[8] Klein opposed the idea, held by some labor leaders, that "women are inferior to men in quickness and understanding, in loyalty and in spirit."[9] Klein used her experience as an organizer in the labor movement to demonstrate the absurdity of popular thinking on gendered attributes: "It was the men in the first days of the strike who constantly wept on my shoulder because they were sure

[7] There is a dispute about whether or not Victorian conceptions of the family were "essentially [...] middle class." Mishler, *Raising Reds*, 19.

[8] Gertrude Weil Klein, "A Woman's Point of View: The Girls Are Stickling Nobly," *The New Leader*, 21 January 1933, 5.

[9] Ibid.

the girls wouldn't stick."[10] Here, she dispels the idea that women were emotional, weak, and liable to jeopardize the success of a strike. The strike, Klein reported, would have been lost had it not been for the support of local socialist women, who were the champions of strike support: "What can Socialists do in a labor struggle? Ask Gertrude Stone and Florence Mulford! How can the Socialist Party come closer to the exploited workers? Ask Comrade Winnie Branstetter, who delivered a beautiful talk."[11] Women, Klein argued, were as capable and committed to the labor movement as men. They, too, and perhaps more so, could wage an effective strike and achieve victory. Gretchen Garrison was not interested in men's assumptions about women capabilities. She pointed to the women's success in activities idealized as men's work: "In business as workers, executives, and investors, women are showing their power and ability."[12] Garrison may have had Violet Thomas in mind when she referenced the business acumen of women.

Socialists drew on broader conceptions of difference to formulate their own arguments about gender. These broader conceptions were, however, translated into socialist terms. Socialists also found themselves engaging with movements that were not necessarily socialist in content or origin. Women employed gender in the socialist press, in labor struggles, and at the local level in the concrete experiences of socialist intentional community. In 1935, amidst much factional discord within the SP, Gertrude Weil Klein wrote an article titled, "It's the Women Who Build While the Men Squabble."[13] Klein argued that men were delinquent comrades and poor stewards of the socialist movement, while arguing that women were more practical and party-minded and, as such, better stewards of the movement. Socialist women employed essentialist notions of gender and drew from their experiences working with men in the Socialist Party to argue that

---

[10]Gertrude Weil Klein, "A Woman's Point of View: The Girls Are Stickling Nobly," 5; Gertrude Weil Klein, "A Woman's Point of View," *The New Leader*, 28 January 1933, 6.

[11]Klein, "A Woman's Point of View: The Girls Are Stickling Nobly," 5.

[12]Gretchen J. Garrison, "Help Wanted—Female," *Eighteenth National Convention of the Socialist Party of America*, May 1934, Box 3, PECSP, 14.

[13]Gertrude Weil Klein, "It's the Women Who Build While the Men Squabble," *The New Leader*, 16 February 1935, 2. Klein was referring to the factional struggles that severely curtailed the party's effectiveness and contributed to the beginning of its effective decline in 1936. Warren, *An Alternative Vision*, 10–15. For a longer exegesis on the fall of the Socialist Party, see Johnpoll, *Pacifist's Progress*, 135–177.

women were the responsible bearers of the socialist torch. "Women," wrote Klein, "are essentially conservative. I mean in a fundamental sense. They are conservers, builders, organizers."[14] While left-wing men belittled women, women answered back with their own gendered claims. Klein was explicit. She believed that the party was being destroyed because "our organizations are run by men."[15] Justifying her claim by invoking essentialist conceptions of masculinity, she pointed to men's lust for power and glory as the cause of discord within the party. Klein was frustrated with her male comrades and with their squabbling.[16] While making her case less forcefully, Gretchen Garrison also considered women "the backbone of the [SP's] membership."[17] Reading Mary Ritter Beard's *On Understanding Women*, as socialist women did, would have reinforced their confidence that they too were the party's architects and builders. In *On Understanding Women*, Beard argued for a more expansive understanding of history that acknowledged the essential role of women in the development of "civilization."[18]

An examination of the socialist movement at the level of personal relationships reveals problems, frustrations, and ultimately a reactionary positioning built on many of the same representations and attitudes that led female communists to demand that their party take action on male domination in the family and the party.[19] When Gertrude Weil Klein reported that her work for the movement, including a column in *The New Leader*, was a tremendous burden, especially with the proposed addition of a full page dedicated to "women's issues" to appear in *The New Leader*, the editor, a

[14] Klein, "It's the Women Who Build While the Men Squabble," 2.

[15] Ibid.

[16] Women, of course, participated in factionalism, too. A number of prominent socialist women signed the Revolutionary Policy Committee's April 1934 "Appeal to the Membership of the Socialist Party," including Zilla Hawes. They were, however, a small minority of the signers.

[17] Gretchen J. Garrison, "Help Wanted—Female," *Eighteenth National Convention of the Socialist Party of America*, May 1934, Box 3, PECSP, 14.

[18] Gertrude Weil Klein, "Girls Battle Starvation in Elizabeth Shirt Strike," *The New Leader*, 27 May 1933, 4; Nancy F. Cott, "Putting Women on the Record: Mary Ritter Beard's Accomplishment," in *A Woman Making History: Marry Ritter Beard Through Her Letters*, ed. Nancy F. Cott (Yale University Press, 1991), 31–32. Beard's argument in *On Understanding Women* fit with the socialist women's ideas about their constitutive role in the movement.

[19] Kate Weigand, *Red Feminism: American Communism and the Making of Women's Liberation* (Baltimore: John Hopkins University Press, 2001), 32.

male comrade, added the following exclamations in brackets to her column: "Nonsense, Gertrude! You look great!"[20] The editor's comment, intended no doubt as a compliment, betrays the depth of concern socialist men had for their female comrades and suggests a superficial view of what women could contribute to the movement. This was not the only occasion when the editor interrupting Klein's column with bracketed comments on her work or appearance.[21] The effect of repeated intrusions was to undermine her independence as a columnist.

Letters written to Klein and the lack of credit socialist women received for their work reveal male socialists' animosity for and condescension toward women's prominence in the party. A letter sent by a male socialist referred to Klein as a "butterfly on a wheel," suggesting that he regarded her as beautiful and ineffective.[22] Klein was not included among the list of "frequent contributions" in advertisements of *The New Leader*, even though lesser-known male socialists were included.[23] Gretchen Garrison was included on the list of contributions to the SP's convention materials, but was last on the list.[24] Pauline Newman resented that her male comrades took much of the credit for good work done by women. In a fatalistic tone, she wrote, "We protest, even though no one cares whether we do

---

[20] Gertrude Weil Klein, "Socialist Women Abroad Can Hail Achievements," *The New Leader*, 21 July 1934, 8. Klein, eventually elected to the New York City Council for the American Labor Party, was one of a large number of impressive Socialist women whose stories remain largely untold. Klein has recently received some notable coverage in the venerable old social-democratic paper *The Jewish Daily Forward*. See Chana Pollack's, "Gertrude Weil Klein's Socialist Yikhes," *The Sisterhood* (blog), *The Jewish Daily Forward*, 11 December 2014, http://blogs.forward.com/sisterhood-blog/210761/gertrude-weil-klein-s-socialist-yikhes/.

[21] Gertrude Weil Klein, "It's the Women Who Build While the Men Squabble," *The New Leader*, 16 February 1935, 2; Gertrude Weil Klein, "An Ex-Governor Wraps Himself in the Red Flag," *The New Leader*, 29 December 1934, 2; Gertrude Weil Klein, "And What Do You Think?" *The New Leader*, 22 September 1934, 2; Gertrude Weil Klein, "Women Socialists Everywhere Lead Fight Upon War," *The New Leader*, 12 January 1935, 2; Gertrude Weil Klein, "A Grave Digger and a Soldier on the Road," *The New Leader*, 8 September 1934, 2; and Gertrude Weil Klein, "Girls Battle Starvation in Elizabeth Shirt Strike," *The New Leader*, 27 May 1933, 4.

[22] Gertrude Weil Klein, "A 'Butterfly on a Wheel' and a 'Little Snip'," *The New Leader*, 19 January 1935, 2.

[23] *The New Leader*, Advertisement, *Eighteenth National Convention of the Socialist Party of America*, May 1934, Box 3, PECSP.

[24] Socialist Party of America, *Eighteenth National Convention of the Socialist Party of America*, May 1934, Box 3, PECSP.

or not! But it is getting tiresome to have celebrations of one organization or another and see the men take all the glory for themselves."[25] Newman lamented that men made up the overwhelming majority of speakers at a celebration commemorating the fortieth anniversary of the United Hebrew Trades, an organization that was built through the hard work of many women. She resented the lack of recognition paid to the sacrifices of heroic socialist women. She ended her protest by striking a positive, hopeful tone: "Some day the men leaders in all organizations will wake up and find that there are many who do care [about women and their contributions]—and then... but let us get there first!"[26] Socialist women experienced gender ideology in different ways. That men like Klein's editor meant well does not mitigate their tones of condescension; men contributed to an assessment of women based on a narrow set of concerns. Other socialist men were openly hostile to women and saw them as nuisances or worse. Some men's hostility seems to have simmered under the surface, perhaps held there by some internal conflict between socialist ideas of equality and a wider, inculcated sense that women were inferior to men. At times, this hostility boiled over in intense episodes.

Condescending references to women's equality, made by male socialists, were not uncommon. Feminism was referred to as a trifling and yet also a dangerous thing.[27] Women were lambasted for their failures, characterized as irrational, depicted as dominating and man-hating, and seen as a force that would subvert the good works of socialism. "This woman's equality is all right as far as it goes," wrote author and former member of the New York State Assembly Sam de Witt in 1928, "but like free speech, there is such a thing as license if it goes too far, and a license is exactly what I would refuse to give most women, after seeing what they did with the vote."[28] Upset that the famous conversation between Susan B. Anthony and Eugene V. Debs in which Anthony said, "Give us suffrage, and we'll give you socialism," and Debs replied, "Give us socialism and we'll give you suffrage," yielded nothing to reality, de Witt blamed women: "we Socialists fought, bled and cried to win for them. They just got up the morning they were enfranchised,

---

[25] Pauline M. Newman, "A Meeting of the Faithful Few," *The New Leader*, 12 January 1929, 6.

[26] Ibid.

[27] S.A. de Witt, "Song for an Impossible Lady," *The New Leader*, 17 March 1928, 8.

[28] Ibid.

walked to the ballot boxes and voted into office the very leather-necks that had been keeping them on a place with idiots and criminals."[29] Sam de Witt's vitriolic characterization of women, professional women in particular, continued with gendered arguments about his socialist comrades and their abilities and motivations. "Sometimes," he wrote, "when I walk through the city or travel through the country, or just sit down and eat at the Rand School Cafeteria, and listen to both conservatives and radical ladies, I fall upon that ancient conclusion that there is something fey [supernatural], or mad, or just abnormal about the fair sex."[30] Taking his argument a step further, de Witt, drawing from mainstream arguments about the women's movement, concluded that women, despite new freedoms, wished to destroy manhood: "I thought that perhaps with this newer life of economic and sex freedom, evolving out of hip-flasks and the Charleston, the mania for possessing, dominating and destroying men would diminish on the part of our womanhood."[31] He went on to lament the sunken status of "mouse-like husbands and boyfriends," who bowed before the manipulative powers of women. Women, he wrote, would "clutch" men, "plot and plan, and whisper and giggle and gossip, and just stir up all the witch-pots in Troubledom to keep what they so outwardly disdain."[32] Anticipating bags full of mail from female comrades, de Witt admitted that there were exceptions, though few in number, to his characterizations of women.[33]

If some male comrades were hostile, flippant, or satirical about feminism and the status of women during the period of socialist revival, other men stood out as advocates for women's equality. In what was perhaps the most comprehensive and articulate statement in support of women, August Claessens, an author and former member of the New York State Assembly, addressed the destructive influence of consumerism on changing standards of beauty. "The intensification," he wrote, "of the element of physical attractiveness by artificial means and its demoralizing effect in the

[29] Anthony and Debs are quoted in Ray Ginger, *The Bending Cross: A Biography of Eugene Victor Debs* (New Brunswick: Rutgers University Press, 1949), 224; de Witt, "Song for an Impossible Lady," 8.

[30] de Witt, "Song for an Impossible Lady," 8.

[31] Ibid.

[32] Ibid.

[33] Ibid.

play of sexual selection [has] bankrupt[ed] many a marriage."[34] Claessens, a social democrat, pointed out that modern marriage was inadequate as a result of "the economic, social and intellectual inequalities of the sexes bred in our social system and that prevent every prospect of marital concord."[35] A good marriage, Claessens argued, was built on equality. His positive view of equality in marriage was conditioned by his own experiences. August Claessens's wife, Hilda, was heavily involved in the party too, though she died in 1932.[36] He dedicated his book *The Logic of Socialism* to Hilda. Indicating the debts he owed his comrade and wife, Claessens wrote, "In dedicating this little work to my comrade and wife, Hilda G. Claessens, I merely give expression to the fact that without her painstaking help my efforts both in speech and in writing would have fallen far short of the success attained."[37] He was unequivocal in his denunciation of the inequitable treatment of women and argued that one of the "degrading elements" of modern marriage was "the anti-social and beastly attitude of men towards women as merely instruments for gratification rather than towards them as fellow human beings."[38] Claessens, unlike some of his comrades, also defended "monogamy, marriage, and the family."[39] Claessens was a proponent of "the struggle for a complete equality of men and women."[40] There was variation in what this could mean for socialists. Claessens was one of the few socialist men to demarcate the lines of his thought on the relationship between women and men. He was atypical. While urging socialists to advocate for equality between women and men, Claessens idealized women as "beautiful, womanly, motherly, and dignified."[41] Claessens liked Dora Russell's proposed "new social status wherein motherhood and the relationship

[34] August Claessens, "An Apostrophe to Sexual Freedom: A Discussion of the Future of Modern Marriage," *The New Leader*, 8 December 1928, 5.

[35] Ibid.

[36] Pauline M. Newman, "The Woman Socialist," *The New Leader*, 12 January 1929, 6; Socialist Party of America, "Necrology," *Eighteenth National Convention of the Socialist Party of America*, May 1934, Box 3, PECSP, 14.

[37] August Claessens, *The Logic of Socialism* (New York: The Leonard Press, 1921), 3.

[38] Claessens, "An Apostrophe to Sexual Freedom: A Discussion of the Future of Modern Marriage," 5.

[39] Ibid.

[40] August Claessens, "Equality of the Sexes," *The New Leader*, 23 May 1925, 9.

[41] August Claessens, "A Debate on Feminism," *The New Leader*, 13 February 1926, 4.

between men, women and children will have its roots in economic security, knowledge, mutual love and wholesome respect."[42] This was a socialist feminism that championed the defense of the family from the economic insecurity of capitalism.[43] It was a feminism that situated women firmly within the family as wife/mother, and a safeguard of domestic morality.

Coupled to this view of the family, as defended by socialists, the bourgeoisie and petty bourgeoisie (gendered as male by Gertrude Weil Klein) were depicted as the true destroyers and subverters of the family. Their lives included a decadent sexuality that was repulsive to the socialist. Whereas the poor might be lured to a life of sexual depravity by their economic circumstances, the rich freely chose such a life and in doing so contributed to the sexual exploitation of the poor and revealed the true contours of bourgeois morality. Klein first pointed to the murder of wealthy lawyer Howard Carter Dickinson, who was the nephew of serving Chief Justice of the Supreme Court Charles Evans Hughes. Dickinson was lured to his death by "party girls," a euphemism for prostitutes.[44] Moving from the particular to a generalization based on class, Klein wrote of the "sordid little merchant [who] takes a holiday when away from his home and family for a few days. A cheap pick-up, a drunken party, a dismal end."[45] Klein concluded, "Men like Dickinson, children who inherit huge fortunes, are just as likely to grow up emotional and mental cripples as are the children who, from a very early age, must use their wits to keep alive. At both ends [of society] we are breeding anti-social characters and characteristics."[46] If bourgeois sexual depravity was castigated so too was free love, though socialists did not universally reject this doctrine. Claessens also wrote off the supposed trend toward "free love" as attributable to "a minority of souls, who are so incapable of compatibility that any sort of constant relationship, sexual, social, vocational and otherwise seems to them utterly hopeless." "In these unhappy folks," he continued, "The incessant pursuit for vari-

---

[42]Ibid.

[43]Paul C. Mishler, *Raising Reds: The Young Pioneers, Radical Summer Camps, and Communist Political Culture in the United States* (New York: Columbia University Press, 1999), 18–19.

[44]Gertrude Weil Klein, "The Poor Little Rich Girl; And Her Poor Little Sister," *The New Leader*, 27 July 1935, 3; "Crime," *Chicago Sunday Tribune*, 29 December 1935, 8.

[45]Weil Klein, "The Poor Little Rich Girl; And Her Poor Little Sister," 3.

[46]Ibid.

ety, their promiscuous sexual proclivities are most often pathological."[47] Claessens's envisioned "sexual revolution" as a feminist revolution, though he avoided using the term feminism, which carried negative connotations for socialists and communists during the 1930s.[48]

Free love was occasionally sneered at in the socialist press.[49] Heywood Broun, a prominent socialist and newspaperman, argued that misconceptions about socialism—including the idea that socialism could be equated with free love—slowed its progress in the American South.[50] This treatment in the socialist press, however, does not mean that all socialists eschewed open sexual relationships, which had roots in socialist thought through the utopian socialists and August Bebel's classic *Women Under Socialism*, a book given away with subscriptions to *The New Leader* in the 1930s.[51] A source of tension for Zilla Hawes and Franz Daniel, Hawes's husband, was that the open relationship that they had agreed upon proved too difficult in practice. John Daniel, their son, reported, "My own parents, it turns out, were experimenting with Free Love a fully thirty years before the hippie culture of the sixties made it a catchphrase and a sporadic way of life."[52] He concluded, "It didn't work out any better for them than it does for most who try it."[53] "My mother" wrote John, "did indeed experiment—and my father, when he found out, raised holy hell in spite of their agreement. My mother, in later years, wasn't sure if he had had other relationships. She thought not, but a woman friend who lived with them in Philadelphia in those days tells me he certainly did."[54] "Free love," which had conflicting meanings, was not a common sexual arrangement among socialists in the 1930s.[55] It is perhaps indicative of the general acceptance

[47]Claessens, "An Apostrophe to Sexual Freedom," 5.

[48]Ibid. For a discussion of the reluctance of the Old Left to identify with "feminism," see Weigand, *Red Feminism*, 7–8.

[49]James Denson Sayers, "Veteran Campaigner Tells How Socialism Can Progress in the South," *The New Leader*, 3 December 1932, 8.

[50]Ibid.

[51]Mishler, *Raising Reds*, 17–18.

[52]Daniel, *Looking After*, 81.

[53]Ibid.

[54]Ibid.

[55]Some socialists sought to define "free love" as companionate marriage, which captured the idea that people should be free to choose and dissolve marriages and dispelled notions that socialists were engaged in promoting an orgy of sexual excess. Despite the

of monogamous marriage that Hawes and Daniel abandoned the permissive type of relationship upon which they had first agreed. Jealousy proved too intense to sanction open marriage.[56]

Women in America looked to their female comrades abroad as examples that affirmed the equity of women and men and their willingness to sacrifice for the socialist movement. The fall of socialist Vienna to the Austrian fascists in 1934 was of great concern to American socialists. Not only were their comrades imprisoned, murdered, or on the run, the greatest, the most civilized socialist city in the world had been conquered by the forces of reaction. Gertrude Weil Klein took to the pages of *The New Leader* to remind her comrades that the socialist women of Austria suffered and "died beside their men." Klein made of a point of eulogizing the women whose names and sacrifices would never be known. She wrote, "All the unknown heroines of the Austrian fight for freedom will also remain enshrined in the hearts of the workers, just as are the heroes of the Commune."[57] Women, too, were committed to socialism. They, too, were willing to pay for freedom and equity with their lives. Klein's forceful ode to Vienna's women carried this point: socialist women were as courageous and as committed to the struggle as socialist men.

Socialist women disapproved of feminism, a movement that carried middle-class, racist connotations in the 1930s.[58] Socialist women opposed the National Women's Party, which was associated with feminism. They did not want to see hard-won legislation that protected women on the basis of difference undermined by the Equal Rights Amendment. Nor did they see much mutual concern for working women from the primary constituents

---

widespread rejection of a more expansive notion of "free love" by socialists, the left would continue to be hounded by critics who claimed that socialists sought to destroy the underpinnings of Christian morality, including monogamous marriage. Socialists, in turn, were keen to point out that bourgeois marriage was a ridiculous ideal and not monogamous. Socialists, turning the tables of the moralists, portrayed capitalists, gendered as male, as sexually deviant hypocrites.

[56]Daniel, *Looking After*, 81. For a cursory introduction to the relationship between socialists and free love see the following works. Karen Hunt, *Equivocal Feminists: The Social Democratic Federation and the Woman Question 1884–1911* (Cambridge University Press, 2002), 114–116; Mishler, *Raising Reds*, 16–20; and Buhle, *Women and American Socialism*, 260–262.

[57]Gertrude Weil Klein, "The Women of Austria Who Died Beside Their Men," *The New Leader*, 31 March 1934, 6.

[58]Weigand, *Red Feminism*, 97–98.

of the National Women's Party.[59] Gertrude Weil Klein declared that she had "never been a feminist."[60] "And of course," she interjected, "I'm not a man-hater." Klein's statements reveal the popular conceptions of feminists, even among her socialist audience, in the 1930s. She added, however, that she had "never been excited about man's inhumanity to women."[61] While careful to diffuse the aspersion "man-hater," perhaps anticipating a critique from male editors or readers, Klein emphasized her disgust with gender-based violence in society. There were good reasons, she argued, for women to be angry and intolerant of "man's inhumanity." Feminism became an expansive movement later in the twentieth century, when left-wing women claimed the label as their own.

If the skeptical social democrats found anything to appreciate in the Soviet Union, it was the improved status of women during the first decade of Soviet rule. While historians have complicated a wholly positive view of the change in the status of women in the Soviet Union in the years after 1917, the social democrats were not wrong to appreciate the general improvement of the conditions of women during the early years of Soviet rule.[62] Zilla Hawes had, as we shall see, a positive view of gender relations (and the opportunities afforded women) in the Soviet Union. The idea that equality existed in the Soviet Union, however much it eventually diverged from reality, was a powerful force in women's minds. There was a place, somewhere tangible, where things were better. This denaturalized gender relations in the United States and gave women a powerful argument to deploy against the limitations imposed by hostile male comrades. While remaining skeptical of the Soviet Union's achievements for women's equality due to the denial of civil liberties in other areas, Claessens, seemingly convinced by positive reports from various sources including Abra-

---

[59] Pauline Newman, "Our Position Justified," *The New Leader*, 29 December 1928; Weigand, *Red Feminism*, 31.

[60] Gertrude Weil Klein, "A Woman's Point of View: The Girls Are Stickling Nobly," *The New Leader*, 21 January 1933, 5.

[61] Ibid.

[62] Gail Warshofsky Lapidus, *Women in Soviet Society: Equality, Development, and Social Change* (Berkeley: University of California Press, 1978), 4, 8, 11.

ham Cahan of the *Jewish Daily Forward*, granted that the Soviet Union completed a feat worthy of celebration.[63]

Gender was central to the experiences of socialist women and men in the 1930s. It shaped how they thought about men and the movement's problems and trajectory. Gender also provided support for arguments about who was responsible for the party's problems. Men discounted the abilities of socialist women, and women blamed men for the party's decline. Women used gender more reflexively. Men wielded it destructively. It shaped abstract arguments and personal experiences in profound ways. For Klein, women found "compensation in being loved, desired, and needed." Thus, women played an emollient, productive role in the party. The "tortuous machinations for power" carried out by socialist men undermined women's best efforts to build a socialist movement, and women found these struggles to be naturally repulsive and hurtful.[64] Klein went so far as to imagine a party in which women were free from the interference of men's destructive habits: "If our women could isolate themselves from the party fracas and had the means, the equipment and the organization to reach women, I think they could create a Socialist movement that would be worth fighting for."[65] Garrison pointed out that "women can promote 'united fronts' which will demonstrate to a laughing world that SOME radicals can work with other groups on specific issues without breaking heads in the process and indulging in undignified quarrels."[66] The inclusion of "SOME" in capital letters was intended for comedic benefit. Garrison's point was that men were excluded from the "SOME" who could do the vital work of coalition building. Garrison and Klein agreed that women could achieve success where men only fostered hostility and indignation.[67] Some male comrades shared these positive gendered assumptions about women. Men in the Australian Labour Party, Klein reported, had acknowledged their errors in "gravely [neglecting] the women of the movement."[68] Klein

---

[63]August Claessens, "An Apostrophe to Sexual Freedom," 5. For a discussion of the reluctance of the Old Left to identify with "feminism," see Weigand, *Red Feminism*, 7–8.

[64]Klein, "It's the Women Who Build While the Men Squabble," 2.

[65]Ibid.

[66]Garrison, "Help Wanted—Female," 14.

[67]Ibid.

[68]Gertrude Weil Klein, "Women Socialists Everywhere Lead Fight Upon War," *The New Leader*, 12 January 1935, 2.

quoted unspecified male "Labour Party leaders" from the Inter-State Conference of Labour Women in Australia: "Had the party taken the women
into its confidence in the early days, it would have advanced further. Women
had to force their way into the movement, and for years their work did
not get the recognition it deserved. There was a time, however, when the
women's organization threatened to become bigger and more powerful
than the men's; and it was at that [moment] that the labor movement
[assumed] its most virile form."[69] There was some truth in the analysis
that women proved more adept than men, if not in the essentialist gender
ideology that Klein and others employed to bolster their points. Women
had made tremendous efforts to revive the party, as the previous chapter
demonstrates. The life of Zilla Hawes is a particularly poignant portrait of
a socialist woman's experiences, frustrations, hopes, and struggles in the
1930s and in the aftermath of that radical decade. Hawes did not articulate
her frustrations as directly as Klein. She did, however, think about her role
in the socialist movement in terms similar to those of Klein. Despite the
differences that set Hawes apart from Klein—Hawes was a member of the
SP's revolutionary faction while Klein was a social democrat—they both
viewed women as a positive, productive force in the SP and challenged the
idea that women and their contributions were inferior. Klein believed that
women were better equipped to build and maintain institutions than men.
If Zilla Hawes did not entirely agree with Klein, she acted as if she did.
Recasting women as the productive members of the community and men
as the destroyers of the socialist movement was a radical redeployment of
gender.[70]

[69] Ibid.

[70] For a discussion of how this idea might be placed in the context of socialist theory,
see Buhle, *Woman and American Socialism*, 27–29. In particular, see Buhle's discussion of August Bebels's idea of "a prehistorical 'Golden Age' of primitive communism
wherein humanity had known peace and harmony under a matriarchal social system."
The idea that women were particularly suited to advance social causes and the construction of these causes around "public motherhood" were central to the Progressive
movement and potentially informed the ways in which socialist women thought about
their capabilities, though each movement was distinctive. See Stromquist, *Re-inventing
"the People"*, 107–108, 119.

HAWES BEFORE HIGHLANDER

Hawes came from a progressive middle-class family. She was born Elizabeth Day Hawes on 8 April 1908 to Oscar Brown Hawes and Anne de Pourtales Day.[71] Anne and Oscar had married in February 1903.[72] Oscar Hawes was the son of George E. Hawes and Adelaide Dunning.[73] George, a dentist, died in 1880 when Oscar was still a child, and Adelaide raised the six young Hawes children.[74] The economic circumstances of the Hawes family after George's death are unclear, yet, whatever these circumstances, they did not limit the success of the Hawes children. Oscar Hawes graduated from Harvard in 1893.[75] His daughter Zilla had an economically secure, even affluent, childhood. When she was two, the family toured Europe.[76] The Hawes family, though not moneyed, was stable and comfortable. They could afford to maintain a summerhouse in Maine.[77] Oscar served as a minister for a Unitarian congregation in Germantown, Pennsylvania.[78] One account of his time in Germantown suggests that he was an adored and respected minister.[79] While the economic position of her family was not tenuous, Zilla would have known of and perhaps accompanied her father in his work for the Nicetown Club for Boys and Girls, which was located in one of Philadelphia's varied manufacturing districts.[80] She

[71] *Harvard College Class of 1893: Fifth Report* (Cambridge: Crimson Printing Company, 1913), 85.

[72] *Harvard College Class of 1893: Third Report* (Boston: Rockwell and Churchill Press, 1903), 223.

[73] *Harvard College Class of 1893: Fifth Report*, 85.

[74] 1880 United States Federal Census Year: 1880; Census Place: Dresden, Washington, New York; Roll: 942; Family History Film: 1254942; Page: 66C; Enumeration District: 131; Image: 0134; *Catalogue of the Alpha Delta Phi* (New York: Executive Council of the Alpha Delta Phi Fraternity, 1899), 489.

[75] "Harvard Scratch Races," *Boston Post*, 1 May 1891, 3.

[76] *Harvard College Class of 1893: Fifth Report* (Cambridge: Crimson Printing Company, 1913), 85.

[77] Daniel, *Looking After*, 13.

[78] "Religious Intelligence," *The Christian Register*, 13 March 1913, 263.

[79] Ibid.

[80] *Harvard College Class of 1893: Fifth Report* (Cambridge: Crimson Printing Company, 1913), 85; Peter Cole, *Wobblies on the Waterfront: Interracial Unionism in Progressive-Era Philadelphia* (Urbana-Champaign: University of Illinois Press, 2007), 11–12.

would have seen a world different from her own comfortable life in the parsonage. In Nicetown, on the teeming streets of an immigrant-populated steel district shaped by the "severity of industrial capitalism," Zilla may have even encountered working-class radicals, whose politics she would one day champion as a radical socialist in Philadelphia in the early 1930s.[81]

Oscar Hawes was an encouraging Unitarian minister who exposed his daughters to political causes. His pronoun use indicates that he was keen to adopt language that included women by 1915.[82] Men did not stand in for the whole of human society in his sermons. Women were included as partners in the search for truth guided by reason. In 1927, he served on the national council of the American Birth Control League.[83] In 1913, he informed his Harvard classmates that he was a man quite satisfied with his family of three daughters.[84] Oscar was far from conventional in his thinking on women and society. His liberal theological and reformist political outlook must have had some influence on his daughter.

And yet, when Zilla Hawes graduated from Vassar in 1929, there was nothing in her life, other than her childhood experiences in Philadelphia, to suggest a socialist course. Oscar Hawes, while a man of conscience and politics, was not a socialist. Nor was their family life steeped in the sort of culture or experience that might lead young people to seek hope and power in the radical left. When she left for Vassar, her father was serving a congregation in Keene, New Hampshire.[85] The family lived in a pleasant stone house situated across the street from the Unitarian church, where

---

[81] Robert M. Zecker, "'Not Communists Exactly, but Sort of Like Non-believers': The Hidden Radical Transcript of Slovak Immigrants in Philadelphia, 1890–1954," *The Oral History Review* 29, no. 1 (2002), 11, 16. Zecker's informants vividly remembered life in the "not-so-nice Nicetown," which they and Zecker then contextualize in "severity of industrial capitalism" of the Progressive Era.

[82] Oscar B. Hawes, "Need of Unity in Religion," *The Ocala Evening Star*, 30 April 1909, 4.

[83] See list of members in the front matter of the *Birth Control Review*, no. 10 (October 1927).

[84] *Harvard College Class of 1893: Fifth Report* (Cambridge: Crimson Printing Company, 1913), 85.

[85] Keene, City Directory, 1928, 142. (New Haven: Price and Lee Company, 1928); 1920 U.S. census, Newton Ward 6, Middlesex, MA. Dwelling 242. Family 257.

Zilla spent her holidays away from Vassar.[86] They had a live-in maid.[87] Their neighbors were managers, assistant managers, and professionals. The family had a comfortable, middle-class life.

It is unclear when Zilla Hawes's commitment to socialism first material- ized. The atmosphere at Vassar during the late 1920s indicates that she was exposed to heterodox ideas about the nature of society that challenged cap- italism's dominance, even if these voices were in the minority.[88] Hawes may have seen her classmates perform George Bernard Shaw's play *Candida*, which was imbued with socialist and feminist content.[89] The most startling fact of Hawes's life at Vassar is that she managed to avoid most campus activities. In her first year at Vassar, Hawes was listed among the first altos in the college choir.[90] By her final year, she was demoted to the second altos.[91] This seems to have been the limit of her involvement with offi- cial organizations. Perhaps official activities were too staid for Hawes. The debates held by Hawes's classmates as part of Vassar's debate council give an indication of the political discussions held on campus. They debated the following proposition: "That an intelligent woman should vote for Hoover rather than Smith." The Smith camp won that debate. Further, and more pertinent for Hawes's socialist trajectory, they debated the issue of publicly owned and operated water supplies. The proponents of public water won.

It must have been difficult for Zilla Hawes, a young woman of intellect and skill, to meet her father's expectations for her future, which came in conflict with her own developing radicalism. A journalist once described him as a "strenuous minister."[92] He was, for instance, a prohibitionist, at least during the 1910s.[93] Zilla was not. She enjoyed alcohol throughout the 1930s. Oscar wanted her to pursue a Ph.D. in English—and presumably a

[86]Dora Cooke (ed.), *Vassarion* (Vassar's Yearbook) (Rochester, NY: The Du Bois Press, 1929), 201.

[87]1920 U.S. census, Newton Ward 6, Middlesex, MA. Dwelling 242. Family 257.

[88]Storrs, *The Second Red Scare*, 30–32.

[89]*Vassarion* (Vassar's Yearbook), 1929, 122; On *Candida*, see Gail Finney, *Women in Modern Drama: Freud, Feminism, and European Theater at the Turn of the Century* (Cornell University Press, 1989), 201–202.

[90]*Vassarion* (Vassar's Yearbook), 1926, 160.

[91]*Vassarion*, 1929, 141. There is no mention of a socialist organization in the year- book.

[92]"A Strenuous Minister," *The Scranton Republican*, 6 February 1905, 1.

[93]"Rev. Billy Sunday and a Square Deal," *The Labor Journal*, 29 December 1916, 4.

professorship at a woman's college, which was, in his perspective a suitably appropriate position for a progressive middle-class woman. Zilla had other ideas. After spending part of 1929 and 1930 at John C. Campbell Folk School (CFS), which was founded, organized, and run by women, she was energized by the possibilities that such a school would allow.[94]

The ideas and experiences that Zilla Hawes would bring from CFS to Highlander animated her expectations about gender relations in a community influenced by socialism. Hawes worked and lived at the CFS in North Carolina when it was run by Olive Campbell, the widow of John C. Campbell who had founded the school in her late husband's honor. Campbell was by all accounts a renaissance woman—teacher, author, traveler, photographer, and able administrator.[95] Hawes's experiences under Olive Campbell at the CFS were fundamentally different from her later experiences at Highlander. Hawes had a fulfilling work life at CFS. She worked outside with livestock, whitewashed buildings, and shoveled silage. Olive Campbell's own example and leadership abilities set the tone for Hawes and fostered her uneasiness with the rigidity of the gendered division of labor at Highlander and with the chauvinistic and dismissive attitudes her male comrades directed at women.[96]

CFS, less overtly political than Highlander, had programs centered on women's experiences, which were never directly addressed by the worker-oriented Highlander. Olive Campbell's interest in rural life and American agriculture spilled over into concerns about rural women and their health.[97] A 1924 report on midwifery in Kentucky made its way into Olive

---

[94] Elizabeth D. Hawes, "Questionnaire for Prospective Brookwood Students," 27 August 1932, Box 67, Folder 28, Brookwood Labor College Collection, Walter Reuther Library and Archives; "Olive Dame Campbell," *Journal of the International Folk Music Council* 7 (1955), 54–55. Evidence suggests that there was an emphasis on domesticity for women at the John Campbell Folk School, though Olive Campbell did claim in one of the school's bulletins, "Days were full of [a] variety [of work] for us all." Olive D. Campbell, "John Campbell Folk School Bulletin," May 1933, Folder 216, The John C. Campbell and Olive D. Campbell Papers [ODC], The Wilson Library, University of North Carolina; Olive D. Campbell, "John Campbell Folk School Bulletin," May 1929, Folder 216, ODC.

[95] Elizabeth Sanders Delwiche Engelhardt, *The Tangled Roots of Feminism, Environmentalism, and Appalachian Literature* (Ohio University Press, 2003), 22.

[96] Zilla Hawes Daniel, "The Plant, a little Café, and Lots of Coffee," in *Refuse to Stand Silently By*, ed. Eliot Wigginton (Doubleday, 1991), 92.

[97] [Olive D. Campbell], Untitled statement of purpose, [1930s], Folder 216, ODC.

Campbell's papers. Mary Breckinridge wrote the report. Melanie Beals Goan, Breckinridge's biographer, regards Olive Campbell as one of Breckinridge's predecessors in the field of women's health in the South. Breckinridge was a pioneer in collecting data on Southern midwifery and a modernizer of birth practices. Women's health in isolated mountain communities was a real concern of Olive Campbell and the staff of CFS, which distinguishes it from Highlander.[98]

CFS was led by women. The director, Olive Campbell, and the assistant director, Marguerite Bidstrup, were women, and CFS was organized around women's social networks. The director of the school's handicraft program was also a woman, Louise Pitman.[99] Various "patronesses" sponsored gatherings on behalf of CFS. Patronesses opened their homes to fundraisers, which featured the school's craft products.[100] Olive Campbell and Marguerite Bidstrup led these events.[101] This suggests that women played an active role in the life and work of CFS, although it does not tell us how the women who worked at the school thought about their position in relation to men. For this, we have to focus on the director's work for she was the public spokesperson for the school and articulated its mission.

Olive Campbell spoke about equality between people including men and women: "We can understand the relationship [between folk school teacher and student] better, if we picture ourselves going out into the mountains and becoming to the people John Smith, or Mary Smith, as they are John Smith or Mary Smith to us - neighbors, friends, equals."[102] While this

---

[98] Mary Breckinridge, "Midwifery in the Kentucky Mountains: An Investigation by Mary Breckinridge," 1923, Folder 161, OCD. See Jack Temple Kirby's "Women, Wedlock, Hearth, Health, and Death," in *Rural Worlds Lost: The American South, 1920–1960* for a discussion of Breckinridge's work. Melanie Beals Goan identifies Olive Campbell as one of Breckinridge's important predecessors in her biography, *Mary Breckinridge: The Frontier Nursing Service & Rural Health in Appalachia.*

[99] Invitation to the sale of handicrafts from Mrs. Albert C. Koch, 8 December 1942, Folder 216, ODC.

[100] List of Patronesses, [1940s], Folder 216, ODC; Revised list of Patronesses, [1940s], Folder 216, ODC.

[101] Invitation to Tea and Motion Pictures from Mrs. Alva Morrison, November 1938, Folder 216, ODC; Invitation to the sale of handicrafts from Mrs. Avery Coonley, 14 April [1942], Folder 216, ODC; Invitation from Mrs. J. Richmond Pitman, 12–13 November [1942], Folder 216, ODC; Invitation to the sale of handicrafts from Mrs. Edward Ballantine, 26 November [1942s], Folder 216, ODC.

[102] Speech by Olive D. Campbell to Southern Mountain Workers Conference, 9 April 1924, Folder 153, ODC.

passage from a speech Campbell delivered in 1924 might seem uncon-
nected to issues of gender, Campbell was emphasizing equality between
men and women at the same time she was advocating for equal relationships between students and teachers in the folk school movement. Further, Campbell pointed out that this emphasis on equality extended to
leisure activities when applied in Danish people's colleges, which she saw
as somewhat analogous to the projects that needed to be undertaken in
the American South. "Almost every school has its daily gymnastic hour,
for the people's college teacher is more interested in raising the average
than in training athletes and winning teams," she wrote, "One sees the
results in the fine up-standing vigorous manhood and womanhood of the
country."[103]

Zilla Hawes must have been frustrated by the shock of moving from a
school run almost exclusively by women, and with an emphasis on gender
equality, to a school where women were a noticeable minority. Life at the
CFS stood in contrast to life at Highlander. Women had more opportunity
to work in a variety of occupations at CFS, which helps to explain some
of Hawes's dissatisfaction with Highlander's stringent structures of work
based on gender.

After her stay at CFS, Hawes went to Philadelphia, worked at a neckwear factory, and joined the Neckwear Union. She also attended Brookwood Labor College beginning in the winter of 1932 and extending into
1933—where a heterodox Marxism became fused with her vision of what
a folk school could be.[104] In 1930, prior to attending Brookwood, Hawes
had been drawn into the Socialist Party when visiting Union Theological Seminary with a friend from Vassar and had been introduced to two
Southerners, Myles Horton and James Dombrowski, by Franz Daniel, her
future husband. In her application to Brookwood, Hawes cited her desire
to work in the South with hosiery workers and at the "Mount Eagle (sic)
Folk School," apparently an early name for Highlander.[105] Roy Reuther,
the brother of Walter and Victor Reuther, attended Brookwood a year after
Hawes. Reuther's writing from his time at Brookwood reveals some of
the content, discussion, and analysis that enraptured Brookwood's student

---

[103] Ibid.

[104] Elizabeth Hawes to A.J. Muste, 12 September 1932, Box 67, Folder 28, BLCC.
"List of Students, 1932–1933," Box 95, Folder 19, BLCC.

[105] Elizabeth D. Hawes to A.J. Muste, 13 August 1932, Box 67, Folder 28, BLCC;
Daniel, *Rogue River Journal*, 28.

body. In one manuscript, he lays out in clear terms his understanding of the materialist conception of history and argues forcefully in its favor—not surprising given that he lived in, "an 'Age of Unemployment,' when sickness, poverty and misery are universal."[106] For Roy Reuther, the materialist argument was palpable. He saw it; he felt it; he lived it. The same arguments likely shaped Hawes's outlook on and embrace of socialism.

HAWES'S CONTRIBUTION TO HIGHLANDER

By the time Zilla Hawes arrived at Highlander, she was an organizer for the Amalgamated Clothing Workers, a vocal SP member, a published journalist in the *Progressive Miner*, and an occasional lunch companion of Jay Lovestone. Her knowledge of and experience in the socialist movement was equal to that of any of her male comrades. She held one of the more revolutionary and influential perspectives at Highlander.[107] Her recommendations became a foundational text shaping the school's educational philosophy of serving the people's needs and developing indigenous knowledge and leadership. She made pointed criticisms of the ways in which Highlander operated, served as a connection to the left-wing of the SP, and held Highlander together by leading the school when Myles Horton and others were away or simply incapable of handling the day-to-day operations. In 1934, Highlander staff members held varying gender ideologies and came into conflict with each other concerning the ways in which these ideologies were expressed and acted upon in the group. These conflicts over gender ideology played out in the formation of the school's work and leisure regimes and were shaped by the socialist politics that were vital to the community's identity. While Hawes did not openly challenge the gender regime at Highlander, she resisted it, and used the restrictive gender ideology held by male staff members to carve out her own space.

Hawes was an ardent advocate of revolution, though Myles Horton and other members of Highlander's staff were rhetorical revolutionaries too. As such, Hawes represented a direct connection between Highlander and the

---

[106]Roy Reuther, "What Is the Materialistic Interpretation of History," Box 1, Folder 32, Roy Reuther Collection [RRC], Walter P. Reuther Library, Archives of Labor and Urban Affairs, Wayne State University, Detroit, MI.

[107]Zilla Hawes to Myles Horton, 20 November 1932, Box 15, Folder 30, HREC; Zilla Hawes to Myles Horton and James Dombrowski, June [1934], Box 15, Folder 31, HREC.

emergence of a strong left-wing tendency within the SP during the early and mid-1930s. In 1932, Zilla Hawes sent a letter to Myles Horton detailing a meeting she had attended along with key communists, not necessarily members of the CP, and SP notables. Roger Baldwin organized the meeting, and those in attendance included Fenner Brockway, King Gordon, Malcolm Cowley, Edmund Wilson, Liston Oak, Scott Nearing, Arnold Johnson, Corliss Lamont, and Franz Daniel. These were influential writers and thinkers. Hawes relayed to Horton that the group decided to form a radical faction within the SP, which Hawes described as "a disciplined, left-wing group within the S.P. but not in its pay, to work… on revolutionary tactics, staying within by not compromising, and if kicked out, being kicked out in a group."[108] Thus, Hawes was part of early discussions that led to the formation of the Revolutionary Policy Committee.

Hawes brought her ideas to internal debates about Highlander's direction, its programs, and the shape of its community life. Her recommendations to the staff members were a blend of practical day-to-day concerns and the revolutionary concerns. Her comments on the governance of Highlander focused primarily on the character of individual staff members and their failure to realize that each task they undertook was part of the overall revolutionary project. This point illustrates the value that Hawes attached to every facet of work at Highlander and the very real contribution of domestic work. Hawes ultimately wanted to create a more coordinated system to ensure that the school ran smoothly.[109]

While maintaining the perspective of the educated intellectual that was common among the staff during this period, Hawes confronted the very real problems that prevented Highlander from making progress in the rural community. She understood that the group had to come to terms with local culture and begin a dialogue that privileged the role of the worker over the proselytizing penchant of the radical intellectual. In the section of her recommendations for the school titled, "Revolutionary purpose," Hawes argued that Highlander's staff members must "meet people on their own ground" and that "this cannot be done by flaunting our standards, even if we consider them an improvement, in people's faces."[110] This could still be done with revolutionary vigor. "The early Russian anarchists and

---

[108]Zilla Hawes to Myles Horton, [1932], Box 15, Folder 30, HREC.
[109]Zilla Hawes, "Recommendations," September 1934, Box 2, Folder 4, HREC.
[110]Ibid.

revolutionists, when they went out to live and propagandize among the peasants," she argued, "followed their purpose with a devotion and perseverance that burned down the suspicion of the backward peasants like fire (Kropotkin)."[111] Hawes acknowledged that Highlander had trouble with a suspicious local community. "There are several things I have done which I now know to have been unwise, but I failed to see the significance they attained the people's eyes."[112] This acknowledgment of fault was likely in reference to a dispute over clothing that the local community regarded as immodest, which was discussed in the previous chapter. Hawes's idea of a convergence between the organizer and the people's "own ground" represents a serious step toward the democratic model of education for which Highlander became known, which suggests that she may have had a greater role in the formulation of this idea than has been credited by previous scholarship. Hawes spoke of the necessity of discipline among the members of Highlander and concluded that staff members had to overcome their own desire for personal freedom and renew their revolutionary intent. Otherwise, she argued, "[their revolution was] better not attempted."[113]

Hawes was an intermediary between Highlander, the SP, and the labor movement. She was a shrewd political commentator, provided solid descriptions of emerging factions within the SP, and situated key personalities according to political allegiance in internal party debates. She also predicted the eventual split in the SP.[114] She conceptualized the struggles at the SP's 1934 convention in terms of capitalists against socialists and saw the Old Guard members as primarily collaborators with the capitalist order. She forwarded this analysis to Horton and the other HFS staff members.[115] Hawes was careful to note SP policies that would be of direct importance to Highlander's efforts. She played up the role of the farmer in the SP and the policies that were adopted to benefit this constituency. Thus, while interested in the broader intellectual discussions of SP policy, Hawes was still deeply concerned about the practicalities of Highlander

[111] Ibid.

[112] Ibid.

[113] Ibid.

[114] Zilla Hawes to Horton, Dombrowski and HFS, 4 June 1934, Box 15, Folder 31, HREC.

[115] Ibid.

as a revolutionary project.[116] She made trade union contacts that would secure employment for staff members outside of Highlander, bring funds to the school, and provide "for straight revolutionary stuff thro'out Tenn."[117] She also used her connections with the SP to find students for Highlander's programs. Hawes was a key organizer for Highlander and had serious intellectual abilities, which she used to shape the development of Highlander along practical, yet revolutionary, lines. The closing lines of her letter to the Highlander staff best express her confidence in these matters: "do the things I have told you."[118]

GENDER AT HIGHLANDER

Interactions between men and women at Highlander were complex, in many cases influenced by the backgrounds of individuals involved and the types of activities undertaken. For instance, there were notable differences between the types of work activities to which women or men were assigned. Politically and intellectually, women and men participated in the community as purported equals. Given the gender biases held by male staff members and the competence and resilience of Zilla Hawes, it is likely that this "equality" was fraught with difficulties and never fully realized. Male staff members may have thought of themselves as forward-thinking men in their relationships with their female counterparts, yet Hawes's commentary on her life at Highlander suggests otherwise.

Myles Horton had a negative view of women and their abilities as students as Highlander. Horton believed that "in the case of girls, particular attention should be given to emotional stability and future usefulness."[119] Hawes was conscious and critical of the position taken by Horton and others. "Of course, I have my prejudices too, on top of a lot of annoying weaknesses," she wrote, "but they can write five letters to my one about them, to the Piebald Steer [one of Hawes's sobriquets for her Highlander comrades, probably Horton]. He'll give them fine consolation. Women

[116][Zilla Hawes to Dorothy Thompson], [24 January 1934], Box 15, Folder 31, HREC.

[117]Zilla Hawes to Horton, Dombrowski and HFS, 4 June 1934, Box 15, Folder 31, HREC.

[118]Ibid.

[119]Myles Horton, "Myles Horton's Criticism," September 1934, Box 2, Folder 4, HREC.

aren't much count, you know."[120] Horton's prejudice toward women went against Hawes's own experience at Highlander, where she was a central pillar for a still-insecure institution.

The work schedules from 1934 reveal that tasks were assigned on a gendered basis. One male staff member was assigned to do the dishes. Women filled the remaining five slots for dish duty.[121] The building crew at the school's second site in Allardt, Tennessee, was made up entirely of men.[122] It does appear that men took a much more active role in dish duty at the Allardt extension only because there were very few female staff members at Allardt.[123] However, the cooking at Allardt was explicitly in the hands of women. "We very gladly welcomed our friends who arrived yesterday," wrote one comrade about a group of several women who came to Allardt. "Now this woman Daniel has been expected around these parts for some time, but has been rather slow in showing up," continued the Allardt comrade, "She is here to help feed this rusty looking bunch of men, and from what I hear she can turn her dough in a wonderful way."[124] The men working to build Highlander's Allardt location were pleased to have a woman to cook for them.

Even as Highlander staff members assigned men to a wider variety of domestic tasks, they continued to define certain types of work as women's work: "We are very glad to see Comrade Och did so well with the washing yesterday. He is fast becoming almost indispensable as a washerwoman."[125] Och's willingness to do the dishes was regarded as "the UNSOLVED MYSTERY!"[126] This was such a mystery because presumably no male staff member would *ever* volunteer for dish duty. This staff member who recorded the meeting minutes also added, "His presence certainly solves one of our dirty problems at present."[127] The "dirty problem" may have represented both the dishes and the problem raised by the

[120] "Staff Meeting," 19 July 1934, Box 2, Folder 4, HREC; [Zilla Hawes to Dorothy Thompson?], [24 January 1934], Box 15, Folder 31, HREC.

[121] "Work Schedule," [January–February 1934], Box 2, Folder 4, HREC.

[122] "The Daily Reminder," 8 August 1934, Box 2, Folder 4, HREC.

[123] "The Daily Record," 10 August 1934, Box 2, Folder 4, HREC.

[124] Ibid.

[125] "Work Schedule," 31 July 1934, Box 2, Folder 4, HREC.

[126] "The Daily Reminder," 8 August 1934, Box 2, Folder 4, HREC.

[127] "Work Schedule," 31 July 1934, Box 2, Folder 4, HREC.

shortage of women staff members and a division of labor that reflected traditional gender norms.

The work schedule shows that more male staff members were doing dishes by August, but two-thirds of the dishwashing was still being assigned to women staff members.[128] Also, the dishwashing teams of two were fairly consistently segregated by gender. At the Allardt soviet, where there were few women staff members, and when a woman did arrive at soviet, she was put on the dishwashing crew.[129] While staff members joked about the possibility of revolution in regards to a decision not to whitewash the chimney, it was clear that there would be no gender revolution at Highlander Folk School, at least not in 1934.[130] While this revolution was not on the horizon, Hawes was very much aware of it and developed her own ideas about gender, which empowered her and highlights her contributions to Highlander.

The success of Highlander was predicated on the substantial intellectual and material contributions of Zilla Hawes. Myles Horton was not the sole dominant figure at Highlander in 1934. Both he and his colleagues acknowledged this fact time and again. While Hawes had always played a central role at Highlander, she had to take on a much heavier burden as Myles Horton became unable to cope with the daily tasks required to run the school. By February 1934, Horton was already "feeling pretty low."[131] Staff members successfully convinced "him to stay at Pleasant Hill in a sanitarium… instead of coming [back] to Monteagle." His comrades were afraid that if he returned to work "he [would] have a collapse."[132] The absence of Horton and the importance of Hawes's leadership during this period were further confirmed in a letter written by Horton to Hawes in which he asked her to take charge of a sensitive legal matter that revolved around a student of Highlander who had turned against the school.[133]

---

[128]"Staff Meeting," 8 August 1934, Box 2, Folder 4, HREC.

[129]"The Daily Record," 9 September 1934, Box 2, Folder 4, HREC.

[130]"The Daily Reminder," 8 August 1934, Box 2, Folder 4, HREC.

[131]Jim Dombrowski to Rubert Hampton, 3 February 1934, Box 15, Folder 31, HREC.

[132]Ibid.

[133]This is mentioned, very briefly, in Adams' *James A. Dombrowski: An American Heretic, 1897–1983* and also in Glen's *No Ordinary School*, 36. Adams downplays Horton's absence, which he suggests spanned only a few weeks. I think it will become clear that Horton was "absent" in one form or another for much longer periods.

The student had been caught stealing by a staff member and had been dismissed. The situation was so dangerous that Horton feared for the life of a staff member involved in the dispute. Hawes blamed Highlander's nonexistent selection process and suggested that interviews and investigations be conducted prior to accepting a student.[134] There was also the question of a prolonged legal battle that would tarnish the reputation of the school.[135] Horton acknowledged his own inability to handle this situation in his closing line to Hawes: "Sorry I am so usless (sic)."[136] Hawes, always one to turn to humor in difficult situations, discussed Horton's decision to recover in a sanitarium and hoped that he would return to the school soon:

> So we'll be back up this week, after Norman Thomas's visit: that is, all except Myles who didn't find his "Tovarischi" [comrades] crazy enough and had to retire to a sanitarium for more interesting company. Or perhaps for less company but more interest: dividends on wrecked health. He must return as soon as he is really able, to go ahead with his work on the educational program for the folk school, where his ideas and ours can clash, spark, and grow.[137]

When Horton was at Highlander, staff members tried to shield him from the stress of operating a school. He was apparently unable to handle very much responsibility even when he did feel more than useless. Staff members went so far as to hold meetings when he could not be present:

> Myles is not at all well; and most of us think he is probably worse than he has been since he came home. The least little things tear him to pieces, and we have all decided it wisest not to have Soviet meetings with him present. Such a little matter as the work schedule would work on his nerves, so we are postponing our next one until Sunday afternoon when he is at rest. The less he has to know about things, the better... he is so darn sensitive about anything we do to try to save him that we have to work on the quiet.[138]

[134]Zilla Hawes to Myles Horton, [February 1934], Box 15, Folder 31, HREC.
[135]Myles Horton to Zilla Hawes, 1934 Thursday night, Box 15, Folder 31, HREC.
[136]Ibid.
[137]Zilla Hawes to [unknown], 13 February 1934, Box 15, Folder 31, HREC.
[138]Dorothy Thompson to Rupert Hampton, 17 April 1934, Box 15, Folder 31, HREC.

According to Hawes, Myles Horton was not the only male staff member in need of care. Hawes emphasized the gendered differences in socialization that separated her from her comrades at Highlander, a distinction that affirmed her view of men in general as helpless and somewhat hopeless. In 1934, Hawes wrote a letter to a female comrade, possibly Dorothy Thompson, detailing her encounters with and thoughts on the male staff members and the differences in social roles relating to house cleaning. Though careful to point out that her male comrades were genuine "radicals," Hawes was frustrated with their lack of cleanliness, their unwillingness to "pick up their clothes a little, and bring their dirty socks downstairs to the laundry." That she felt the need to reaffirm her male comrades' radicalism in a conversation about cleaning suggests the degree to which gender was present at Highlander. They did not clean, she said, but they were still good radicals. To make this connection implies that Hawes was conscious of tensions between the sexual division of labor and radicalism. Hawes wanted her male colleagues to do the basic work of cleaning so that she "could clean their god-forsaken barracks up a little more for them so they wouldn't have to breathe dust all night." In the end, however, she did not blame them, arguing that their mothers had probably spent years "trying to get them to pick up, and never succeeded." Discouraged by the state of affairs and the ways in which gendered expectations shaded the community, she asked, "How can one make any impression on the eternal junk piles, when six contribute?"[139] We begin to see not only the organizational tasks that confronted Hawes, but also the weight of gender. Hawes was cleaning up men's messes both metaphorically and literally.

Hawes took a complex view of her work role at Highlander. She consciously used her male comrades' prejudice as a means to maintain space for herself, and, at the same time, she was unhappy with the division of labor at the school. She took charge in the kitchen at Allardt and ensured that she would have autonomy. "It's a shame the way I'm just coddling the boys along so as to get my kitchen," she wrote, adding, "excuse me, I should say 'the' kitchen, since it belongs to the soviet, but the funny thing about that is, the boys are so used to woman's place being by the fireside, they can't get into the notion of building a kitchen for themselves."[140] Hawes used

[139]Zilla Hawes to [Dorothy Thompson?], [24 January 1934], Box 15, Folder 31, HREC.

[140]Ibid.

her male comrades' ideas about women to carve out some autonomy for herself, though she was ultimately dissatisfied with the restrictive nature of these same expectations. She validated the importance of domestic work in an intentional community by noting that the community did not function well in her absence; nonetheless, she imagined more freedom in her work life. In doing so, Hawes asserted that she wished to flee to the Soviet Union where she imagined that she would be able to free herself from expectations of gender. "Well, when I go to Soviet Russia and become an expert tractor driver, on a kolkhoz or whatever that unpronounceable word is," she wrote, "they'll [her male comrades] see the difference."[141]

An examination of Highlander yields a better understanding of gender ideology among a left-wing cohort that was part of the SP. It also clarifies the role that women played in shaping a legendary institution of the American left, Highlander Folk School. Hawes articulated core ideals that would come to shape the school. This contribution cannot be overlooked in favor of an idealized vision of Highlander robbed of its political and gendered contexts and an equating of Highlander with Horton. Hawes shaped Highlander by advocating for a revolutionary, yet pragmatic, approach to workers' education. At the same time, she failed to openly advocate for a similar revolution in gender ideology, though she privately yearned for such a revolution.

[141] Ibid.

CHAPTER 8

The Great Transition: Channeling "A Mighty River"

From the second half of the 1930s onward, socialists transitioned from independent political action under the banner of the Socialist Party of America (SP) to an embrace of the Democratic Party as an electoral vehicle. As part of this process, they forged what one contemporary called, "a new conception of democratic socialism."[1] Their utopian aspirations faded, and they accepted social democracy, or what one commentator called "mature" socialism.[2] Socialists no longer insisted there was a "correct" road to socialism.[3] They recognized that "democratic capitalism [was] not totally evil."[4] The movement of socialists into the ranks of the Democratic Party confounds claims that socialism failed in the United States because socialists

George Edward, Sr. to George Edwards, Jr., 21 September 1938, Box 98, Folder 14, George Edwards Jr. Papers [GEJP], Walter P. Reuther Library, Archives of Labor and Urban Affairs, Wayne State University, Detroit, Michigan.

[1] Richard Lowenthal, "Socialism's New Look," *The New Leader*, 3 September 1951, 12.

[2] Denis Healey, "European Socialism Today," *The New Leader*, 16 September 1957, 14.

[3] Lowenthal, "Socialism's New Look," 15.

[4] Liston Oak, "Communism Versus Social Democracy," *The New Leader*, 15 June 1946, 2.

© The Author(s) 2019   167
J. Altman, *Socialism before Sanders*,
https://doi.org/10.1007/978-3-030-17176-6_8

were too ideological in their outlook and could not accept the pragmatic demands required in politics. Perhaps the SP was too dogmatic, rigid, and unwilling to accept the demands of participation in a political system that required compromising ideals to achieve power and bring change. Ultimately, however, American socialists proved they could compromise. They adopted a pragmatic approach to political action and achieved some success. "If Socialist theory has made no inroads upon the American mind," wrote one editorialist in the early 1950s, "Socialist demands have. In addition, the Socialist movement has been an excellent training ground for some of the foremost men in public life—witness the CIO's [Congress of Industrial Organizations] new President, Walter Reuther."[5] The shift to the Democratic Party was not a capitulation of socialism in favor of liberalism. Rather, it was a process by which socialism was rethought and remade while maintaining itself as distinct from liberalism. Its history was different, its vision of the future was broad, and its attentions were focused on social class.[6]

In 1934, many socialists were revolted by "capitalist parties" (Democrat and Republican) and class collaboration. After the midterm elections and 1934 gubernatorial election in California, George Edwards, Sr., a longtime member of the SP and an attorney, made known his distaste for Democratic candidate Upton Sinclair's abandonment of the Socialist Party. Sinclair, a socialist, had broken with the Socialist Party in an attempt to win broader appeal on the Democratic ticket. "This is no time for rejoicing," Edwards told his son, "so far as I know, for any radical who contemplates the election results. But I still think the remark old Mr. Giddens made to me is sound: 'The only thing worse than trying as we do and getting beat as

---

[5]David Liberson, "The Minor Parties Hit Low Ebb," *The New Leader*, 29 December 1952, 11.

[6]Boyle, *The UAW and the Heyday of American Liberalism, 1945–1968*, 259. Boyle explores this distinction and the tension between the social democrats and liberals. Some works tend to blur the distinction between reformist socialists who joined the New Deal coalition and liberals. See Warren, *An Alternative Vision*, 117. Daniel Bell's closing statement on what happened to socialism in the United States is too tepid a description: "In the form of a set of ideas, socialism has, as a pale tint, suffused into the texture of American life and subtly changed its shadings." Bell also referred to "quondam socialists," stressing a break with socialism and claimed, "by 1950 American socialism as a political and social fact had become simply a notation in the archives of history." Bell's closing epigraph about the Rabbi of Zans further emphasizes a closing of socialist tradition rather than a remaking. See Bell, *Marxian Socialism*, 191–193.

we do, would be not to try at all, or to vote with the Democrats.'"[7] In 1934, socialists accepted the maintenance of their political independence as an article of faith—a principle that could only be repudiated by apostates. Better to lose, they argued, than compromise with the perceived class enemy. Even if Sinclair achieved electoral success, Norman Thomas argued, his plans to create cooperative competition for capitalism would fail. "The capitalist system," Thomas wrote to Sinclair, "will either defeat you or your plan outright or ruin it."[8] Edwards used Upton Sinclair's loss in the general election—although Sinclair *had* won the August Democratic primary—as proof of the futility of bargaining with the capitalist parties. "Certainly the results in California made it clear that it was not the name Socialist the capitalists hated but the reality behind even as compromising a person as Sinclair," Edwards, Sr. told Edwards, Jr., "after they decided they could not wholly handle him."[9] If there was no hope for a compromiser such as Sinclair, socialists could not expect to win through such dilution of their principles. All the forces of capital had, after all, aligned against Sinclair. Edwards, Sr. wrote, "But I think that Sinclair was beat by the combination of Eastern money, Roosevelt's shiftiness, and the lying newspapers."[10] The suspicion Edwards placed on the compromisers and reformers of capitalism extended to President Roosevelt: "I wouldn't trust any statement of Roosevelt as far as I could throw the Adolphus hotel [a prominent feature of the Dallas skyline in 1934]."[11] Roosevelt was just another capitalist and many Socialists had difficulty accepting that meaningful change, even in the midst of economic crisis, could be achieved through the old, corrupt capitalist parties.

By 1938, however, a remarkable transformation had occurred within the American socialist movement. George Edwards, Sr. had changed his mind about Roosevelt, the New Deal, and the sacred pillar of political independence. Warming to the New Deal, Edwards wrote, "[Oscar] Ameringer, a week a or so ago had an article in which he listed the SP immediate

[7] George Edwards, Sr. to George Edwards, Jr., 7 November 1934, Box 97, Folder 1, GEJP.

[8] "Thomas Tells Sinclair Some Socialist Truths," *The New Leader*, 2 June 1934, 2.

[9] George Edwards, Sr. to George Edwards, Jr., 7 November 1934, Box 97, Folder 1, GEJP.

[10] Ibid.

[11] Ibid.

demands of 1916 and said all seventeen of them, except two have been wholly or in substantial part put into operation, since then, the exceptions being government ownership of the railroads and popular voting on war."[12] Edwards, still voicing some inward turmoil over his conversion, could speak approvingly of New Deal officials: "If we can keep out of war the ferment of new ideas that has been started in the government by the numerous liberal officials and employees like Elliot of Ft. Worth and Corcoran and Cohen of Washington is very hopeful."[13] For Edwards, there was now reason for optimism. "The Wagner act, the CIO, and the UAW [United Automobile Workers]," he wrote, "all are far beyond anything that was in sight ten years ago."[14] Edwards's assessment of a successful long-term strategy was changing, too: "We can in time get the positions of power, but the knowledge of the game we can get sooner, and it will aid to the power."[15] Socialists could rise through the labor movement and the New Deal and reach commanding heights. Cooperation with reform elements in the mainstream parties could yield future victory and give the socialists skills and experiences necessary to exercise power effectively.[16]

The shift from an earlier thinking about the role of politics and engagement with the Democratic Party was stark. In 1936, George Edwards, Sr. had wondered, "what can come of the ILGWU [The International Ladies' Garment Workers' Union] and the Auto workers, whose leaders have come out frankly for Roosevelt after they have pretended to be Socialists."[17] He added with a note of disdain for the labor compromisers of the era, "How can anyone [by which he meant socialists] be willing to work for

[12]George Edward, Sr. to George Edwards, Jr., 21 September 1938, Box 98, Folder 14, GEJP.

[13]George Edward, Sr. to George Edwards, Jr., 13 December 1938, Box 98, Folder 15, GEJP.

[14]George Edward, Sr. to George Edwards, Jr., 13 December 1938, Box 98, Folder 15, GEJP.

[15]George Edward, Sr. to George Edwards, Jr., 21 September 1938, Box 98, Folder 14, GEJP.

[16]Norman Thomas supported this sentiment as early as 1933 in some select circumstances. See the conversation between Thomas and Felix Cohen outlined in Storrs, *Second Red Scare*, 22.

[17]George Edward, Sr. to George Edwards, Jr., 29 May 1936, Box 97, Folder 11, GEJP.

Dubinsky or Perlstein as superiors, or for John L. Lewis?"[18] Edwards was not, however, convinced that there was an alternative. He signaled his ambivalence. "And yet," he wrote, "even as I write that, I wonder how one can get a chance to work anywhere where men of that type are not at the top – the top being attainable by the things people like Lewis and Dubinsky and Jack Altman are willing to do."[19] The compromises necessary to achieve power were made, in Edwards's view, at the expense of principle. He still wondered how this way of things might be overturned.

The scope of this change cannot be overemphasized. Socialists were abandoning their own political institutions and becoming increasingly hopeful that the offerings of the New Deal were, in fact, a step for nascent socialism, even if in their most guarded moments they considered it a small step. Positive engagement with the New Deal coalition became nearly universal among socialists, who benefitted from the patronage of the New Deal's leading figures. By October 1940, Highlander Folk School's staff had asked Eleanor Roosevelt "to serve as patroness and to attend" the school's winter benefit in Washington, D.C. Roosevelt agreed.[20]

Revision was mandated by socialists' inability to make appreciable gains during a moment of crisis for capitalism and their desire, as expressed by Edwards, to "get a chance to work" on behalf of their ideals. Frustrated electoral ambitions and practical necessities led socialists toward greater engagement with the New Deal. With expectations inflated by the Depression, socialists' eventually faced electoral reality, as they realized that their party was not an effective vehicle. Highlander Folk School's efforts through Labor's Non-Partisan League to mobilize workers on behalf of New Deal candidates were part of this shift.[21] George Edwards, Sr. relayed frustrations with socialism to his son. He quoted a railroad worker that the SP hoped would run for the office of railroad commissioner. The worker, a man named Hembree, told Edwards, "I have spent years cussing out everything as a socialist, and I have isolated myself. Now I am working as the chairman of the grievance committee and am trying to do what I can with immediate

[18] Ibid.
[19] Ibid.
[20] James Dombrowski to Franz Daniel, 29 October 1940, Box 10, Folder 8, HREC.
[21] Glen, *No Ordinary School*, 63.

tasks and evils."[22] The change in tactics made sense by 1938. A focus on the "immediate tasks and evils" was no longer chastised as collaborationism. Edwards, Sr. agreed with Hembree: "I do not quote him accurately for I have not his letter here," Edwards told his son, "but the cussing and the isolation are the points I wanted to mention to you, because he also was lamenting the futility of his efforts [emphasis in original]."[23] Edwards shared his desires for his son's future, which included a path different from his own and a break with the perceived purism and outsider status of the SP. "I do not want you to be less radical than I have been for I have not been too radical. I do not want you to accept as right any of the injustices of law and property and business," Edwards, Sr. confessed, "But I want you to see that they are not things that can be ended by denunciation. We do not need to denounce. We need to explain. There is almost no strong position that can be taken by frontal attack, sensibly. Frontal attack means the enemy has the full advantage of his position."[24] Socialists should be sensible. Perhaps, Edwards argued, the approach of Upton Sinclair had merit after all. Capitalism had to be reformed from within not assailed or disbanded by means of revolution. He now saw a path to the height of power for men like his son who would abandon neither principle nor practicality in a world that seemed so full of possibilities for change, even if it was not of a utopian magnitude. It was simply more efficacious to work within the political structures, as these offered labor some protection, and on the national stage such a strategy yielded real benefits for those who opposed capitalism's brutish irrationality.

Practical demands dictated a shift in strategy, too. The labor movement occupied socialists' attentions in the late 1930s and 1940s. The immensity of labor's endeavors, the amount of work to be done in order to maintain the labor movement, and the fierce resistance that organizers encountered were beginning to take a toll on their idealism and unbridled enthusiasm, which, in turn, limited their vision for the future. The scale of human suffering witnessed and endured in the attempt to organize the South powerfully affected participants. Victories were often delayed, transitory, and dependent on government intervention. Socialists could no longer believe that

---

[22]George Edward, Sr. to George Edwards, Jr., 21 September 1938, Box 98, Folder 14, GEJP.

[23]Ibid.

[24]Ibid.

the old world would be completely swept away and that cooperation with the old capitalist parties did not matter. It was clear to most people in the movement that they were now settling in for a long, complicated fight that would require powerful allies and not be centered on a Socialist Party that was fading into irrelevant internal struggles. It must have been ultimately satisfying that the Textile Workers' Union of America was retained in some of the mills—though only through the intervention of the National Labor Relations Board (NLRB). Organizers who had only a few years before been tepid or hostile to the New Deal realized its importance.[25] The war, too, boosted organizing success. Yet it also reaffirmed the structural problems that labor faced, including recalcitrant employers and Democratic office-holders who used their power to obstruct federal intervention.[26]

Socialists active in the labor movement increasingly needed to endorse New Deal candidates to secure continued protection for their unions. This pressure was greatest for newly successful socialist labor leaders who now depended on broad and potentially fragile coalitions for support. The 1938 gubernatorial race in Michigan created clear divisions in the socialist movement that affirmed the notion of a broader shift in many socialists' approach to politics, a shift which split the SP in the late 1930s and left it without many of its most talented organizers and administrators.[27] Democratic Governor Frank Murphy had resisted pressure to use the National Guard to break the UAW's sit-down strikes at GM plants in Flint, Michigan.[28] Walter Reuther resigned from the SP in 1938 to support Murphy.[29] "It seems to me that the SP is wrong and the CP [Communist Party] is right in reference to Murphy," George Edwards, Sr. concluded, "He is not going to bring in Utopia but neither is the SP candidate, and most of the union men are bound to vote for Murphy because it is a better gamble for their wages and hours and the wholeness of their heads. If this is true, why not recognize it, and vote frankly for Murphy by no means stating an

---

[25] George Brown Tindall, *The Emergence of the New South, 1913–1945* (Baton Rouge: Louisiana State University Press, 1967), 520.

[26] Nelson Lichtenstein, *Labor's War at Home: The CIO in World War II* (Temple University Press, 2003), 209–210.

[27] Lichtenstein, *Walter Reuther*, 127–128.

[28] Sidney Fine, *Sit-down: The General Motors Strike of 1936–1937* (University of Michigan Press, 1969), 294; Dubofsky and Van Tine, *John L. Lewis*, 195.

[29] Lichtenstein, *Walter Reuther*, 127.

exaggerated opinion of his importance?"[30] The alienation of socialists who favored American intervention against fascism also furthered this rift. This dual pressure ensured the destruction of the SP as an effective institution and with it the loss of a generation of talented people capable of sustaining it.

Twin pressures exerted themselves on the socialists. Socialists needed help from sympathetic elected officials, though some officials the CIO had supposed were sympathetic proved unreliable, to pressure employers into negotiations and prevent the state from using violence to break strikes. Workers lost strikes when elected officials sided with employers at the expense of the labor movement.[31] Socialists in the labor movement also had to be responsive to their rank and file or they risked losing their access to power and their ability to influence events. Explaining his own shift from the SP to the Democratic Party and Roosevelt, while reaffirming his commitment to socialism, Philip Van Gelder said, "I sort of drifted away. In 1936, when your union was 100 percent behind Roosevelt, it just didn't make any sense to say, 'Well that's OK for you guys, but I'm for Norman Thomas.'"[32] Disagreements formed between socialists in and outside the labor movement. "Norman Thomas felt that if you didn't vote for him for president," Van Gelder clarified, reaffirming his socialism, "then you weren't a socialist. I think that was a big mistake. He kept aloof from the labor movement, and he expected its members to agree with our ideology before they were ready for it."[33] Socialists who held leadership positions in the labor movement had a duty to follow a course that would yield benefits for their members while recognizing the limitations of both the Democratic and Socialist parties. Edwards, Sr. grudgingly admitted the CP's members were correct about their support for Roosevelt and Murphy: "I hate to admit any good thing about the CP because their hypocrisy and double-dealing and lying and boasting and bossism make me sick."[34] Even though socialists and communists were deeply at odds with one another, both were,

[30] George Edward, Sr. to George Edwards, Jr., 21 September 1938, Box 98, Folder 14, GEJP.

[31] Dubofsky and Van Tine, *John L. Lewis*, 231.

[32] Levinson and Morton, "An Interview with Philip Van Gelder," 463.

[33] Ibid.

[34] George Edward, Sr. to George Edwards, Jr., 21 September 1938, Box 98, Folder 14, GEJP.

for a time, part of a growing social-democratic consensus. This was a time for moderation, securing what was offered in the face of crisis, and working to build and maintain a new movement around a pragmatic working class. Compromise was necessary, and socialists found that it was not altogether distasteful.

This thinking was expanding through the late 1930s and early 1940s, as younger, once-radical socialists began to see the SP's policies as problematic and its national campaigns as fruitless. In 1940, Paul Porter confided to Newman Jeffrey, "I'm not decided about the Washington trip. I rather hate to attend the convention, because I think it would be a big mistake to nominate a candidate [for the US presidential race]."[35] Porter argued that the SP should not run a candidate against Roosevelt. Porter's cohort also disagreed with Thomas's position against US intervention in WWII and supported Roosevelt's programs to aid the British. The SP did run Norman Thomas for president again. The result was embarrassing.[36] The dissident Old Guard, now outside of the SP, helped form the American Labor Party, which ran Roosevelt on its ballot line and thus overcame local resistance to voting Democrat.[37] In 1936 Thomas had won the support of 86,000 voters in New York. In 1940, Thomas's votes in New York dropped to 18,950, less than half a percent of the total vote.[38] Thomas garnered over 70,000 fewer votes nationally in 1940 than in 1936.[39] When compared with Thomas's high point in 1932, the decline was larger still, and yet 1940 had a particular sting when longtime comrades publicly and unequivocally supported Roosevelt over Thomas.[40]

If Thomas's loss of some important supporters in 1936 could be explained by the demands placed on labor leaders, the defection of longtime allies in 1940 had more to do with the solidification of support behind Roo-

---

[35] Paul Porter to Newman Jeffrey, 17 May 1940, Box 60, Folder 41, Mildred Jeffrey Collection [MJC], Walter P. Reuther Library, Archives of Labor and Urban Affairs, Wayne State University, Detroit, Michigan.

[36] Gregory, *Norman Thomas*, 184; W. A. Swanberg, *Norman Thomas: The Last Idealist* (Charles Scribner's Sons, 1976), 200.

[37] Cecelia Bucki, *Bridgeport's Socialist New Deal, 1915–36* (University of Illinois Press, 2001), 190.

[38] "Election Results," *The New Leader*, 7 December 1940, 1.

[39] Gregory, *Norman Thomas*, 184.

[40] "Comparison of the Official Socialist Vote, 1928 and 1932," [1932–1933], Box 5, PHP.

sevelt and the redefinition of socialism. Abandoning the SP was no longer a fraught choice. Frank Crosswaith was one of the leading socialists who switched from Thomas to Roosevelt. "I have never voted any other but a Socialist ticket," explained Crosswaith, "because of my conviction that democratic Socialism offers to mankind the only way out of the midnight of capitalism onto the noonday of economic and political freedom." Support for Roosevelt, argued Crosswaith, was not a repudiation of socialism. "I am more convinced today than ever before," he said, "that society can no more escape the logic of Socialism then can life escape the logic of death." Crosswaith cited the "enlightened achievements" of Roosevelt's administration as proof that socialism's logic was, in fact, inescapable—even the mainstream capitalist parties had to yield. Not only did Crosswaith support Roosevelt, he also constructed this support as *the* appropriate choice for good socialists.[41]

Interactions with government officials strengthened socialists' burgeoning belief that government was not necessarily a natural extension or tool of the capitalist class. They adopted a more pluralistic view. Socialists' anti-communism contributed to this shift by allying with CIO anti-communists. In June 1941, the US government took over operation of North American Aviation in Inglewood, California after a controversial strike halted production of one-fifth of American military aircraft and local police had been unable to establish order and drive pickets away from the plant's gates.[42] Franz Daniel provided support for the International UAW as it struggled to gain control of the situation. His reports to his friends were positive—the Army took charge, cleared pickets, and production resumed.[43] "The army wants to get the hell out of the plant," Franz Daniel wrote to Mildred Jeffrey in 1941, "[Colonel] Branshaw is a very able man and he has handled this situation with a lot of sense."[44] Daniel, who was sent to Los Angeles by Sidney Hillman to troubleshoot the strike situation, did not support the strike and argued that the CP was responsible for what he regarded as an illegitimate action designed to undermine the defense preparations in

---

[41]Frank Crosswaith, "I Support Roosevelt: Labor Leader Discusses the Candidates," *New York Amsterdam News*, 2 November 1940, 17.

[42]John H. Ohly, *Industrialists in Olive Drab: The Emergency Operation of Private Industries During World War II*, ed. Clayton D. Laurie (U.S. Government Printing Office, 1999), 19, 24.

[43]Ibid., 24.

[44]Franz Daniel to Mildred Jeffrey, 23 June 1941, Box 55, Folder 9, MJC.

service of the Nazi-Soviet Pact.[45] "There seems to be no real CP control on the loyalties of the vast majority [of workers]," Daniel wrote while arguing that the CP had manufactured the strike by importing CP members from other unions to bolster support.[46] Daniel's interpretation of the situation was mediated by his anti-communism and support for US war mobilization. Daniel viewed the crisis as "our [the anticommunists in the CIO] chance to take over the CIO."[47] The achievements of a state-directed economy during the wartime mobilization also buoyed socialists' hopes for the future.

The transformation—the movement away from independent socialist politics—was not an unconscious one and was the subject of much inner deliberation and rationalization. Socialism had been a core component of the intellectual lives of many thousands of people. It could not be lightly tossed aside and was not altogether abandoned. George Edwards, Sr. explained his support for reformism as part of a new realization that capitalism, while still potentially cruel, could be mastered and controlled by those who championed the common good. "The capitalist system," he wrote, "is no more lovely to me than it used to be, but I know more about it and I know that it is more like a mighty river that must have its waters diverted and utilized for the common good than it is like a fort that is to be taken by fighting."[48] Capitalism could be rationalized, mixed with more ameliorative forms of economic organization, and controlled,

---

[45]Franz Daniel to Mildred Jeffrey, 11 June 1941, Box 55, Folder 9, MJC; For an exploration of historical examinations of the North American strike see James R. Prickett, "Communist Conspiracy or Wage Dispute?: The 1941 Strike at North American Aviation," *Pacific Historical Review* 50, no. 2 (May 1981), 215–233. Prickett challenges Daniel's (and many historians') interpretations of the strike. The strike, Prickett argues, was about wages and the failings of the government mediation, which alienated workers. Nelson Lichtenstein reaches a similar conclusion and adds union competition between the UAW and IAM to the set of circumstances that led to a strike at North American Aviation. See Nelson Lichtenstein, *Labor's War at Home: The CIO in World War II* (Temple University Press, 2003), 59–60. Lichtenstein concludes that the strike was only possible because the rank-and-file workers in the plant were willing to engage in militant action to increase their wages. Daniel and his allies were keen to play up the CP link for their own political advantage. The CP, according to Lichtenstein, used its appeal to militancy and its potential rewards in the same way.

[46]Franz Daniel to Mildred Jeffrey, 11 June 1941, Box 55, Folder 9, MJC.

[47]Franz Daniel to Mildred Jeffrey, 10 June 1941, Box 55, Folder 9, MJC.

[48]George Edward, Sr. to George Edwards, Jr., 21 September 1938, Box 98, Folder 14, GEJP.

ideally by socialist planners who were conscious of its evils. This was a fundamental redefinition of socialism that would become widely accepted by American socialists, and those who came to occupy a more ambiguous space, from Norman Thomas to Reinhold Niebuhr.[49] The acceptance of gradualism and the continued existence of capitalism in some reduced and controlled form became the foundational tenet of the new social democracy and it represented a major intellectual shift, perhaps the most important intellectual legacy of the left in the twentieth century.[50] Socialists abandoned the dream of a perfect world for the prospect of a much better one.

The changes in socialists' thinking about revolution matched their acceptance of reformism as a path to improving human societies. Revolutionary rhetoric was no longer a currency among those socialists who had earlier in their lives used it to prove their credentials and their masculinity. By the early 1940s—and with the continuation and intensification of anti-communism—revolution had become a joke. "Come the revolution," Myles Horton wrote to Roger Baldwin, "I propose that you be made Commissar of Birds. Zilphia [Horton] had put in her bid to be Commissar of Wild Flowers. Certainly, if, as the enclosed Chattanooga Free Press editorial says, we are to do the job, there is no reason why we shouldn't have something to say about our own futures."[51] Revolution-as-joke was all the more radical a transformation given that less than a decade earlier such an upheaval was regarded as perfectly serious, impending, and necessary by the same people who now spoke of it facetiously.[52]

---

[49] Merkley, *Reinhold Niebuhr*, 179.

[50] The importance, scale, and speed of this change cannot be overstated. Few other movements of the era had proven so open and adaptable while maintaining its core purpose for being and basic intellectual premise. Roosevelt, for instance, did not even represent a coherent political tradition so much as help to invent a new one. It took many European socialist movements with much more access to power and institutional strength far longer to arrive at the same conclusions as the bulk of the American socialist movement. It is possible that the shift toward social democracy in the United States helped other socialist movements understand their own limits. See, for instance, Lichtenstein's discussion of Walter Reuther's support for Willy Brandt in *Walter Reuther*, 343.

[51] Myles Horton to Roger Baldwin, 24 October 1942, Box 6, Folder 4, HREC.

[52] Luff, *Commonsense Anticommunism*, 112.

The Labor Movement and the End of Utopianism

The labor movement no longer seemed a perfect vehicle for social advancement and liberation. It too was a product of human frailty. If fear and employers' ruthless exercise of power were not enough to tarnish the hopefulness of the early 1930s, the labor movement provided a check on the utopianism of the early to mid-1930s. Franz Daniel's idiomatic confession to Newman Jeffrey in 1939 highlighted his frustrations. "I'm up to my ears," Daniel told Jeffrey. "Last Friday," he continued, "the cops picked up two of our business agents for the Queens Local. One confessed to shaking down the bosses—he was caught with marked money on him—and implicated the other."[53] Hillman or Jacob Potofsky increasingly tasked Daniel with trouble shooting problematic locals. "It's one hell of a mess," he reported, "and I have the beautiful job of supervising the cleanup of the local."[54] Two years later and Daniel was again faced with alleged union corruption. "We have a mess on our hands here in L.A.," Franz Daniel told Mildred Jeffrey, "and I'm now back in laundries up to my neck."[55] He was speaking of the Amalgamated Clothing Workers of America's (ACWA) laundry manager in LA, who had been arrested for extortion. The official had reportedly "held a conference with a woman owner of a laundry he was organizing in his apartment and when she left the cops rushed in and found $500 in marked money on him."[56] Daniel was not certain about the facts and considered the possibility of an anti-union frame-up, but the laundry owner claimed that "she had purchased protection from the union from [the union official] for two grand and that the 5 c in notes were the first payment."[57] "He's still in jail being held in 25 thousand dollar bail," Daniel reported, "and we aren't going to get him out until we know more about the case."[58] Daniel was concerned about how the arrest would hurt the union. "It was a sweet mess," he said, "The papers are going to town and you can imagine what the comrades are doing to Leo and me."[59]

---

[53] Franz Daniel to Newman Jeffrey, 12 July 1939, Box 11, Folder 57, NJC.
[54] Ibid.
[55] Franz Daniel to Mildred Jeffrey, 23 June 1941, Box 55, Folder 9, MJC.
[56] Ibid.
[57] Ibid.
[58] Ibid.
[59] Ibid.

Corruption was an opening that the CP used to attack their more established enemies. Daniel was more upset by the additional work that the case meant for him: "But the worst thing is that I'm having to take over the goddamned union and hold it together for a while. They were in the middle of wage conferences and I have to pick those up and carry them on. Nice."[60] Nice, indeed—corruption took its toll on the idealistic industrial unionists who had fought and fought only to realize that their integrity, passion for the movement, and willingness to serve was not universal.

As his comment about the "comrades" implied, Daniel was also fighting the communists for control of local unions. The internecine warfare that characterized the labor movement through the 1940s took a toll on those who fought it. They expended much energy on control and stability at the expense of unity and growth, though there may not have been any other way forward. It was a high stakes battle that placed organizers under great stress: "At the Queens mass meeting last night," Daniel wrote, "which I called to establish some order in the local the CP tried to break it up. I smacked the hell out of them and then opened up and blasted away."[61] Daniel was apprehensive about the constant strife at the level of the local union: "The heat will be turned up on me in no uncertain terms now. The C.P. business agents are sabotaging the union.... So we have our own troubles."[62] By the late 1940s, Daniel told a colleague that he had lost his faith.[63] If Daniel blustered and roared outwardly, he was less confident in unguarded moments. Still a committed socialist anti-communist, he nonetheless wondered if the labor movement was floundering and whether the movement was well led. He had gone from the pinnacle of absolute belief to the despair of uncertainty in a decade.

There were new and old battles to fight and these preoccupied socialists, orienting them back toward the labor movement and the practical considerations of the moment. The new concern was winning control of the CIO, the jewel of a renewed labor movement. Franz Daniel was traveling around the United States doing his best to preserve and protect, as he saw it, the movement he had helped to build. He traveled to Pennsylvania, New York, Wisconsin, and California all in the service of the movement.[64]

---

[60] Ibid.

[61] Franz Daniel to Newman Jeffrey, 12 July 1939, Box 11, Folder 57, NJC.

[62] Ibid.

[63] David S. Burgess, *Fighting for Social Justice: The Life Story of David Burgess* (Wayne State University Press, 2000), 81.

[64] Franz Daniel to Newman Jeffrey, 12 July 1939, Box 11, Folder 57, NJC.

Daniel reported in 1939, "Everything is breaking at once—the bosses are in a definite campaign to weaken the union before negotiations for the new contract open up."[65] Employers continued their often-fierce resistance to the labor movement throughout the period, aided, in part, by divided unions. On top of the ordinary concerns that required the near constant care of the organizer, Daniel was fighting what he regarded as a hostile force. "The C.P. is raising hell," he told his friend Newman Jeffrey.[66] There was always some new emergency that required immediate attention, and the men who stood at the top of the great industrial unions were allies of convenience who frequently warred with each other. "I had a long talk with Hillman last week," Franz Daniel reported, "He's sore at Lewis but there isn't a chance of Hillman pulling a Dubinsky."[67] David Dubinsky, leader of the ILGWU, had initially supported John L. Lewis's efforts to make industrial unionism a priority for the AFL and was a founder of the Committee for Industrial Organization. Dubinsky, however, was reluctant to break from the American Federation of Labor (AFL) and returned with the ILGWU to the AFL in 1940.[68] Daniel confirmed that rather than part from the CIO, as Dubinsky had done, Hillman planned to capture it for his social-democratic wing of the labor movement. "On the contrary," Daniel wrote to his comrade Newman Jeffrey, "Hillman is out to build up a big following within the CIO in order to fight [Lewis and the far left] with."[69] Daniel was one of Hillman's operatives in the field, who was tasked with carrying out Hillman's vision for the labor movement. "In that direction," Daniel concluded, "[Hillman] wants to get control again of the Dept Store Clerk organization and I'm to be used in that move. So it looks like I'll be around New York for some time to come. But before that we've

---

[65] Ibid.

[66] Ibid.

[67] Ibid.

[68] Parmet, *The Master of Seventh Avenue*, 122–128, 133–137, 146–152, 170–173, 184–185. Even before the suspension from the AFL of the union that had formed the CIO in September 1936, Parmet demonstrates Dubinsky's reluctant break from the AFL. Jurisdictional disputes and fears of CP influence in the CIO were factors mediating the ILGWU's return to the AFL.

[69] Franz Daniel to Newman Jeffrey, 12 July 1939, Box 11, Folder 57, NJC; On this conflict between Lewis and Hillman, see Dubofsky and Van Tine, *John L. Lewis*, 235–236; Fraser, *Labor Will Rule*, 432–433, 442–447.

got to pull this damn Laundry Union of out the woods."[70] The battles raged. There was little respite for the tired warriors of Hillman's social-democrat faction. In this atmosphere, the specific battles of the moment (rather than a larger, ideological image of socialism) took precedence and encouraged the adoption of pragmatism. This pragmatism's socialist origins and social-democratic basis ensured that it was not, however, a wholly "bread-and-butter pragmatism" focused on increasing the wage packet.[71]

HIGHLANDER: CONFRONTING CHANGE

The shift from revolutionary socialism to a more staid social-democratic outlook was evident in disagreements between Zilla Hawes and Franz Daniel and Highlander's staff. Eventually, Hawes and Daniel came to see the labor movement, and a certain vision of the labor movement, as much more central to the unfolding struggles of working people than Highlander, which they regarded as insular, unresponsive, increasingly mired in its own dramas, and too susceptible to the influence of communists.[72] This view was consistent with their labor roots in the ACWA.[73] As early as 1937, Zilla Hawes regarded the reluctance of Highlander's staff to accept immediate and paid positions organizing textile workers as an abrogation of responsibility: "However, on the basis of the facts, especially that in the incident [the unanswered call for members of Highlander's staff to become temporary organizers at Cleveland, TN] I dealt with," she wrote, "the staff failed to show decisive and concerted action, I am afraid that my confidence in Highlander as a responsible labor school is seriously impaired."[74] Daniel and Hawes became increasingly hostile toward Highlander as differences in labor policy developed into accusations of communist sympathy.

The issues ran deeper than just "the incident" regarding textile organizers. She and Daniel questioned the very nature of the school's existence, challenging its reasons for being. These issues had been actively debated

[70]Franz Daniel to Newman Jeffrey, 12 July 1939, Box 11, Folder 57, NJC.

[71]Simeon Larson and Bruce Nissen, *Theories of the Labor Movement* (Wayne State University Press, 1987), 132. See the editors' introduction to part three of their survey.

[72]Franz Daniel to Rose Bush, 4 August 1941, Box 55, Folder 9, MJC.

[73]Fraser, *Labor Will Rule*, 508–509.

[74]Zilla Hawes to Jim [Dombrowski] and staff, 28 February 1937, Folder 14, Box 29, HREC.

amongst staff throughout the existence of the school and now a growing divide again exposed questions that had remained in dispute. Hawes referenced the discourse that had shaped Highlander and told her friend James Dombrowski, "Perhaps the whole affair will make it possible to clarify our divergent beliefs as to what a labor school is, although that cannot repair the damage done." The differences, Hawes claimed, without remembering her own revolutionary ideals and her tendency to assume impending upheaval, had been with them from the beginning. "It goes back," she told Dombrowski, "repeatedly to the old dilemma we have discussed so often: the necessity for practical experience in the trade union movement, for which a temporary capacity on picket lines, or leading workers education, is no adequate substitute." Hawes, quite understandably, wanted Highlander's staff to have practical experience in the labor movement—by practical she meant experience running campaigns, administering a union, and learning about the institutional practices at the heart of the labor movement. This was all valuable experience, but not perhaps what drew Highlander's high-minded educators to the labor movement. It was, however, immensely practical advice and highlights the shift in emphasis within the labor movement—a shift that accompanied the rise of social democracy—toward professional, managed campaigns and away from the old prairie-fire style of organizing at Highlander and elsewhere or the more feudal loyalties of the United Mine Workers.[75]

Hawes identified the growing importance of large institutions in shaping union policy at the local level. "The American, including the Southern, labor scene," she wrote, "is becoming rapidly one of national scope, and a job in which international unions are more and more taking initiative."[76] This was change that she and Daniel embraced.[77] Hawes argued, "one has to have the utmost cooperation between central bodies and internationals, plus intelligent radical leadership, to achieve the soundest and most lasting results."[78] This was responsible, social-democratic trade unionism as it filtered down to the one-time revolutionary organizers of the early to mid-1930s. Highlander, she admitted, had made progress, though it

---

[75] Ibid.

[76] Ibid.

[77] They were eventually disheartened by the neglect of the Southern field.

[78] Zilla Hawes to Jim [Dombrowski] and staff, 28 February 1937, Box 14, Folder 29, HREC.

needed to cooperate more directly with international unions (and not only local branches of the labor movement).[79] Speaking of the lost opportunity for a Highlander staff member to work as an ACWA organizer in Cleveland, Tennessee, Hawes concluded, "that was the hard blow I felt; when the first real opportunity was offered to work with an international union, [and] it was muffed."[80] Some of the disagreement must have been personal. Daniel had said Highlander would help and when no help came from Highlander, he would have been stung or even embarrassed by the absence of a much-needed organizer. Hawes regarded Highlander's strategic orientation toward unions as inherently flawed: "A labor school, to my mind, should be able to respond to emergency calls from those unions whom it expects to win over to workers education: conversely, workers education, even in the process, should allow for those readjustments which, if responded to and ably met, would entitle it to a deserved reputation for leadership in the field of activity."[81] "Without this proven competency," Hawes concluded," I can see no validity to workers education of an academic and in-itself-nature."[82] Hawes wrote to Highlander's staff after the incident, "it is certain that none of us connected with the Amalgamated [ACWA] will either be in a position, nor be willing, to help open up another such opportunity in the near future, since even a legitimate excuse was not offered by HFS [Highlander Folk School]."[83] Hawes and Daniel were unimpressed by Highlander's reluctance to engage with the labor movement on a more concrete basis.

Hawes saw her break with Highlander as a choice between the labor movement or Highlander. She acknowledged a desire to fight for labor in the South: "If need for organizers remains imminent in the Southern field, that is where my work will be done in the near future, and possibly for the next few years." "This is a natural development," she told her comrades, "but one which this recent episode accentuates, since without confidence one cannot honestly make an effort to participate in school activities; although I want it understood that I will continue to do whatever I can to help work out an effective medium of workers education, with the need for

[79] Ibid.
[80] Ibid.
[81] Ibid.
[82] Ibid.
[83] Ibid.

it becoming increasingly pressing, to my intimate knowledge." Hawes was willing to continue to work with Highlander, if the staff would give way to Hawes and Daniel's position and reform. Otherwise, she was not willing. She was also direct about her critique of the way in which the school was mismanaged: "As far as Highlander is concerned, I am afraid that the theory of cooperative staff control has so far proved little more than a theory: in practice, strong individual opinions dominate, which is as much the fault of weaker members who possibly dare not exert themselves." Hawes told James Dombrowski and the other staff members, "a clear sense of direction, based upon the needs of a growing labor movement, is what Highlander lacks, as a foundation for quick as well as deliberative decisions, on the initiative of any staff member." She also critiqued the intellectual atmosphere that pervaded the school: "If theoretical analysis could achieve [action and direction], we would have it; if trial-and-error by experience could achieve it, or the combination of both, we would have it." This was an argument that went to the very core of Highlander's early model. The theory and even the efforts to work out some communal program—to live their early interpretations of socialist values—had failed to produce the results that Hawes (and others) had expected. Highlander's communal experience had demonstrated this unequivocally.[84]

Hawes was clear-minded enough to concede that even the shift she detailed as necessary for Highlander to become useful was not enough to guarantee new successes in the South. The problems of the South went beyond the lack of efficacious union action. She had undoubtedly learned much during her years as an organizer. Hawes emphasized "pragmatism" and "action" coupled with "philosophical analysis of the existing movement," though she warned that labor organizers and educators should not be too "ideological." They had to convince international unions of their worth and work within a labor culture that mediated against their efforts. Hawes still, perhaps to help ease her own transition from rebel to reformer, claimed "that without a radical approach, in the literal sense of the word, workers education would only serve to promote the immediate and less lasting phases of the existing movement." Her need to clarify the meaning of "radical" and define its context indicates that she was interested in demarcating the meaning from her earlier uses of word. Hawes was still concerned with the origins of the crises of the 1930s, though her concern

---

[84] Ibid.

was more studied than in years earlier. She no longer spoke of the revolution or the proletariat. In three years, Hawes's language has undergone a near total transformation. Hawes argued that Highlander's "staff failed to show decisive and concerted action" when confronted with a request for assistance from the organizing campaign in Cleveland, Tennessee. Highlander's utility for the labor movement and willingness to take direction from the ACWA were her primary concerns.[85]

The dispute over Highlander's role in the broader movement was part of a longer debate about the school that dated from 1934, when an influx of new staff reinvigorated the school.[86] Staff reached no clear conclusions between 1934 and 1937 because the political and social world was constantly shifting. The instability and unpredictable nature of economic and political life in the United States changed with the New Deal. A package of important reforms, including the Wagner Act, the Social Security Act, the Works Progress Administration, and the Fair Labor Standards Act, provided stability and some security, and Horton recalled his own realization that "capitalism was more viable than I had thought." He no longer believed "capitalism was on its last legs." To paraphrase Horton, Roosevelt had made capitalism work again. "That's when I started trying to calm myself down," he wrote, "and grasped that the revolution had to be built step by step, that it wasn't going to come as a great explosion automatically."[87] Highlander's prospects changed with the rise of the CIO and the official integration of Highlander into the CIO beginning in 1937.[88] Work with the CIO, acceptance of social democracy, and improvements in Highlander's financial status stabilized the school and gave it a clear focus that it had hitherto lacked. These changes were accompanied by a new discipline that had been lacking in Highlander's dreamier early years.[89] The school's educational program took a decidedly practical turn.[90] Its outward activism also shifted to the political field, where the labor forces supported by Highlander and working through Labor's Non-Partisan League won victories

[85] Ibid.

[86] For a discussion of the incident and its institutional context, see Glen, *No Ordinary School*, 43–44.

[87] Horton, *The Long Haul*, 81.

[88] Horton, *The Long Haul*, 87, 88–95; Glen, *No Ordinary School*, 45.

[89] Glen, *No Ordinary School*, 48.

[90] Ibid.

in local elections in 1938. These victories were undermined by the elite's ability to severely curtail the financial resources of local officials.[91] The sheriff's salary and budget were cut dramatically.[92] WPA programs were delayed and then canceled. This experience highlighted the failings of a WPA that remained under the control of officials keen to maintain the social order over which they had long presided.[93]

Having followed Hawes's suggested course, Highlander's staff found themselves still at odds with Hawes and Daniel. The convergence of the left around support for Roosevelt, the labor movement (the CIO in particular), and an abandonment of the revolutionary radicalism of the early to mid-1930s masked the tension between those who embraced the popular front, those who saw tolerance of the CP as temporary and tactical, and those who outright opposed the CP. Highlander was in the first group. Hawes and Daniel were in the final group. If the CIO's anti-communist leaders began to consider Highlander suspect in the late 1940s and early 1950s, Highlander's staff were skeptical of the CIO's "reactionary" drift.[94] The break between the two may have been mutual and Highlander increasingly turned its attentions to the black freedom movement and the fight against segregation.[95] Its staff remained reluctant to adopt an official anti-communist position.[96]

Eventually, however, consensus with the social democrats was complete with Highlander's effective, public embrace of anti-communism in the 1950s. Though Horton denied that Highlander was "communistic" as early as 1936, his turn toward an aggressive anti-communism came much later.[97] In 1954, when testifying before the U.S. Senate Internal Security Subcommittee—which was attacking the Southern Conference Education Fund, headed by former Highlander staffer James Dombrowski—Horton abandoned Highlander's previous position. Horton told Senator James Eastland, "We accept no students from the Communist Party and never

[91] Thomas, "The Highlander Folk School," 363; Price, "The New Deal in Tennessee," 116–117.

[92] Price, "The New Deal in Tennessee," 117.

[93] Glen, *No Ordinary School*, 50.

[94] Adams, *Unearthing Seeds of Fire*, 84–86; Glen, *No Ordinary School*, 153.

[95] Glen, *No Ordinary School*, 153–154.

[96] Ibid., 147.

[97] Glen, *Highlander*, 38.

have."[98] A few years later in 1957, when state officials from Georgia leveled charges of communist infiltration at Highlander Folk School, Myles Horton again went on the record against communism. Horton told a reporter from *The Washington Afro American*: "We can only say that Highlander did not and does not welcome enrollment of anyone with a totalitarian philosophy whether from the extreme right or from the extreme left." He finished his statement to the reporter by drawing a direct comparison between the Communist Party and White Citizens' Councils. "In these troubled times, nothing but more trouble can come from the White Citizens' Councils and the Communist Party's infiltration into groups earnestly seeking a democratic solution to our problems," he said. Horton's statement was politically strategic as state officials were eager to discredit Highlander's work in the civil rights movement by painting the school as a font of Communist teaching. Stalin's crimes had gained increasing attention in the United States after his death.[99] When Horton equated the Soviet Union with the Citizens' Councils and their advocacy of physical and structural violence, it resonated with anti-Stalinist sentiments of the time. Horton's critical view of the Communist Party would immediately gain renewed credence when the Soviet Union destroyed the burgeoning movement for socialist democracy that found voice in Hungarian workers' councils. *The Pittsburgh Courier*'s John Rousseau published an exposé that brought the "pro-Fascist" White Citizens' Councils and their violent rhetoric to the public's attention.[100] The ACWA, which had given jobs and support to Highlander and its socialist allies, unequivocally denounced the White Citizens' Councils.[101] In response, Horton reaffirmed the democratic critique

---

[98] United States Senate, *Hearings before the Subcommittee to investigate the administration of the internal security act and other internal security laws of the Committee on the Judiciary on Subversive Influence in Southern Conference Education Fund, Inc.* (Government Printing Office, 1955), 150. For a full summary and analysis of this hearing see Adams, *An American Heretic*, 222–232. Adams states that Dombrowski was surprised by Horton's statement about the exclusion of Communist Party members at Highlander.

[99] "Text of Speech on Stalin by Khrushchev as Released by the State Department," *New York Times*, 5 June 1956, 13.

[100] John Rousseau, "EXPOSE—White Citizens Councils' Hate Crusade: Part I," *Pittsburgh Courier*, 18 August 1956, B7; John Rousseau, "EXPOSE—White Citizens Councils' Hate Crusade: Part II," *Pittsburgh Courier*, 15 August 1956, B7.

[101] "Textile Union Condemns White Citizens Councils," *Atlanta Daily World*, 26 May 1956, 2; "Textile Union Rebuffs Dixie to Condemn Citizens Councils," *The Atlanta Constitution*, 19 May 1956, 1; "Textile Workers Blast White Citizen Coun-

of communism and fascism that had been so characteristic of socialism during the 1930s and 1940s. "Both are morally bankrupt and have nothing to offer," Horton told the report, "We want only those at Highlander who do their own thinking."[102] This was not mere lip service. Horton's comments to the *The Washington Afro-American* were a reaffirmation of democratic socialism in the face of interrogators who tried to smear Highlander and blur the distinctions between Stalinism and the democratic left.[103]

Highlander's political history, however, was not as simple as the narrative that Horton spun for reporters. The socialist view of communism, while always skeptical of communist actions and claims, had shifted through the 1930s, 1940s, and into the 1950s, as political and economic possibilities changed and as revelations about the Soviet Union called into question its sometimes-exalted status. This was complicated by the reality that the communists took many "correct" and principled positions on trade union politics, positions with which many democratic socialists could agree or at least understand.[104] Highlander's staff and former RPCer Philip Van Gelder sided, in broad terms, with John L. Lewis and militants in the labor movement. For this, they were accused of consorting with communists by their social-democratic comrades, who wanted to restrict militancy and impose rationalized labor relations.[105] Daniel, Hawes, and most others sided with Hillman, who favored the regimentation and formalization of labor

cils," *The Washington Post* and *Times Herald*, 19 May 1956, 18; and Bernard D. Nossiter, "Potofsky Scores White Councils," *The Washington Post* and *Times Herald*, 21 May 1956, 15.

[102] "Tenn. School Head Raps Red Charges," *The Washington Afro-American*, 15 October 1957.

[103] This did not help Highlander escape a state-level red scare directed at the school's desegregation work. John Glen recounts these episodes in incredible and terrifying detail. See Glen, *No Ordinary School*, 207–248.

[104] Historians focus on rank-and-file revolts within the UMW and the alternative organizations these revolts engendered. There is, of course, overlap between this history and the history of Highlander. Franz Daniel, who played an important role in connecting Highlander to the textile unions in the South, considered Powers Hapgood a close comrade of similar politics. Hapgood unlike Daniel never abandoned the position that the CP had a right to be heard. Hapgood arguably had more prescience and regarded a reheated red scare as a political problem for the entire left, not just for the CP. See Robert Bussel's *From Harvard to the Ranks of Labor: Powers Hapgood and the American Working Class* (Penn State Press, 2010), 193–195. Hapgood's position had much in common with the position of James Dombrowski.

[105] Franz Daniel to Rose Bush, 4 August 1941, Box 55, Folder 9, MJC.

relations that had characterized the ACWA's relationship with employ-ers.[106] Militant strains within the socialist and labor movements challenged the broad consensus developing around the New Deal. Yet, outright con-frontation between communists and noncommunists was delayed due to strategic consensus around major issues of the day. For example, in WWII, the CP changed its position from opposition to intervention and fully embraced the necessity of subordinating labor to war production. This put them in agreement with socialists and the CIO, and allowed uneasy coexistence to continue.[107]

Well-intentioned rank-and-file communists with whom Highlander's staff intersected in their struggles for socialism in the South further com-plicate narratives about Highlander's political sympathies. Highlander's journey from revolutionary socialist commune to the popular front and finally to socialist anti-communism was a circuitous one. The 1950s, and the Cold War hysteria that shaped American politics was familiar to Hor-ton—as Highlander had faced red-baiting in the early 1930s from the AFL, state officials in Tennessee, and from Works Progress Administration offi-cials. Yet in the 1950s, as the Cold War hysteria grew, Horton found it more difficult to deflect such criticisms without fundamentally disavowing cooperation with communists.

DEMOCRATS AND SOCIALISTS

Socialism's shift to the Democrats was by no means a clear-cut process. Doubts were common and support was initially contingent. Even with WWII fervor in full swing, Zilla Hawes was skeptical about the labor movement's efforts "to implicate itself inextricably with the Democratic party."[108] Hawes and Daniel were considering the merits of working within the Democratic Party or pursuing third-party efforts. Vice President

---

[106] Zieger, *The CIO*, 143.

[107] The social democrats and Christian democrats in coalition would see the CP extir-pated from the CIO. The war had only briefly subordinated this desire. See Levenstein, *Communism, Anticommunism, and the CIO*, 150–152. The delay of the reckoning with the CP was ensured as the Communists embraced much of Hillman's program on war mobilization—even if there was dissent in individual CIO unions. John L. Lewis con-tinued to represent an alternative to Hillman's program, which some dissenters in the CIO found attractive. See Philip Van Gelder to John L. Lewis, 10 October 1952, Box, 2, Folder 11, PVGC.

[108] Zilla Hawes to Franz Daniel, 24 July 1943, Box 3, Folder 5, FDC.

Wallace was the hope of the left inside the Democratic Party. This view was shared across labor's factions. Zilla Hawes, who believed that Wallace's "caliber rates very high," told Franz Daniel, "I'm convinced that Wallace is becoming a focal and vocal power of progressive ideas."[109] Hawes understood the exigencies of the war, though she continued to have great hope in the future of the New Deal. "The President," she wrote of Roosevelt, "no doubt inevitably, has lost something, in my estimation: running a world war he can hardly help it, but the inspiration is gone, and I feel more than heretofore that he talks down a wee bit, and skips a little too glibly over the home front. Perhaps his next message will clear that up. At any rate it is significant that the purposes behind the New Deal caught hold firmly enough to find espousal through another personality, and Roosevelt's subtle pat on the back to Wallace indicates that FDR intends it that way."[110] Labor, Hawes argued, had a "responsibility for affirmative, vigorous action."[111] Wallace would not get the Democrat's nomination for vice president for the 1944 election, though labor supported his nomination.[112] The bulk of the labor movement, including Hawes and Daniel, would not support Wallace's Progressive Party bid for the presidency four years later because of the Wallace campaign's association with the CP. For the socialists, anti-communism was an ideological imperative. Yet, socialists also faced pressure from right-wing anti-communists who were eager to undermine their work.

If socialists needed no help distancing themselves from the CP, fear of congressional investigations conditioned a shift away from explicitly embracing the language of socialism. Even Daniel by early 1940 now referred to his group not as socialists, but as "honest radicals" and "realistic radicals," though he did acknowledge that his goal was to reach out to people who had "in the past been associated with the Socialist Party."[113] Daniel was eager to organize those former SP members who had broken with the party because of their support for New Deal Democrats and as a result of their support for war mobilization. He wrote, "In my opinion the [Reuther] brothers are a bit too cagy about putting things in writing. After

---

[109] Ibid.
[110] Ibid.
[111] Ibid.
[112] Fraser, *Labor Will Rule*, 530–533.
[113] Franz Daniel to Newman Jeffrey, 13 January 1940, Box 11, Folder 57, NJC.

all, the Dies, Smith, etc. Committees have too much on all of us for us to worry about one more letter." Nonetheless, a tone of carefulness *had* set in. Even Daniel's old friends Newman and Mildred Jeffrey were reluctant to give Daniel a straightforward response. He told them, "I would feel a hell of a lot more certain that I'm not wasting my time if you would write direct."[114]

While they endorsed the New Deal and dropped the socialist label, socialists saw the New Deal as a beginning. As Walter Reuther told the 1948 convention of Americans for Democratic Action, they conceptualized the New Deal as a jumping off point not as an end, and looked across the Atlantic for their vision of the good society.[115] American socialists cited Scandinavian countries, Britain, and Israel as countries that they wished the United States to emulate. More than ten years later, at a hostile 1959 meeting with Nikita Khrushchev, leader of the Soviet Union, in the United States, Walter Reuther "cited Israel as the 'country nearest to the democratic socialism in the free world.'"[116] Emil Rieve argued that the Scandinavian nations demonstrated that socialism was not at odds with political democracy, and, in fact, demonstrated that the two were inextricably linked.[117] Khrushchev retorted, "An instrument doesn't exist that could measure the insignificant amount of socialism there."[118] At the 1948 convention of Americans for Democratic Action, Reuther connected the movement for social democracy in the United States with the efforts of socialists in Europe. "We witness the struggle of Europe's non-Communist left," Reuther told his audience, "to create a third force independent of the Communist and Fascist extremes. This third force will fail if we in America fail to steer this nation on a consistently progressive course at home and abroad."[119] Social democracy was his vital "third force."

Social-democratic thought in the United States retained much of its socialist content, even as socialists entered the Democratic Party. Social

[114]Franz Daniel to Newman and Mildred Jeffrey, 31 January 1940, Box 11, Folder 57, NJC.

[115]Walter R. Storey, "The ADA Convention: A New Liberal Frontier," *The New Leader*, 6 March 1948, 5.

[116]John Herling, "U.S. Labor vs. Khrushchev," *The New Leader*, 5 October 1959, 17.

[117]Ibid.

[118]Ibid.

[119]Storey, "The ADA Convention," 5.

democrats advocated limited nationalization and continued to view imperialism with suspicion and through an anti-communist lens. By the middle of the 1950s, social democrats could speak of at least some nationalization as "inevitable." Reinhold Niebuhr understood the nationalization of British coal mines as such. He held that this was "so inevitable that the whole nation [Tories included] agreed with the policy."[120] Such programs, Niebuhr argued, were possible in the United States, too. In 1955, Niebuhr believed that a comprehensive system of public health care would come to the United States. Niebuhr continued to identify broadly with the social-democratic impulse, arguing that only the Labour Party could shepherd Britain through the tempestuous seas of the post-war world. Referring to the immediate post-war years, Niebuhr argued, "Only a Labor government could have 'tightened the belt' of an impoverished nation without special resentment." He further held that Labor alone "would have been willing to liquidate the British Empire and thus save the cause of democracy."[121] The French, who pursued a quite different strategy, argued Niebuhr, had inadvertently strengthened the communist hand. "The tardiness of the French," he wrote, "in yielding to nationalist aspirations has given Communism its greatest victory."[122] Social-democratic thinking in 1950s was not robbed of its vitality by compromise with the Democratic Party. Social-democratic anti-communism, in particular, turned conventional logic about domestic and foreign policy on its head. "Until America puts its own [economic] house in order and proves that democracy works," argued Walter Reuther as he advocated for "a full-employment, full-production, [and] full-distribution economy," "it will not sell democracy to the world no matter how fancily we dress it up. Herein lies the key to a positive foreign policy."[123]

The lives of these socialists did not spin on an academic axis. There was no formal period of hurried intellectual effort designed to help struggling labor organizers come to grips with the changes they were witnessing and experiencing. They did not read Ferdinand Lassalle or Eduard Bernstein and his defenders in the intelligentsia and decide that social democracy suddenly had great merit. Social democracy was not rediscovered in books; it was made anew. Theirs was a reinvention, of sorts, as they were broadly

---

[120]Niebuhr, "The Fate of European Socialism," 6.

[121]Ibid.

[122]Ibid., 7.

[123]Walter Reuther, "Wanted: A Positive Social Program," *The New Leader*, 15 April 1950, S-3.

aware of their positions in relation to others, but they were not so concerned with placing themselves in some grand intellectual tradition. Hence, they were new social democrats by accident or through experience rather than by design. They reacted to their changing circumstances and adopted new positions that were broadly in line with basic socialist principles. They continued to see capitalism as deeply flawed and continued to place class —sometimes now engulfed by the metonymy or synecdoche "labor"—at the center of their analysis.

CHAPTER 9

Epilogue: Norman Thomas Nostalgia

As the era of mid-century American socialism began to fade beyond memory, it experienced a last resurgence of attention both from commentators and from those shaped in the intensity of the 1930s. Norman Thomas, in particular, stood in as the face of a now-respectable American socialism, admired, at last, even by those who held socialism in distain. "I think that Thomas was a hero," William F. Buckley, Jr. allowed shortly after Thomas's death in 1968.[1] Thomas had been the inaugural guest on Buckley's show *Firing Line*, where the two had debated the war in Vietnam.[2] Martin Luther King, Jr. told Thomas, "All that we hear of the Great Society seems only an echo of your prophetic eloquence."[3] Thomas's *New York Times* obituary concluded, "Once scorned as a visionary, he lived to be venerated as an institution, a patrician rebel, an idealist who refused to despair, a moral man who declined to permit age to mellow him."[4] Thomas received praise from

---

[1] William F. Buckley, Jr., "Norman Thomas a Hero, But...," *Los Angeles Times*, 7 January 1968, B8.

[2] Gregory, *The Great Dissenter*, 273. Gregory concludes that Thomas did well against Buckley: 'Buckley clearly had his hands full in dealing with the "grand old man" and probably hoped that future guests would cause him less anguish.'

[3] Gregory, *The Great Dissenter*, 271.

[4] Alden Whitman, "Norman Thomas, Socialist, Dies," *New York Times*, 20 December 1968, 43.

© The Author(s) 2019
J. Altman, *Socialism before Sanders*,
https://doi.org/10.1007/978-3-030-17176-6_9

the highest representatives of the nation. including, on his death, President Lyndon Johnson.[5]

Thomas's ideas, many argued, had been thoroughly, if not completely, integrated into the mainstream of American political thought. He was hailed as a fount of much social policy. "Franklin Roosevelt was astute enough to have paid attention to Mr. Thomas," wrote one Thomas admirer responding to an article on Thomas in the *Washington Post*, "The New Deal was not much more than a scheme to put into practice virtually every social program that Mr. Thomas had been espousing."[6] *The New York Times* carried a similar argument:

> Mr. Thomas lived to see many of his specific prescriptions for social ills filled by other parties. Running for President in 1932, in one of six such races, Mr. Thomas had a platform calling for such Depression remedies as public works, low-cost housing, slum clearance, the five-day week, public employment agencies, unemployment insurance, old-age pensions, health insurance for the aged, minimum-wage laws and the abolition of child labor.[7]

Thomas himself contributed to the narrative that the New Deal—at least partially—fulfilled his social vision, but only years after its highpoints, during which he had remained skeptical and critical.[8] Norman Thomas the individual both stood in for and obliterated the Socialist Party in this narrative, which would have been unrecognizable to socialists, Norman Thomas included, in the mid-1930s.

Despite its lack of complexity (or perhaps because of it) this narrative became commonplace. "Norman Thomas knew that his campaigns were not futile," *The New York Times* reported in 1972, "Very many of the

---

[5]Gregory, *The Great Dissenter*, 269–270, 271–272; Alden Whitman, "Norman Thomas, Socialist, Dies," *New York Times*, 20 December 1968, 1.

[6]L.J. Fiskin, letter to the editor, "Remembering Norman Thomas," *Washington Post*, 5 December 1982, C6.

[7]Alden Whitman, "Norman Thomas, Socialist, Dies," *New York Times*, 20 December 1968, 43.

[8]Gregory, *The Great Dissenter*, 109; Whitman, "Norman Thomas, Socialist, Dies," 43. Whitman's article included the following insightful anecdote about Thomas's relationship to the New Deal: "Each of these then-radical proposals [those adopted by New Dealers] is now a generally accepted part of the fabric of American life. Mr. Thomas once acknowledged this state of affairs. 'It was often said by his enemies that [Franklin D.] Roosevelt was carrying out the Socialist party platform.' He said in a bitter moment. 'Well, in a way it was true—he carried it out on a stretcher.'"

specific programs he advocated were adopted by Democrats, imbedded in the law of the land and subsequently defended by Republicans."[9] Private memory and public remembrance were deceptive. Insider reminiscences hinted that socialists (and Thomas) had once had broader ambitions. When the faculty of Princeton, Thomas's alma mater, had challenged a ban on his speaking at campus by voting him an honorary degree, John Herling, a Thomas confidant, recalled, "One of the younger members of his small staff noted wryly that the abolitionist Wendell Phillips did not deliver the Phi Beta Kappa oration at Harvard until after the slaves were freed."[10]

The difficulty in reconciling the radicalism of past belief and the once broader ambitions that accompanied it with the social-democratic present was not confined to commentary on Norman Thomas. In the 1970s, Andrew Biemiller, former congressman from Wisconsin and lobbyist for the AFL-CIO, commenting on a question that a British comrade had asked him and Franz Daniel in the early 1930s, reported that in those days the answer had been easy. The question was about whom Biemiller and Daniel supported in British politics: the *collaborator* Ramsay MacDonald, who formed a national government reliant on Conservative support, or the *revolutionary* James Maxton, who was very critical of MacDonald and in the 1930s pursued a radical form of socialism.[11] Biemiller and Daniel had supported Maxton and viewed MacDonald as a traitor. Biemiller's remembering of the incident and how easy their support for Maxton had been in the 1930s suggested just how much socialism had changed, though the content of this change was open to the interpretation of the audience, and the references lost to anyone who had not participated in the events. The question that had been so easy to answer in the 1930s no longer solicited such a simple answer. The fiery and revolutionary spirit of the 1930s had not only been tamed, but it was nearly forgotten. Despite the occasional suggestion to the contrary, socialists remembered themselves and Thomas in selective ways, as did the arbiters of public knowledge.

Paeans to Thomas in the press were often formulaic. Traits and narratives developed relatively late in Thomas's life were engrained forever in

[9]"Thomas School," *New York Times*, 26 July 1972, 36.

[10]John Herling, "Where Is Norman Thomas When We Really Need Him?" *The Washington Post Outlook*, 28 November 1982, C4.

[11]"Memorial Service for Franz Daniel," 29 September 1976, Box 15, Folder 19, FDC; Austen Morgan, *J. Ramsay MacDonald* (Manchester University Press, 1987), 200; and William Knox, *James Maxton* (University of Manchester Press, 1987), 90.

testimonials to the treasured man of principle. Obligatory differentiation between Thomas and his communist foes was followed by an admission of Thomas's importance in shaping the social policy of the United States. "He abhorred violence," read one eulogy's differentiation.[12] It concluded with the most restrained version of the panegyric formula: "he lived to see early derision of his views converted, not into universal acclaim, but at least into respectable consideration."[13] *The Washington Post*'s obituary adhered to the standard. First it reminded readers of the difference, this time more explicitly, between Thomas and the communists. "Although often equated with Communists," it informed, "Mr. Thomas had a profound contempt for their philosophy."[14] *The Post* conceded only that Thomas was "brilliant to the end."[15] Commentators interpreted Thomas's past comments to indicate his prescience and to differentiate his socialism from Soviet Communism.[16] *The New York Times*, on the one-hundredth anniversary of Thomas's birth, quoted from his 1918 application to join the Socialist Party of America, affirming Thomas's anti-communist credentials: "When Mr. Thomas joined the Socialist Party in 1918, he noted in his application his 'fear of the undue exultation of the state and a profound faith that the new world we desire must depend upon freedom and fellowship, rather than any sort of coercion whatsoever.'"[17] Thomas's "fundamental ethical precepts" were emphasized over "the Marxist idea of class conflict."[18]

[12]"Norman Thomas, a Good Man," *Boston Globe*, 20 December 1968, 28.

[13]Ibid.

[14]"Socialist Norman Thomas Dies at 84," *The Washington Post*, 20 December 1968, A1.

[15]"Socialist Norman Thomas Dies at 84," A1; A lengthier article in *The Washington Post* also set out the basic historical trajectory of Thomas's career as a socialist (warts and all), thought it too focused heavily on Thomas's anticommunist credentials. It also concluded that was something of a widely admired national treasure. "Norman Thomas: An American Rebel," *The Washington Post*, 20 December 1968, C14. *The Los Angeles Times*'s article on Thomas's death contained similar themes of anticommunism and broader relevance in shaping social policy, though it touched on his work for the "early civil rights movement." Robert J. Donovan, "Norman Thomas Dead at 84: Norman Thomas, Socialist Leader for 40 Years, Dies," *Los Angeles Times*, 20 December 1968, 1, 6.

[16]Walter Goodman, "A Giant of Socialism is Hailed On 100th Anniversary of Birth," *New York Times*, 19 November 1984, B8. The article was carried in other publications too.

[17]Ibid.

[18]Ibid.

By highlighting Thomas's ethical core, commentators endeavored to place Thomas in a safe category, free from the politics of the Cold War. The narrative from newspapers and public officials affirmed that Thomas had, in the words of New York's Mayor Abraham Beame, argued for policy that was later enacted: "Many of the reforms we now take for granted were advocated by Norman Thomas long before others took up the cause."[19] Norman Thomas was safe for Americans, though Thomas himself, when he was alive, contested this effort to sanitize him, to turn him into a "grand old man," a sobriquet applied to Thomas by William F. Buckley, Jr.[20] Thomas told Buckley: "I thought we were going to debate Vietnam and not discuss me and my life and miracles." He continued, "I would point out that while I have not achieved many of the things that I cared most about I have come nearer hitting the nail on the head of what the people would adopt later than most candidates for president or other office. I am no Don Quixote tilting at windmills when I was the pioneer on so much social legislation that this country now has."[21] Thomas, defusing Buckley's glowing, if acerbic, introduction, told the audience, "after all, I've been around a long time and it is an old, old trick to kill an opponent by kindness." He claimed the social legislation of the twentieth century as partially his own and also contested the idea that he was harmless national treasure.

Tributes and fondness for Thomas (and for the socialist movement for which he often stood in) grew more important when he had passed from the American political scene. There were fierce defenses of Thomas's memory. When George Will, a columnist for the *Washington Post*, compared James Buckley, a Republican candidate for Senate and sibling of William F. Buckley, Jr., to Norman Thomas, John Herling told Will a story to illustrate the absurdity of the comparison. "Once campaigning in one of the poorest neighborhoods of Pittsburgh, where rags were stuffed in tenements windows to keep out the cold, Thomas knocked on the door of a flat," began Herling, "'Good evening, sir,' he said to the man who confronted him. 'I'm the Socialist candidate for president.' The man drew back in abhorrence. 'Oh,' he said, 'So you're the son of a bitch who wants to change our system.' Obviously, nobody could or should accuse Jim Buckley of being

---

[19] Fowler, "Dedication Hails Norman Thomas," 28.

[20] William F. Buckley, Jr., "Vietnam: Pull Out? Stay In? Escalate?" *Firing Line*, WOR-TV (New York, NY, 8 April 1966).

[21] Ibid.

that kind of a 'son of a bitch.'"[22] Norman Thomas remained incompara-
ble for his younger followers. John Herling recalled, "Voting for Norman
Thomas always represented a choice that only the young in heart and clear
in head were capable of making. It is he who first urged men and women
to 'vote their hopes rather than their fears.'"[23] He stood apart, and efforts
to sanitize his past or use it for political ill were not to be tolerated.

By the 1970s, even the old labor right, embodied in Thomas's near-
opposite George Meany, was surprisingly nostalgic for a bit of old-fashioned
socialism. Other old socialists who clung to their anticommunism above
almost all else and refused to wrestle with realities of American military
"intervention" in Southeast Asia also yearned for Thomas.[24] The nostalgia
for socialism was growing—particularly among older labor leaders who had
come to oppose wars of "intervention," even against communists. They
often packaged this opposition as sound anti-communist policy.[25] Intervention bred communism, they argued.[26] Ironically enough, it was the
very moment of labor's internal political strife in 1972 that elicited what
John Herling called "a nostalgic sigh" from the AFL-CIO President George
Meany, who told reporters, "if only Norman Thomas were alive."[27] Meany
kept the AFL-CIO officially neutral in the presidential race between Nixon
and McGovern, an indication of the growing fragmentation of American
politics and the continuing frustrations that confronted the Democratic

[22]John Herling, letter to the editor, "Foolish Comparison," *Washington Post*, 17
October 1980, A12.

[23]Herling, "Where Is Norman Thomas When We Really Need Him?" C1.

[24]Sidney Hook, "Democratic Socialist Tells Why He's for Nixon," *Los Angeles Times*,
19 October 1972, C7; Also see Michael Harrington's response, "A Socialist Explains
Reasons for His Support of McGovern," *Los Angeles Times*, 20 October 1972, B7.
Harrington's analysis that American support for "reactionary dictators" fueled support
for Communists was similar to that of Philip Van Gelder, Franz Daniel, and Newman
Jeffrey. When Jeffrey derided old YPSLs who voted for Nixon, he may have had people
like Sidney Hook in mind.

[25]Franz Daniel to Gerald Bonham, 2 March 1976, Box 15, Folder 2, FDC.

[26]Franz Daniel to Gerald Bonham, 2 March 1976, Box 15, Folder 2, FDC.

[27]Quoted in John Herling, "Where Is Norman Thomas When We Really Need Him?"
The Washington Post Outlook, 28 November 1982, C1; Meany's comment is not apocryphal. See Sidney Hook, "Democratic Socialist Tells Why He's for Nixon," *Los Angeles Times*, 19 October 1972, C7; Bernard K. Johnpoll, "George Meany and Morris
Hillquit," *New York Times*, 19 August 1972, 23.

coalition.[28] Norman Thomas would have disapproved, and Meany's comment, if wistful, was probably insincere.[29] Socialism, which had come to mean social democracy for many by the mid-twentieth century, continued to hold a certain cachet for the generation that had entered the labor movement in the 1930s and who, by the 1960s and 1970s, had labored for more than three decades on behalf of that movement and its progeny. Even though the relationship was sometimes difficult, social democrats in the labor movement offered aid to the new social movements of the 1960s and 1970s.[30]

In a more thoughtful and genuine tribute to Norman Thomas, the Board of Education in New York City decided to name a public school in Thomas's honor in 1972.[31] The school was finally dedicated in 1976.[32] Glowing tributes, coupled with much misrepresentation and simplification, followed. To say, as a writer for the *New York Times* did, that Norman Thomas always "worked within the system" ignored the complexities of the 1930s.[33] Socialists came to see that accommodations could be made with "the system" as it was reformed and hoped that they would make further progress still. In the red-hot fury of the early to mid-1930s, this was hardly the default position of most socialists, including Thomas.

Veteran socialists still spoke, or again began to speak, of themselves as *socialists*. That label had regained some of its luster, due, in part, to the arid political landscape that greeted unionists in the last decades of the twentieth century. Reclamation of the socialist label was also a response to lingering divisions that had long characterized the labor movement, divisions exacerbated in the late 1960s and in the 1970s by the AFL-CIO's continued support for American policies in Vietnam and rejection of the

---

[28] Boyle, *The UAW and the Heyday of American Liberalism*, 5, 206–207.

[29] Alden Whitman, "Norman Thomas, Socialist, Dies," *New York Times*, 20 December 1968, 43.

[30] Boyle, *The UAW and the Heyday of American Liberalism*, 159–160, 194–196; Maurice Isserman, *The Other American: The Life of Michael Harrington* (Public Affairs, 2000), 207.

[31] "Thomas School," *New York Times*, 26 July 1972, 36.

[32] Glenn Fowler, "Dedication Hails Norman Thomas: Ceremony at High School Named for Him Recalls Reforms He Urged," *New York Times*, 28 May 1976, 28.

[33] "Thomas School," 36.

"New Politics."[34] The major social-democratic unions backed McGovern in 1972 while the AFL-CIO remained "neutral." Those backing McGovern included UAW, AFSCME, UE, the ACWA, ILGWU, District 65, and others.[35] Norman Thomas nostalgia was for some merely a rhetorical device, certainly an ironic one for George Meany, to deploy in order to highlight their heightened frustrations and affirm the existence of their own values. There had long been a division within the labor movement between the inheritors of Debs and Thomas—those who remained deeply critical and uneasy over American capitalism, including the racial divisions on which it was built and maintained, and its corrosive, undemocratic effects—and the inheritors of a more conservative trade unionism.[36] These divisions came increasingly into the open in 1972, when the still-visionary social democrats endorsed McGovern and then participated, along with Michael Harrington, in reorganizing American socialism on terms that had shaped the most influential elements of the socialist movement since the mid-1930s.[37] Despite Meany's remarks about Norman Thomas as an alternative to Nixon or McGovern, the labor socialists had finally had their way, as the movement reorganized, with labor support, around an idea that they had long put into practice: a "'socialist caucus' within the Democratic party."[38]

A more substantive and emotive yearning for the days of Norman Thomas took shape among some socialists. By the mid-1970s, Franz Daniel had taken to signing his letters to comrades, "Keep the Faith."[39] When Daniel died in 1976, his old friends from Soviet House in

---

[34]Tensions existed for many years after the merger of the AFL and the CIO and boiled over into personal and political struggles within the labor movement. Walter Reuther and George Meany, for instance, once had a public quarrel in a restaurant about Franz Daniel's position in the CIO. It was as much about union politics as it was about personnel (and personal) matters. See Daniel, *Rogue River Journal*, 116. On Vietnam and the evolution of the social-democratic trade unionists and on the AFL-CIO's rejection of the New Politics see Levy, *The New Left and Labor*, 53, 55–56, 180–181.

[35]Boyle, *The UAW and the Heyday of American Liberalism*, 258. See note 41 for a list of the unions that endorsed McGovern.

[36]Lichtenstein, *The Most Dangerous Man in Detroit*, 353.

[37]Peter Levy, *The New Left and Labor in the 1960s* (University of Illinois Press, 1994), 179–182; Boyle, *The UAW and the Heyday of American Liberalism*, 258.

[38]Peter Kihss, "Socialists Plan Founding Parley," *New York Times*, 10 September 1973, 21.

[39]Franz Daniel to Newman Jeffrey, 13 April 1974, Box 11, Folder 61, NJC.

Philadelphia sent condolences. Peg and Franklin McCurdy signed their card, "Old Socialists & Unitarians."[40] Socialism was again something to take pride in, to remember, to preserve, and to defend. Daniel, serving as a board member of the Public Utilities Commission in Springfield, Missouri, in the 1970s was quite open about his socialist allegiance. "One thing is sure," he reported to his comrade Newman Jeffrey, "the simplistic faith I once had in idealistic socialism is valuable to me in talking about policies—but it is far from the answer to the day by day problems."[41] If idealism still had its place when framing and advocating policy, as Daniel suggested, socialism could be used as an attractive explanatory device: "The rest of the board is aware of my socialistic base and ideology and they like to talk to me about it. And I've been of very practical help [in] getting the board to understand the workers problems and reactions." As a socialist serving on the Springfield, Missouri, utilities board, Daniel was rehabilitating the faith of his youth, and, if his fellow board members really did "like to talk" about socialism, he was evangelizing, too.[42] A renewed openness about socialism—still often misremembered in the wake of the Second Red Scare and the vicious infighting that had wracked the labor movement in the late 1940s—characterized the later decades of the twentieth century.[43] A disquiet in American political life brought on by Vietnam, economic crisis, Watergate, the rise of the political right and Reaganism, and the decline of the labor movement fueled an increasing nostalgia for Norman Thomas, who often stood in as symbol for a robust social-democratic critique.

In 1975, there was a reunion of the Young People's Socialist League in Philadelphia. The event caused much thoughtful reminiscing for Newman Jeffrey. "I never had a real childhood, first or second," he wrote to his friend Franz Daniel, "I was never a Ypsil [a member of the Young People's Socialist League]. I was born a mature socialist and have remained one all my life. I was not one of the Ypsils who supported Nixon or one of the modern

[40] Peg and Franklin McCurdy to Margaret and Georgia, 26 August 1976, Box 4, Folder 17, FDC.

[41] Franz Daniel to Newman Jeffrey, 13 April 1974, Box 11, Folder 61, NJC.

[42] "Springfield City Utilities: Red! Red! Red!" *Dallas County Courier*, 29 January 1976, Box 11, Folder 59, NJC.

[43] There certainly was not much talk of the Revolutionary Policy Committee or the Militant factions of the Socialist Party of America by the 1960s and 1970s. Alice Cook's memoir is the exception. Cook, *Lifetime of Labor*, 76.

Ypsils who have gone so fat with years."[44] His examples of the latter of these types were Solomon Barkin and Andrew Biemiller, a former congressman and top political operative for the AFL-CIO.[45] In part, Jeffrey's missive to Daniel must be read as a reclaiming of radical fire. He was not going to attend the reunion in Philadelphia. His animosity was fierce. He did not want to be one of "the present day Ypsil who have gone to fat with Meany, Barkin, Biemiller, who seem hell bent on a repeat performance of their 1972 imitation of Martin, Barton, and Fiske [Fish]."[46] Martin, Barton, and Fish had been FDR's isolationist foils in the Congress. It is possible that Jeffrey was referring to Meany's opposition to McGovern in 1972, which had split the labor movement (and fractured what remained of the organized American socialist movement).[47]

By the 1970s and 1980s the limitations of McCarthyism were being cast off. Myles Horton was an open radical again, an anti-capitalist.[48] Franz Daniel, a delegate to the 1976 Democratic National Convention, was again trumpeting socialism. His comrades voiced some concern about Carter's politics, and Daniel may have had his own reservations about Carter.[49] Zilla Hawes, too, had continued appreciation for socialism. Living with her son John and her daughter-in-law Marilyn before her death in 1992, Hawes had her "most satisfying friendship... [with] a young Socialist and labor activist."[50] Newman Jeffrey was still an old socialist, though he claimed always to have been a "mature socialist."[51] Forty or fifty years had passed since its last revival, yet socialism still held much meaning for them all.

[44]Newman Jeffrey to Franz Daniel, 11 November 1975, Box 11, Folder 61, NJC.

[45]Saxon Wolfgang, "Solomon Barkin, 92, Economist in Labor Movement and Teacher," *New York Times*, 6 April 2000, C25; Michael Norman, "Andrew J. Biemiller Dies at 75," *New York Times*, 4 April 1982, 36; and "Andrew J. Biemiller," *The Washington Post*, 10 April 1982, A14.

[46]Newman Jeffrey to Franz Daniel, 11 November 1975, Box 11, Folder 61, NJC.

[47]"Meany Trying to Decide, 2 Other Unions Pick Nixon," *The Atlanta Constitution*, 15 July 1972, 6A; Philip Shabecoff, "Meany Criticizes 'Elite' Democrats," *New York Times*, 19 September 1971, 38.

[48]"The Adventures of a Radical Hillbilly: An Interview with Myles Horton," *Bill Moyer's Journal*, 1981.

[49]"Memorial Service for Franz Daniel," 29 September 1976, Box 11, Folder 19, FDC.

[50]Daniel, *Looking After*, 88.

[51]Newman Jeffrey to Franz Daniel, 11 November 1975, Box 11, Folder 61, NJC.

It may have meant more as careers ended and reflections began, and it continued to define important aspects of their lives.

Personal nostalgia and loss carried political meaning. Ursula Niebuhr wrote to the old socialist John Herling about the political crises of the early 1980s that challenged post-WWII liberalism: "I wonder what you think about the present situation? How long is this wretched house of cards going to last? If it were not so obscene, it would be funny."[52] Making her own position clear, she told Herling, "I have a particular distaste for the neo-conservatives who strike me as weasel-like in this period of crisis. At times, I wish Reinhold were here to be a contemporary Jeremiah."[53] The sense that something had gone terribly awry in American politics was rooted in the absence of the old as much as the presence of new, frightening forces:

> So many of the neo-conservatives seem to me to be like the false prophets, and it needs a real prophet to say, "Woe unto them." Reinhold would have used some of the words of the last chapter of the First Book of Kings, a passage which he loved, where the true prophet is in jail and the false prophets prophesy good, for they are yes men. ...But alas, there are not prophets at this moment, alas.[54]

Nostalgia indeed. Ursula Niebuhr was referencing the 1982 economic crisis that gripped America and the truth tellers, the fiery prophets, Thomas and Niebuhr, were gone.

Historians, particularly those who came of political age in the 1960s and 1970s, have demonstrated a renewed appreciation for social democracy and the complexities that confronted social-democratic labor leaders.[55] Much of this comes in the face of successful efforts in the late twentieth and twenty-first centuries to destroy the achievements of social democrats

---

[52] Ursula Niebuhr to John Herling, 25 March 1982, Box 63, RNP.

[53] Ibid.

[54] Ibid.

[55] An uneasy consensus—what Lichtenstein has called, "a kind of popular front between the new union leadership and the left academy"—has emerged around the value of social democracy. See Nelson Lichtenstein, "Historians as Public Intellectuals," in *A Contest of Ideas: Capital, Politics, and Labor* (University of Illinois, 2013), 40–42.

and their allies on the liberal left.[56] Tony Judt's work can be read as a mournful eulogy to the lost world of social democracy in the United States and in Western Europe. In Britain, panegyric defenses of social democracy and warnings about its long intellectual decay are voiced with increasing urgency.[57] The displacement of socialist parties by the "radical" left or by the rise of "left" factions within old social-democratic parties are manifestations of the desire to return to social democracy, and a recognition that what remains of the socialist vision is social democratic. The economic policies of Jeremy Corbyn and John McDonnell's Labour Party or Bernie Sanders's campaign for the Democratic nomination in 2016 have much more in common with traditional social democracy than with those adventurers, utopians, and party-builders who advocated and implemented more radical transformations in the early to mid-1930s. It is simply that the conventional leaders of social-democratic parties had given so much ground in accepting the neoliberal consensus that they are no longer distinguishable as social democrats.[58] This is the great rub at the heart of the rupture in Western politics at present. The right faces its own problems—conditioned, at least in part, by the erosion of social democracy—as its base has found angry voices in populist candidates from Farage to Trump and Le Pen.

The problem for socialists has always been finding a way to reconcile inspiration with the compromised art of politics. American socialists were not unsuccessful at reconciling their dream of socialism with the immediacy

[56]Tony Judt, *Ill Fares the Land* (Penguin Press, 2010), 98–99; Jamie Peck, *Constructions of Neoliberal Reason* (Oxford University Press, 2010), 42–46.

[57]Evgeny Morozov, "Does Silicon Valley's Reign Herald the End of Social Democracy?" *The Guardian*, 20 September 2015; Patrick Diamond, "Social Democracy Is on the Ropes—It Needs a New Vision," *The Guardian*, 4 June 2014; The popularity of the nonagenarian Harry Leslie Smith's writings in both *The Guardian* and *The Newstatesman* are further indication of this phenomenon. Smith describes himself as "an activist for the preservation of social democracy." See Harry Leslie Smith, *Harry's Last Stand: How the World My Generation Built Is Falling Down, and What We Can Do to Save It* (Icon Books, 2014). There is also a revival of intellectual attention to social democracy and its possibilities as a new alternative to the failure of neoliberalism. See Andrew Gamble, "Moving Beyond the National: The Challenges for Social Democracy in a Global World," in *Social Justice in the Global Age*, eds. O. Cramme and P. Diamond (Cambridge: Polity Press, 2009); Olaf Cramme and Patrick Diamond, eds., *After the Third Way: The Future of Social Democracy in Europe* (London: I.B. Tauris, 2012); and Lane Kenworthy, *Social Democratic America* (Oxford University Press, 2014).

[58]David Harvey, *A Brief History of Neoliberalism* (Oxford University Press, 2005), 62–63.

capitalism's exploitative reality.[59] The problem of the socialist movement in the twenty-first century is to regain power without sacrificing basic principles. Bernie Sanders has found a way forward with a relatively conservative, social-democratic message. Social democracy in America seems to be so "revolutionary" because it has never had a consistent hold in the United States.

Socialists have lacked a lightening-rod leader for decades. Debs, Thomas, and Harrington have found few inheritors in an era when much of the left embraced the "third way," an accommodation with neoliberalism most closely associated with Bill Clinton in the United States and Tony Blair in the United Kingdom. The movement survived, nourished by aging pragmatists and fresh-faced recruits. With neoliberalism under increasing strain for its perceived superficiality and shallowness, Bernie Sanders, who has surpassed Debs, Thomas, and Harrington in popular appeal, has emerged to breathe new life into the movement. In the turbulent and unpredictable twenty-first century, the future of American socialism is unknowable. If there is one sentiment developed by the socialists who carried their ideals through much of the twentieth century that deserves emulation, it is not to trust those who claim to know the future, be they market, Marxist, or technocratic utopians. As Norman Thomas reminded in 1953, "The working class is not the Messiah which some of us thought."[60] Thomas certainly never regarded the market as a Messiah. There was no anointed savior, Thomas concluded, though democracy offered a path to redemption.[61]

---

[59] Boyle, *The UAW and the Heyday of American Liberalism*, 4; Halpern, *UAW Politics in the Cold War Era*, 123.

[60] Norman Thomas, *Democratic Socialism: A New Appraisal* (League for Industrial Democracy, 1953), 38.

[61] Ibid., 20–21.

BIBLIOGRAPHY

ARCHIVAL SOURCES

Duke University Library, Durham, N.C.
Socialist Party of America Papers (microfilm edition)
Manuscript Division, Library of Congress, Washington, D.C.
Reinhold Niebuhr Papers
Manuscript, Archives, and Rare Book Library, Robert W. Woodruff Library, Emory University, Atlanta, Georgia.
Raoul Family papers (digital collection)
Miriam and Ira D. Wallach Division of Art, Prints and Photographs, New York Public Library, New York, NY.
WPA Federal Art Project Images, Photography Collection (digital collection)
State Historical Society of Wisconsin Library, Wisconsin Historical Society, Madison, Wisconsin.
Highlander Research and Education Center Papers
Swarthmore College Peace Collection, Swarthmore, Pennsylvania.
A.J. Muste Papers (microfilm edition)
Tamiment Library and Robert F. Wagner Labor Archives, New York University, New York, NY.
Socialist Party Printed Ephemera Collection
League for Industrial Democracy Papers
Walter P. Reuther Library, Archives of Labor and Urban Affairs, Wayne State University, Detroit, Michigan.
Brookwood Labor College Papers

Franz E. Daniel Collection
George Clifton Edwards, Jr. Papers
George Clifton Edwards, Sr. Papers
Herman Wolf Papers
Mildred Jeffrey Collection
Newman Jeffrey Collection
Philip H. Van Gelder Collection
Roy Reuther Papers
Wilson Library, University of North Carolina, Chapel Hill, N.C.
    The John C. Campbell and Olive D. Campbell Papers (digital collection)

GOVERNMENT PUBLICATIONS

Massachusetts. Middlesex County. 1920 U.S. Census, population schedule. Digital images. Ancestry.com. http://ancestry.com.

New York. Washington County. 1880 U.S. Census, population schedule. Digital images. Ancestry.com. http://ancestry.com.

Pennsylvania. Allegheny County. 1900 U.S. Census, population schedule. Digital images. Ancestry.com. http://ancestry.com.

Pennsylvania. Allegheny County. 1920 U.S. Census, population schedule. Digital images. Ancestry.com. http://ancestry.com.

Pennsylvania. Allegheny County. 1930 U.S. Census, population schedule. Digital images. Ancestry.com. http://ancestry.com.

United States Senate, *Hearings before the Subcommittee to investigate the administration of the internal security act and other internal security laws of the Committee on the Judiciary on Subversive Influence in Southern Conference Education Fund, INC.* (Government Printing Office, 1955).

NEWSPAPERS AND MAGAZINES

The American Scholar
The Atlanta Constitution
Atlanta Daily World
The Boston Globe
Chicago Daily Tribune
The Christian Century
Dallas County Courier
The Florence Times-News
Harper's Magazine
The Labor Journal
The Lewiston Daily Sun
The Los Angeles Times

Manchester Guardian
The Milwaukee Journal
The New Leader
The New Republic
New York Amsterdam News
New International
The New York Times
The North American Review
The Pittsburgh Courier
The Pittsburgh Press
Reading Eagle
The Scranton Republican
The Wall Street Journal
The Washington Afro-American
The Washington Post
The World Tomorrow

PUBLISHED PRIMARY SOURCES

Browder, Earl. *The Meaning of Social-Fascism: Its Historical and Theoretical Background*. New York: Workers Library Publishers, 1933.
Burgess, David S. *Fighting for Social Justice: The Life Story of David Burgess*. Detroit: Wayne State University Press, 2000.
Claessens, August. *The Logic of Socialism*. New York: The Leonard Press, 1921.
Cook, Alice. *A Lifetime of Labor: The Autobiography of Alice H. Cook*. New York: The Feminist Press at the City University of New York, 1998.
Daniel, John. *Looking After: A Son's Memoir*. Washington, D.C.: Counterpoint, 1996.
———. *Rogue River Journal: A Winter Alone*. Washington, D.C.: Shoemaker & Hoard, 2005.
Daniel, Zilla Hawes. "The Plant, A little Café, and Lots of Coffee." In *Refuse to Stand Silently By*, edited by Eliot Wigginton, 89–101. New York: Doubleday, 1991.
Dombrowski, James. *The Early Days of Christian Socialism in America*. Octagon Books, 1966 [1936].
Horton, Myles with Judith Kohl and Herbert Kohl, *The Long Haul: An Autobiography*. New York: Teachers College Press, 1998.
Kempton, Murray. *Part of Our Time: Some Ruins and Monuments of the Thirties*. New York: New York Review Books, 1998 [1955].
Marx, Karl and Friedrich Engels, *Communist Manifesto*. New York: Rand School of Social Sciences, 1919.

Maurer, James Hudson. *It Can Be Done: The Autobiography of James Hudson Maurer*. New York: The Rand School Press, 1938.

Mills, C. Wright. "Letter to the New Left." *New Left Review* 1, no. 5 (1960): 18–23.

Mitchell, H.L. *Mean Things Happening in this Land: The Life and Times of H.L. Mitchell, Co-Founder of the Southern Tenant Farmers Union*. Norman: University of Oklahoma Press, 2008 [1979].

Niebuhr, Reinhold. *Moral Man and Immoral Society: A Study in Ethics and Politics*. New York: Charles Scribner's Sons, 1932.

Oneal, James. *Socialism Versus Bolshevism*. New York: The Rand School Press, 1935.

Porter, Paul R. Transcript of an oral history conducted 1992 by Morris Weisz, Association for Diplomatic Studies and Training Foreign Affairs Oral History Project, Labor Series, State Department, George P. Shultz National Foreign Affairs Training Center, Arlington, Virginia. http://www.adst.org/OH%20TOCs/Porter,%20Paul%20R.toc.pdf.

Ware, Caroline Farrar. *Greenwich Village, 1920–1930: A Comment on American Civilization in the Post-War Years*. Berkeley: University of California Press, 1935.

Thomas, Norman. *Democratic Socialism: A New Appraisal*. New York: League for Industrial Democracy, 1953.

West, Don. *No Lonesome Road: Selected Prose and Poems*. Urbana: University of Illinois Press, 2004.

TELEVISION PROGRAMS

Buckley Jr., William F. "Vietnam: Pull Out? Stay In? Escalate?" *Firing Line*, WOR-TV (New York, NY: 8 April 1966).

Moyers, Bill. "The Adventures of a Radical Hillbilly: An Interview with Myles Horton" *Bill Moyer's Journal*, PBS (5 June and 11 June 1981).

SECONDARY SOURCES: ARTICLES, BOOKS, AND DISSERTATIONS

Adams, Frank T. *James A. Dombrowski: An America Heretic, 1897–1983*. Knoxville: University of Tennessee Press, 1992.

———. *Unearthing Seeds of Fire: The Idea of Highlander*. Winston-Salem: John F. Blair, 1975.

Alexander, Robert Jackson. *The Right Opposition: The Lovestoneites and the International Communist Opposition of the 1930's*. Westport: Greenwood Press, 1981.

Andersen, Kristi. *After Suffrage: Women in Partisan and Electoral Politics Before the New Deal*. Chicago: University of Chicago Press, 1996.

Bell, Daniel. *Marxian Socialism in the United States.* Princeton: Princeton University Press, 1967.

———. *The End of Ideology.* Cambridge: Harvard University Press, 2000 [1960].

Bernstein, Irving. *The Turbulent Years: A History of the American Worker, 1933–1940.* Chicago: Haymarket Books, 2010 [1969].

Bingham, June. *Courage to Change: An Introduction to the Life and Thought of Reinhold Niebuhr.* Lanham: University Press of America, 1992.

Boyle, Kevin. *The UAW and the Heyday of American Liberalism, 1945–1968.* Ithaca: Cornell University Press, 1995.

Brecher, Jeremy. *Strike! Revised, Expanded, and Updated Edition.* Oakland: PM Press, 2014.

Bronner, Stephen Eric. *Socialism Unbound: Principles Practices, and Prospects.* New York: Columbia University Press, 2013.

Brown, Susan Love. *Intentional Community: An Anthropological Perspective.* Albany: State University of New York Press, 2002.

Brustein, William. *Roots of Hate: Anti-Semitism in Europe Before the Holocaust.* Cambridge: Cambridge University Press, 2003.

Bucki, Cecelia. *Bridgeport's Socialist New Deal, 1915–36.* Urbana: University of Illinois Press, 2001.

Buenker, John D. "The Politics of Mutual Frustration: Socialists and Suffragists in New York and Wisconsin." In Sally Miller, ed., *Flawed Liberation: Socialism and Feminism.* Westport: Greenwood Press, 1981.

Buhle, Mari Jo. *Women and American Socialism, 1870–1920.* Urbana: University of Illinois Press, 1983.

Buhle, Paul. *From the Knights of Labor to the New World Order: Essays on Labor and Culture.* New York: Garland, 1997.

Bussel, Robert. *From Harvard to the Ranks of Labor: Powers Hapgood and the American Working Class.* University Park: The Pennsylvania State University Press, 2010.

Cashman, Sean Dennis. *America in the Twenties and Thirties: The Olympian Age of Franklin Delano Roosevelt.* New York: New York University Press, 1989.

Childs, David. *The Two Red Flags: European Social Democracy and Soviet Communism since 1945.* London: Routledge, 2000.

Cobble, Dorothy Sue. *The Other Women's Movement: Workplace Justice and Social Rights in Modern America.* Princeton: Princeton University Press, 2011.

Cohen, Gidon. *The Failure of a Dream: The Independent Labour Party from disaffiliation to World War II.* London: Tauris Academic Studies, 2007.

Cohen, Robert. *When the Old Left Was Young: Student Radicals and America's First Mass Student Movement, 1929–1941.* New York: Oxford University Press, 1993.

Cole, Peter. *Wobblies on the Waterfront: Interracial Unionism in Progressive-Era Philadelphia.* Urbana: University of Illinois Press, 2007.

Collins, Robert M. *The Business Response to Keynes, 1929–1964.* New York: Columbia University Press, 1981.

Coodley, Lauren. *Upton Sinclair: California Socialist, Celebrity Intellectual.* Lincoln: University of Nebraska Press, 2013.

Cott, Nancy F. "Putting Women on the Record: Mary Ritter Beard's Accomplishment." In *A Woman Making History: Marry Ritter Beard Through Her Letters,* edited by Nancy F. Cott. New Haven: Yale University Press, 1991.

Cottrell, Robert. *Roger Nash Baldwin and the American Civil Liberties Union.* New York: Columbia University Press, 2000.

Cowie, Jefferson and Salvatore, Nick. "The Long Exception: Rethinking the Place of the New Deal in American History." *International Labor and Working-Class History* 74, no. 1 (Fall, 2008): 3–32.

Cowie, Jefferson. *Capital Moves: RCA's Seventy-year Quest for Cheap Labor.* New York: The New Press, 2001.

Cramme, Olaf and Diamond, Patrick, eds., *After the Third Way: The Future of Social Democracy in Europe.* London: I.B. Tauris, 2012.

Crosland, Anthony. *The Future of Socialism.* New York: Schocken Books, 1963 [1956].

Cultice, Wendell W. Youth. *Battle for the Ballot: A History of Voting Age in America.* New York: Greenwood Press, 1992.

Curl, John. *For All The People: Uncovering the Hidden History of Cooperation, Cooperative Movements, and Communalism in America,* 2nd ed., Oakland PM Press, 2002.

Denning, Michael. *The Cultural Front: The Laboring of American Culture in the Twentieth Century.* London: Verso, 1998.

Dubofsky, Melvyn and Van Tine, Warren R., *John L. Lewis: A Biography.* Urbana: University of Illinois Press, 1986.

———. *Hard Work: The Making of Labor History.* Urbana: University of Illinois Press, 2000.

Duke, David Nelson. *In the Trenches with Jesus and Marx: Harry F. Ward and the Struggle for Social Justice.* Tuscaloosa: University of Alabama Press, 2003.

Dunbar, Anthony P. *Against the Grain: Southern Radicals and Prophets, 1929–1959.* Charlottesville: University of Virginia Press, 1981.

Durham, Frank. "Opposition in process: The press, Highlander Folk School, and radical social change, 1932–1961." PhD diss., University of Wisconsin – Madison, 1993.

Eagleton, Terry. *Ideology: An Introduction.* London: Verso, 1991.

Eisenberg, Carolyn Woods. *Drawing the Line: The American Decision to Divide Germany, 1944–1949.* Cambridge: Cambridge University Press, 1996.

Engelhardt, Elizabeth S. D. *The Tangled Roots of Feminism, Environmentalism, and Appalachian Literature.* Athens: Ohio University Press, 2003.

Faue, Elizabeth. *Community of Suffering & Struggle: Women, Men, and the Labor Movement in Minneapolis, 1915–1945.* Chapel Hill: University of North Carolina Press, 1991.

Feurer, Rosemary. *Radical Unionism in the Midwest, 1900–1950.* Urbana: University of Illinois Press, 2006.

Filippelli, Ronald L. and Mark D. McColloch, *Cold War in the Working Class: The Rise and Decline of the United Electrical Workers.* Albany: State University of New York Press, 1995.

Finnegan, Mary. *Selling Suffrage: Consumer Culture & Votes for Women.* New York: Columbia University Press, 1999.

Fleischman, Harry. *Norman Thomas: A Biography, 1884–1968.* New York: W.W. Norton, 1969.

Forman, James. *The Making of Black Revolutionaries.* Seattle: University of Washington Press, 1997 [1972].

Fraser, Steve. *Labor Will Rule: Sidney Hillman and the Rise of American Labor.* New York: Free Press, 1991.

Fraser, Steve and Gerstle, Gary, eds., *The Rise and Fall of the New Deal Order, 1930–1980.* Princeton: Princeton University Press, 1989.

Frost, Richard H. *The Mooney Case.* Palo Alto: Stanford University Press, 1968.

Galenson, Walter. *The CIO Challenge to the AFL: A History of the American Labor Movement, 1935–1941.* Cambridge: Harvard University Press, 1960.

Gamble, Andrew. "Moving beyond the National: the challenges for social democracy in a global world." In *Social Justice in the Global Age,* edited by Olaf Cramme and Patrick Diamond, 117–135. Cambridge: Polity Press, 2009.

Ginger, Ray. *The Bending Cross: A Biography of Eugene Victor Debs.* New Brunswick: Rutgers University Press, 1949.

Glen, John M. *Highlander: No Ordinary School.* Knoxville: University of Tennessee Press, 1996.

Goan, Melanie Beals. *Mary Breckinridge: The Frontier Nursing Service & Rural Health in Appalachia.* Chapel Hill: University of North Carolina Press, 2008.

Gordon, Colin. *New Deals: Business, Labor, and Politics in America, 1920–1935.* Cambridge: Cambridge University Press, 1994.

Green, James R. *Grass-Roots Socialism: Radical Movements in the Southwest, 1895–1943.* Baton Rouge: Louisiana State University Press, 1978.

Greenberg, Cheryl. *"Or Does it Explode?": Black Harlem in the Great Depression.* New York: Oxford University Press, 1997.

Greene, Julie. "Historians of the World: Transnational Forces, Nation-States, and the Practice of U.S. History." In *Workers Across the Americas: The Transnational Turn in Labor History,* edited by Leon Fink, 12–17. New York: Oxford University Press, 2011.

Gregory, James N. "Upton Sinclair's 1934 EPIC Campaign: Anatomy of a Political Movement." *Labor: Studies in Working-Class History of the Americas* 12, no. 4 (2015), 51–81.

Gregory, Raymond F. *Norman Thomas: The Great Dissenter.* New York: Algora Publishing, 2008.

Grubbs, Donald H. *Cry from the Cotton: the Southern Tenant Farmers' Union and the New Deal.* Chapel Hill: University of North Carolina Press, 1971.

Gruber, Helmut. *Red Vienna: Experiment in Working-Class Culture, 1919–1934.* New York: Oxford University Press, 1991.

Gutman, Herbert G. *Work, Culture, and Society in Industrializing America: Essays in American Working-Class and Social History.* New York: Vintage Books, 1977.

Halpern, Martin. *UAW Politics in the Cold War Era.* Albany: State University of New York Press, 1988.

Harrington, Michael. *Socialism, Past and Present.* New York: Arcade Publishing, 1989.

Harvey, David. *A Brief History of Neoliberalism.* New York: Oxford University Press, 2005.

Hewitt, Nancy A. introduction to *No Permanent Waves: Recasting Histories of U.S. Feminism,* ed. Nancy A. Hewitt, 1–12. New Brunswick: Rutgers University Press, 2010.

Horowitz, Daniel. *Betty Friedan and the Making of the Feminine Mystique: The American Left, The Cold War, and Modern Feminism,* paperback ed. Amherst: University of Massachusetts Press, 2000.

Howe, Irving. *Socialism and America.* New York: Harcourt Brace Jovanovich, 1986.

Hunt, Karen. Equivocal Feminists: *The Social Democratic Federation and the Woman Question 1884–1911.* Cambridge: Cambridge University Press, 2002.

Iriye, Akira. *Global and Transnational History: The Past, Present and Future.* New York: Palgrave Macmillan, 2013.

Isserman, Maurice. "Michael Harrington and the Debs-Thomas tradition." *Dissent* 43, no. 4 (Fall 1996): 100–108.

———. *The Other American: The Life of Michael Harrington.* New York: Public Affairs, 2000.

———. *Which Side Were You On?: The American Communist Party During the Second World War.* Urbana: University of Illinois Press, 1982.

James, C.L.R. *Modern Politics.* Oakland: PM Press, 2013.

Jensen, Joan M. *Calling This Place Home: Women on the Wisconsin Frontier, 1850–1925.* St. Paul: Minnesota Historical Society Press, 2006.

Johnpoll, Bernard K. *Pacifist's Progress: Norman Thomas and the Decline of American Socialism.* Chicago: Quadrangle Books, 1970.

Judd, Richard William. *Socialist Cities: Municipal Politics and the Grass Roots of American Socialism.* Albany: State University of New York Press, 1989.

Judt, Tony. *Ill Fares the Land.* New York: Penguin Press, 2010.
———. *Postwar: A History of Europe Since 1945.* New York: Penguin Press, 2005.
Katznelson, Ira. *Fear Itself: The New Deal and the Origins of Our Time.* New York: W.W. Norton & Company, 2013.
Kazin, Michael. *American Dreamers: How the Left Changed a Nation.* New York: Vintage Books, 2011.
Kelley, Robin D.G. Hammer and Hoe: Alabama Communists during the Great Depression. Chapel Hill: University of North Carolina Press, 1990.
Kent, Hazel. "'A paper not so much for the armchair but for the factory and the street': Fenner Brockway and the Independent Labour Party's New Leader, 1926–1946." *Labour History Review* 75, no. 2 (2010): 208–226.
Kenworthy, Lane. *Social Democratic America.* New York: Oxford University Press, 2014.
Kessler-Harris, Alice. "Gender Ideology in Historical Reconstruction: A Case Study from the 1930s." *Gender & History* 1, no. 1 (1989): 31–49.
Kipnis, Ira. *The American Socialist Movement 1897–1912.* Chicago: Haymarket Press, 2005 [1952].
Kirby, Jack Temple. *Rural Worlds Lost: The American South, 1920–1960.* Baton Rouge: Lousisana State University Press, 1987.
Kollontai, Alexandra. "The Social Basis of Woman Question." In *Selected writing of Alexandra Kollontai,* edited by Alix Holt, 58–73. New York: W.W. Norton, 1980.
Korstad, Robert and Nelson Lichtenstein, "Opportunities Found and Lost: Labor, Radicals, and the Early Civil Rights Movement," *The Journal of American History* 75, (1988): 786–811.
Koscielski, Frank F. "Divided Loyalties: American Unions and the Vietnam War." PhD diss., Wayne State University, 1997.
Kutulas, Judy. *The American Civil Liberties Union and the Making of Modern Liberalism, 1930–1960.* Chapel Hill: University of North Carolina Press, 2006.
———. *The Long War: The Intellectual People's Front and Anti-Stalinism, 1930–1940.* Durham: Duke University Press, 1995.
Lapidus, Gail Warshofsk. *Women in Soviet Society: Equality, Development, and Social Change.* Berkeley: University of California Press, 1978.
Large, David Clay. *Between Two Fires: Europe's Path in the 1930s.* New York: W.W. Norton, 1991.
Larson, Simeon and Bruce Nissen. *Theories of the Labor Movement.* Detroit: Wayne State University Press, 1987.
Levenstein, Harvey A. *Communism, Anticommunism, and the CIO.* Westport: Greenwood Press, 1981.
Levy, Peter. *The New Left and Labor in the 1960s.* Urbana: University of Illinois Press, 1994.

Lewis-Colman, David. *Race Against Liberalism: Black Workers and the UAW in Detroit*. Urbana: University of Illinois Press, 2008.

Lichtenstein, Nelson. "Historians as Public Intellectuals." In *A Contest of Ideas: Capital, Politics, and Labor*. Urbana: University of Illinois Press, 2013.

———. *Labor's War at Home: The CIO in World War II*. Philadelphia: Temple University Press, 2003 [1982].

———. *State of the Union: A Century of American Labor*. Princeton: Princeton University Press, 2002.

———. *The Most Dangerous Man in Detroit: Walter Reuther and the Fate of American Labor*. New York: Basic Books, 1995.

Lindemann, Albert S. *A History of European Socialism*. New Haven: Yale University Press, 1984.

Linebaugh and Rediker. *The Many-Headed Hydra: Sailors, Slaves, Commoners, and the Hidden History of the Revolutionary Atlantic*. Boston: Beacon Press, 2000.

Lipset, Seymour Martin and Gary Marks, eds. *It Didn't Happen Here: Why Socialism Failed in the United States*. New York: W.W. Norton, 2000, 205.

Loew, Raimund. "The Politics of Austro-Marxism." *The New Left Review* 1, no. 118 (1979): 15–51.

Luff, Jennifer. *Commonsense Anticommunism: Labor and Civil Liberties between the World Wars*. Chapel Hill: University of North Carolina Press, 2012.

Lynd, Staughton and Andrej Grubacic. *Wobblies and Zapatistas: Conversations on Anarchism, Marxism and Radical History*. Oakland: PM Press, 2008.

Mark, Eduard. "October or Thermidor? Interpretations of Stalinism and the Perception of Soviet Foreign Policy in the United States, 1927–1947." *The American Historical Review* 94, no. 4 (1989): 937–962.

Mayer, Arno. *The Persistence of the Old Regime: Europe to the Great War*. New York: Pantheon, 1981.

McDaniel, Charles. *God & Money: The Moral Challenge of Capitalism*. Lanham: Rowman & Littlefield, 2007.

McGreen, J. Dennis. "Norman Thomas and the Search for the All-Inclusive Socialist Party." PhD diss., Rutgers University, 1976.

Merkley, Paul. *Reinhold Niebuhr: A Political Account*. Montreal: McGill-Queen's Press, 1975.

Messer-Kruse, Timothy. *The Yankee International: Marxism and the American Reform Tradition, 1848–1876*. Chapel Hill: University of North Carolina Press, 1998.

Miller, Sally M., ed. *Flawed Liberation: Socialism and Feminism*. Westport: Greenwood Press, 1981.

———. "Socialism and Women." In *Failure of a Dream? Essays in the History of American Socialism*, edited by John H. M. Laslett and Seymour Martin Lipset, 291–317. Berkeley: University of California Press, 1984.

———. *Victor Berger and the Promise of Constructive Socialism, 1910–1920.* Westport: Greenwood Press, 1973.

Miller, Timothy. *The Quest for Utopia in Twentieth-century America: 1900–1960.* Syracuse: Syracuse University Press, 1998.

Minchin, Timothy J. *What Do We Need a Union For? The TWUA in the South, 1945–1955.* Chapel Hill: University of North Carolina Press, 1997.

Mishler, Paul C. *Raising Reds: The Young Pioneers, Radical Summer Camps, and Communist Political Culture in the United States.* New York: Columbia University Press, 1999.

Montgomery, David. "Labor and Political Leadership in New Deal America." *International Review of Social History* 39, no. 3 (1994): 335–360.

———. "The Mythical Man." *International Labor and Working-Class History* 74 (Fall 2008): 56–62.

Morgan, Ted. *A Covert Life: Jay Lovestone, Communist, Anti-Communist, and Spymaster.* New York: Random House, 1999.

Mosse, George L. *The Image of Man: The Creation of Modern Masculinity.* New York: Oxford University Press, 1996.

Myers, Constance Ashton. *The Prophet's Army: Trotskyists in America, 1928–1941.* Westport: Greenwood Press, 1977.

Nadel, Stan. "The German Immigrant Left in the United States." In *The Immigrant Left in the United States,* edited by Paul Buhle and Dan Georgakas, 45–76. Albany: State University of New York Press, 1996.

Nichols, John. *The "S" Word: A Short History of an American Tradition…Socialism.* London: Verso, 2011.

Norwood, Stephen H. *Strikebreaking and Intimidation: Mercenaries and Masculinity in Twentieth-Century America.* Chapel Hill: University of North Carolina Press, 2002.

Orleck, Annelise. *Common Sense and a Little Fire: women and working-class politics in the United States, 1900–1965.* Chapel Hill: University of North Carolina Press, 1995.

Ottanelli, Fraser M. *The Communist Party of the United States: From the Depression to World War II.* New Brunswick: Rutgers University Press, 1991.

Palmer, David. "'An Anarchist with a Program': East Coast Shipyard Workers, the Labor Left, and the Origins of Cold War Unionism." In *American Labor and the Cold War: Grassroots Politics and Postwar Political Culture,* edited by Robert W. Cherny, William Issel and Kieran Walsh Taylor, 85–117. New Brunswick: Rutgers University Press, 2004.

———. *Organizing the Shipyards: Union Strategy in Three Northeast Ports, 1933–1945.* Ithaca: Cornell University Press, 1998.

Pastorello, Karen. *A Power Among Them: Bessie Abramowitz Hillman and the Making of the Amalgamated Clothing Workers of America.* Urbana: University of Illinois Press, 2008.

Payne, Stanley G. *Spain's First Democracy: The Second Republic, 1931–1936*. Madison: University of Wisconsin Press, 1993.

Peck, Jamie. *Constructions of Neoliberal Reason*. New York: Oxford University Press, 2010.

Pedersen, Vernon L. *The Communist Party in Maryland, 1919–57*. Urbana: University of Illinois Press, 2001.

Peel, Mark. "Male Social Workers and the Anxieties of Women's Authority: Boston and Minneapolis, 1920–1940." *Journal of Men's Studies* 15, no. 3 (2007): 282–294.

Pierce, Robert Clayton. "Liberals and the Cold War: Union for Democratic Action and Americans for Democratic Action, 1940–1949." PhD diss., University of Wisconsin Madison, 1979.

Pimlott, Ben. *Labour and the Left in the 1930s*. Cambridge: Cambridge University Press, 1977.

Pittenger, Mark. *American Socialists and Evolutionary Thought, 1870–1920*. Madison: University of Wisconsin Press, 1993.

Pitzer, Donald E. *America's Communal Utopias*. Chapel Hill: University of North Carolina Press, 1997.

Pratt, William. "'Jimmie Higgins' and the Reading Socialist Community." In *Socialism and the Cities*, edited by Bruce Stave, 141–156. Port Washington: Kennikat Press, 1975.

———. "Women and American Socialism: The Reading Experience." *Pennsylvania Magazine of History and Biography* 99, no. 1 (1975): 72–91.

Price, Michael E. "The New Deal in Tennessee: The Highlander Folk School and Worker Response in Grundy County," *Tennessee Historical Quarterly* 43 (1984): 99–120.

Quadagno, Jill. *One Nation, Uninsured: Why the U.S. Has No National Health Insurance*. Oxford: Oxford University Press, 2006.

Radford, Gail. *Modern Housing for America: Policy Struggles in the New Deal Era*. Chicago: University of Chicago Press, 1996.

Raphael, D. D. *Hobbes: Morals and Politics*. London: Routledge, 2014.

Rasmussen, Larry. "A Few Facets of Niebuhr's Thought." In *Reinhold Niebuhr: Theologian of Public Life*. Minneapolis: Fortress Press, 1991.

Rice, Daniel F. *Reinhold Niebuhr and His Circle of Influence*. Cambridge: Cambridge University Press, 2012.

Riley, Dylan. "Southern Questions." Review of *Fear Itself: The New Deal and the Origins of Our Time* by Ira Katznelson. *The New Left Review* 85 (2014): 147–160.

Rodgers, Daniel T. *Atlantic Crossings: Social Politics in a Progressive Age*. Cambridge: Harvard University Press, 1998.

Rosenzweig, Roy. "'Socialism in Our Time': The Socialist Party and the Unemployed, 1929–1936." *Labor History* 20, no. 4 (1979): 485–509.

Ross, Jack. *The Socialist Party of America: A Complete History.* Lincoln: Potomac Books, 2015.

Ruotsila, Markku. "Leftward Ramparts: Labor and Anticommunism between the World Wars." In *Little "Red Scares": Anti-Communism and Political Repression in the United States, 1921–1946,* edited by Robert Justin Goldstein, 165–194. Burlington: Ashgate, 2014.

Ryan, James G. *Earl Browder: The Failure of American Communism.* Tuscaloosa: University of Alabama Press, 1997.

Sanders, Bernard, and Huck Gutman. *Outsider in the House.* London: Verso, 1997.

Sassoon, Donald. *One Hundred Years of Socialism: The West European Left in the Twentieth Century.* New York: The New Press, 1996.

Schatz, Ronald W. *The Electrical Workers: A History of Labor at General Electric and Westinghouse, 1923–60.* Urbana: University of Illinois Press, 1983.

Schlesinger Jr., Arthur M. *The Crisis of the Old Order: 1919–1933, The Age of Roosevelt.* New York: Houghton Mifflin Harcourt, 2003.

———. "Some Lessons from the Cold War." In *The End of the Cold War: Its Meaning and Implications,* edited by Michael J. Hogan, 53–62. Cambridge: Cambridge University Press, 1992.

Schuyler, Lorraine Gates. *Weight of Their Votes: Southern Women and Political Leverage in the 1920s: Southern Women and Political Leverage in The 1920s.* Chapel Hill: University of North Carolina Press, 2008.

Schwartz, Bonnie Fox. *The Civil Works Administration, 1933–1934: The Business of Emergency Employment in the New Deal.* Princeton: Princeton University Press, 1984.

Seidler, Murray B. *Norman Thomas: Respectable Rebel.* Syracuse: Syracuse University Press, 1961.

Sidorick, Sharon McConnell. "Silk Stockings and Socialism: Class, Community, and Labor Feminism in Kensington, Philadelphia, 1919–1940." PhD diss., Temple University, 2010.

Simon, Bryant. *A Fabric of Defeat: The Politics of South Carolina Millhands, 1910–1948.* Chapel Hill: University of North Carolina Press, 1998.

Simon, Rita, ed. *As We Saw the Thirties.* Urbana: University of Illinois Press, 1967.

Smith, Harry Leslie. *Harry's Last Stand: How the World My Generation Built is Falling Down, and What We Can Do to Save It.* London: Icon Books, 2014.

Stolberg, Mary M. *Bridging the River of Hatred: The Pioneering Efforts of Detroit Police Commissioner George Edwards.* Detroit: Wayne State University Press, 1998.

Stone, Ronald H. *Professor Reinhold Niebuhr: Mentor to the Twentieth Century.* Louisville: Westminster and John Knox Press, 1992.

Storch, Randi. "'The Realities of the Situation': Revolutionary Discipline and Everyday Political Life in Chicago's Communist Party, 1928–1935." *Labor: Studies in Working-Class History of the Americas* 1, no 3 (2004): 19–44.

————. *Red Chicago: American Communism at its Grassroots, 1928–35.* Urbana: University of Illinois Press, 2007.

Storrs, Landon R. Y. "Left-Feminism, the Consumer Movement, and Red Scare Politics in the United States, 1935–1960." *Journal of Women's History* 18, no. 3 (2006): 40–67.

————. "Red Scare Politics and the Suppression of Popular Front Feminism: The Loyalty Investigation of Mary Dublin Keyserling." *The Journal of American History* 90, no. 2 (2003): 491–524.

————. *The Second Red Scare and the Unmaking of the New Deal Left.* Princeton: Princeton University Press, 2012.

————. *Civilizing Capitalism: The National Consumers' League, Women's Activism, and Labor Standards in the New Deal Era.* Chapel Hill: University of North Carolina Press, 2000.

Stromquist, Shelton. *Labor's Cold War: Local Politics in a Global Context.* Urbana: University of Illinois Press, 2008.

————. *Reinventing "The People" The Progressive Movement, the Class Problem, and the Origins of Modern Liberalism.* Urbana: University of Illinois Press, 2006.

Swanberg, W. A. *Norman Thomas: The Last Idealist.* New York: Charles Scribner's Sons, 1976.

Thomas, H. Glyn. "Highlander Folk School: The Depression Years," *Tennessee Historical Quarterly* 23 (1964): 358–371.

Thomas, Paul. *Marx and the Anarchists.* London: Psychology Press, 1980.

Tindall, George Brown. *The Emergence of the New South, 1913–1945.* Baton Rouge: Louisiana State University Press, 1967.

van Elteren, Mel. *Labor and the American Left: An Analytical History.* London: McFarland, 2011.

Venkataramani, M.S. "Leon Trotsky's Adventure in American Radical Politics, 1935–1937." *International Review of Social History* 9, no 1 (1964): 1–46.

Warren, Frank A. *An Alternative Vision: The Socialist Party in the 1930's.* Bloomington: Indiana University Press, 1974.

Weigand, Kate. *Red Feminism: American Communism and the Making of Women's Liberation.* Baltimore: John Hopkins Press, 2001.

Weinstein, James. *Ambiguous Legacy: The Left in American Politics.* New York: New Viewpoints, 1975.

————. *The Decline of Socialism in America: 1912–1925.* New Brunswick: Rutgers University Press, 1984.

Williams, Raymond. *Culture and Society, 1780–1950.* New York: Penguin Books, 1963.

Zecker, Robert M. "'Not Communists Exactly, but Sort of like Non-Believers': The Hidden Radical Transcript of Slovak Immigrants in Philadelphia, 1890–1954." *The Oral History Review* 29, no. 1 (2002): 1–37.

Zieger, Robert H. *The CIO, 1935–1955.* Chapel Hill: University of North Carolina Press, 1995.

INDEX

© The Editor(s) (if applicable) and The Author(s),
under exclusive license to Springer Nature Switzerland AG 2019
J. Altman, *Socialism before Sanders*,
https://doi.org/10.1007/978-3-030-17176-6